DATE DUE

11/29/05			
12-19			
10-29-08			

D0866585

The European Union
Economy, Society, and Polity

DISCARDED

Andrés Rodríguez-Pose

London School of Economics

OXFORD
UNIVERSITY PRESS

OXFORD

UNIVERSITY PRESS

Great Clarendon Street, Oxford OX2 6DP

Oxford University Press is a department of the University of Oxford.
It furthers the University's objective of excellence in research, scholarship,
and education by publishing worldwide in

Oxford New York

Auckland Bangkok Buenos Aires Cape Town Chennai
Dar es Salaam Delhi Hong Kong Istanbul Karachi Kolkata
Kuala Lumpur Madrid Melbourne Mexico City Mumbai Nairobi
São Paulo Shanghai Singapore Taipei Tokyo Toronto

and an associated company in Berlin

Oxford is a registered trade mark of Oxford University Press
in the UK and in certain other countries

Published in the United States
by Oxford University Press Inc., New York

© Andrés Rodriguez-Pose 2002

Library of Congress Cataloging in Publication Data

(Data applied for)

ISBN 0-19-874286-X

Typeset by RefineCatch Limited, Bungay, Suffolk
Printed in Great Britain on acid-free paper by
Biddles Ltd, www.biddles.co.uk

To my parents, José Luis and Josefina

Preface

When I, somewhat foolishly, accepted Andrew Lockett's offer to write a compendium of current issues in the European Union, little did I imagine the time and the amount of work this would take. Three and a half years after Andrew Lockett's first approach and almost three after he left Oxford University Press, the book finally comes to light. It has been a long and somewhat intermittent task, but it has certainly been worth it, because in writing this book I have learned a great deal and benefited from the advice, guidance, and criticism of colleagues. Paul Cheshire, Gilles Duranton, Henry Overman, and Diego Puga gave generous guidance in the economic topics. The social section owes much to the support of Ian Gordon and Claire Kilpatrick and to the suggestions of Murray Low. The political section has been thoroughly discussed with John Tomaney. Some of these friends have read drafts of chapters and commented on them. But just as important as the input of colleagues has been the impact on the book of interaction with students. My students at the LSE and those of the Caja Madrid/LSE globalization masterclasses in Madrid have been—unbeknown to them—the guinea pigs of most of the chapters included in the book. My gratitude goes to them. A large percentage of the data presented in the book is EUROSTAT data made available to academics at no cost by the University of Durham and ESRC r.cade gateway. The successive editors involved in the project at OUP (Angela Griffin, Jonathan Crowe, and John Grandidge) have also provided valuable insights and assistance. Research support from the Royal Society–Wolfson Research Merit Award and from the Philip Leverhulme Research Prize is gratefully acknowledged. Finally I would like to thank Leticia for her support. This book is dedicated to my parents, José Luis and Josefina.

Contents

List of tables

List of figures

Glossary of terms

ANZERTA	Australia and New Zealand Closer Economics Relations and Trade Agreement
CAP	Common Agricultural Policy
CEECs	Central and Eastern European Countries
CEFTA	Central European Free Trade Area
CIS	Commonwealth of Independent States
CMEA	Council for Mutual Economic Assistance
CSF	Community Support Framework
EAGGF	European Agricultural Guidance and Guarantee Fund
EC	European Communities
ECUs	European Currency Units
EFTA	European Free Trade Association
EMU	European Monetary Union or Economic and Monetary Union
ERDF	European Regional Development Fund
ESF	European Social Fund
EU	European Union
FDI	Foreign Direct Investment
GDP	Gross Domestic Product
GNP	Gross National Product
IMF	International Monetary Fund
IRAP	*Imposta Regionale sulle Attività Produttive*
JHA	Justice and Home Affairs
LAIA	Association for Latin American Integration
M&As	Mergers and Acquisitions
MERCOSUR	*Mercado Común del Sur*
NAFTA	North American Free Trade Association
NATO	North Atlantic Treaty Association
OECD	Organization for Economic Co-operation and Development
Ops	Operations Programmes
Phare	*Pologne-Hongrie: Assistance à la Restructuration des Economies*
PPS	Purchasing Power Standards
R&D	Research and Development
RPR	*Rassemblement pour la République*
SEA	Single European Act
SMEs	Small and Medium-sized Enterprises
SNP	Scottish National Party
SPDs	Single Programming Documents
TFR	Total Fertility Rate
UDF	*Union Démocratique Française*
UK	United Kingdom

UN	United Nations
US	United States
VAT	Value-Added Tax
WTO	World Trade Organization

Prologue

The challenges to the European Union

The recent processes of globalizaton of the world economy and socio-economic restructuring are transforming our societies and generating new challenges and opportunities for the whole of Europe, in general, and the European Union (EU), in particular. The challenges are of different kinds: some are economic, some social, and others fundamentally political. On the economic side, the EU faces greater competition from the rest of the world. The US has been growing at a faster rate than the EU during the last few decades and has recently fostered the creation of the North American Free Trade Association (NAFTA), the largest regional economic bloc in the world. Japan, despite having suffered a long economic crisis throughout the 1990s, is still the second largest economy in the globe. And the rising economies of South East Asia and Latin America are becoming key world economic players. The EU needs to improve its competitiveness in order to keep up with other dynamic spaces. Economic integration may prove to be the answer in order to achieve this goal. Yet, greater economic integration could prove harmful for internal economic cohesion in western Europe. Within its borders, the EU harbours substantial economic disparities among member states and among its regions. Any increase in the level of disparities, as a result of differential growth rates or of the enlargement to the East, is likely to become an issue of unpredictable economic and political consequences.

Social challenges are also growing. Europe is ageing. No other society in the world has such a large percentage of senior citizens and, given its low levels of fertility, the ageing problem is unlikely to recede in the future. But while Europe is ageing, economic hardship in neighbouring states—and particularly in eastern Europe, Africa, and Latin America—is putting greater migratory pressure on the EU's borders. Migrants, if allowed into the EU in large numbers, could contribute to increase competitiveness and drive down ageing, but would also enter a relatively rigid labour market that for more than the last two decades has been characterized by high levels of structural unemployment.

Finally, the political challenges are dominated by the issue of enlargement and by regionalization. On one side, the expansion of the EU towards the East and the addition of several new—and poorer—members will have a profound effect on the structure of the EU. On the other, the nation state is coming under great pressure from two parallel forces. At the top end, economic and political integration is scooping some of the traditional functions performed by nation states. At the bottom end, a regionalization and regional devolution wave is further transforming the way European nation states have traditionally functioned and operated.

Despite the different nature of these challenges, all challenges are interconnected and influence each other. The future capacity of the EU to compete in a globalized world and the measures adopted to foster greater competitiveness will have important implications for the level of cohesion, unemployment, and the degree of social polarization. They will also affect the capacity of the EU to assimilate larger contingents of foreign workers and poorer members into the EU. A higher or lower competitiveness may even have an effect on fertility rates. Similarly, the decisions adopted on migration will contribute to lessen or increase the ageing problem, and will influence unemployment, social exclusion, and economic cohesion. And the process of regionalization and regional devolution is likely to be fuelled by greater regional inequalities, the degree of regional competitiveness, employment levels, and even by ageing and enlargement.

The only certainty is that the EU that will emerge form this set of economic, social, and political challenges, will be very different from the current EU. The degree of transformation and adaptation to the new conditions will be, to a large extent, determined by the depth and scope of the reforms undertaken across Europe. Reforms need to be carried out at the internal (i.e. institutional) level. Eastern enlargement and the complexity of economic integration require a thorough rethinking and restructuring of the institutions of the EU in order to accommodate a series of countries whose population almost equals that of the current EU and a degree of economic governance which is much more complex than anything the EU has experienced before. But, as demanding as the internal reform—if not more demanding—are the structural changes that the EU and its members have to undertake in order to face these global and European challenges. If in the future Europe is a competitive and cohesive economy; if it is a dynamic society capable of assimilating migrant workers and preventing the increase of racism and xenophobia; if it is a society where unemployment is low and social polarization a thing of the past, it will be basically down to the success of the reforms carried out. If, on the contrary, Europe fails to take on reforms or to cope with the challenges, the best-case scenario presented above will be nothing but a pipe dream.

Some reforms are already in place. The process of economic integration has been under way for some time. The completion of the Single Market and the launch of Economic and Monetary Union (EMU) have been designed and implemented with European competitiveness in mind. In migration, policing, justice, or foreign affairs, the EU is trying to give a unified European response to global challenges. In other policy areas, the degree of co-ordination is much lower. Labour markets, employment, family and social security policies, or regional devolution, despite their increasing European and global nature, still fall within the policy realm of the nation state.

This textbook about the European Union deals with some of the challenges stemming from the processes of globalization and socio-economic restructuring and how they are being dealt with at the European and at the national level. It examines the EU in spatial terms from a thematic perspective. The book is structured in three parts which reflect the different economic, social, and political challenges to the EU. Part I on the economy of the EU looks first at the issue of competitiveness. It addresses the European problems of competitiveness and how the process of European economic integration is tackling them. The early impact of the process of economic integration is also presented. The discussion on competitiveness is followed by the study of economic cohesion. Issues like the possible impact of European economic integration on economic growth and imbalances and the effectiveness of European development policies are covered.

Consideration of the European economy is followed in Part II by three chapters on social challenges. The chapters cover the issues of ageing, migration and xenophobia, unemployment and social polarization. The chapter on ageing presents the demographic trends behind the formation of inverted demographic pyramids and the increase in the number of senior citizens across Europe, before studying the measures that are being adopted to combat the problems of ageing by different EU member states. The chapter on migration looks at past and present migration in Europe and at the differences between the present migration wave and earlier waves. It then turns to the analysis of the Europeanization of migration policies and the link between the increase in migration and the emergence of xenophobic and racist attitudes and movements across Europe. The trade-off between unemployment and social polarization in the EU is analysed in Chapter 5. This chapter studies the evolution of unemployment since the crisis of the 1970s and the array of national measures used to combat it. The description of how the reforms aimed at increasing the flexibility of labour markets are resulting in greater social polarization and in the emergence of atypical forms of employment follows.

The final part covers the political challenges to the EU. Two challenges are addressed. The first one is that of enlargement. The transition from communism and central planning to democracy and market economies in central and eastern Europe and the difficulties of the process are discussed. Section 6.4 deals with the implications of enlargement for the new member states and for the EU itself. Chapter 7 covers the issue of regionalization and regional devolution in the EU. It presents how western Europe has been transformed from a continent where centralized states prevailed to one in which most states have been regionalized in just a few decades. Different national forms of regionalization are discussed, as well as the challenge regional devolution represents for the future of the European nation state and of the EU.

I
ECONOMY

1

Competitiveness

1.1 Introduction

European economic integration has come a long way in recent years but is still far from completion. The late twentieth century and early twenty-first century have seen the onset of the Single Market and of the single currency. Yet, total economic integration will not be completed without a much greater degree of economic harmonization and political integration. Reaching the present level of economic integration in the European Union (EU) has been a slow and somewhat spasmodic process. Despite being commonly known as the Common Market throughout much of the 1970s and 1980s, the European Community (EC) was only a customs union during much of its existence. The pace of economic integration increased during the 1990s. The EC became a real common market, in which free mobility of factors of production is allowed, on 1 January 1993. The introduction in January 1999 in eleven of the fifteen member states of the Euro—the common European currency—represented a further step towards full economic integration.

The acceleration of the process of European integration during the 1990s has been mainly driven by the desire to make the EU more competitive in a globalized economy. But to what extent has this been achieved? This chapter looks at the evolution of the EU economy as a whole, and compares it with the evolution of other world economies. The first section is devoted to the stages of economic integration and economic integration in the EU. The second section deals with economic integration as a means to achieve competitiveness and studies the expected benefits of economic integration. Finally, the last section examines the impact of European economic integration on trade, economies of scale, productivity, and growth.

1.2 The stages of economic integration

Economic integration among different nations or regions rarely happens overnight. The progressive removal and ultimate eradication of economic barriers between different states is often a lengthy and winding process, whose rhythm is determined by economic as well as political bargaining and compromise. Political resolution also determines the intensity of economic integration. From the simple elimination of trade tariffs to the total unification of monetary and fiscal policies and institutions, there are numerous stages of economic integration. These stages, first described by Balassa in 1961, represent the different levels which may be adopted in the process towards full economic integration. Most processes of economic integration however rarely go beyond the two initial stages of integration.

The simplest level of integration is the **free trade area**. In a free trade area, free movement of goods is allowed among its members. This implies the abolition of tariffs and quotas for imports from area members, although members of the area keep their own quotas and tariffs *vis-à-vis* third countries. In essence the free trade area is a preferential trade agreement, which may include just a series of products or expand to the whole manufacturing sector and even services. One of the disadvantages of the free trade area is that since members maintain their own tariffs and quotas *vis-à-vis* third parties, countries outside the area may redirect their trade and target the country with the lowest tariffs or highest quotas in order to access the markets within the area. In order to prevent this and other problems, which may ultimately lead to tensions among members of the free trade area and to the demise of the agreement, most free trade areas go beyond the simple elimination of tariffs and adopt some timid form of policy integration or institutional co-ordination.

A more advanced stage of economic integration is the **customs union**. In a customs union, the eradication of internal tariffs and quotas is accompanied by some common external trade restriction and/or the harmonization of external tariffs and quotas. The establishment of common external tariffs and quotas necessarily implies a much greater level of institutional co-ordination than in the free trade area. Members of the customs union not only have to give up their capacity to set up external tariffs, but often also harmonize and make compatible other aspects of their respective national trade policies. Custom unions frequently result in the creation of common regulatory bodies and institutions which police and control trade within the union and, in some cases, even implement policies whose main aim is to foster and to regulate trade within the union.

The **common market**, also known as **single market**, is usually the next stage of economic integration. The common market shares with a customs union the eradication of internal and the harmonization of external tariffs, but it also implies the removal of all non-tariff barriers to free factor mobility. The outcome is the free mobility of goods, capital, labour, and services across the territory of the common market. The eradication of all obstacles to free factor and asset mobility usually requires a much greater level of regulation than in customs unions. Institutions are set up in order to monitor and guarantee that decisions adopted by the authorities of the member states do not affect competition and the free mobility of factors across the common market.

A further stage of integration occurs when members of a common market begin to harmonize their economic policy. At this stage the common market starts to become an **economic union**. National economic authorities of the member states, under the aegis of a common or a series of central institutions, resort to coordinating certain areas of economic policy until they ultimately give up their national control over them to a supranational body. The harmonization of economic policy generally occurs in the fields of monetary and/or fiscal policies.

When all areas of economic policy in the member states are harmonized the economic union gives way to the stage of **complete economic integration**. In this final stage of the process of economic integration the capacity of individual states to implement their own independent economic policies disappears completely. Central institutions substitute national ministries of the economy and national central banks as the centres of economic decision-making. In a complete economic integration the economies of the members states are regulated as if they were the economies of a unified nation: there is a common currency and common fiscal and financial system and national economic institutions become mere branches of the central institutions.

1.2.1 Economic integration in the EU

Any process of economic integration is difficult to achieve and requires not only an economic rationale, but also a strong political will. The fact that free trade areas only include the abolition of tariffs and quotas among members states and demand little or almost no economic harmonization make them attractive for groups of countries willing to share some of the benefits of free trade, but wary of giving up their economic independence. Indeed, most processes of economic integration in the past have been limited to the free trade area stage. This is the case, for example, of the European Free Trade Association (EFTA) and of many of the current multinational regional economic associations such as the North American Free Trade Association

(NAFTA), the Australia and New Zealand Closer Economic Relations and Trade Agreement (ANZCERTA), or the Association for Latin American Integration (LAIA). The original EC, at the time of the signing of the Treaty of Rome in 1957, was also a free trade area which gradually developed into a customs union as common foreign tariffs and quotas were agreed and common policies implemented in the early years of its existence (Table 1.1).

Few free trade areas lead to the establishment of customs unions. The fact that customs unions usually imply a much greater degree of institutional coordination than free trade areas and that the former are often regarded as a significant step towards economic union deters many nations from venturing into further integration. Only when one of the members with economic and political ascendancy in the free trade area pushes the others in that direction or when there is the political will in all member states to strengthen economic ties, are customs unions completed. The German *Zollverein* is an example of the former. In 1834 a series of German states set up a customs union which became the embryo of what was to be full economic integration a few decades later. The *Zollverein* was however a union of unequals. Prussia's political, military, and economic might in nineteenth century Germany allowed it to shape the *Zollverein* according to its own economic and political interests. The EC represented a form of customs union in which economic and political determination by all member states played a capital role. The signature of the Treaty of Rome in 1957, by which the EC was established, represents a negotiated agreement among equals to set up a customs union. However, the EC is the exception to the rule.

More often than not, free trade areas fail to make the passage to a customs union. Outside the EC, few economic associations have succeeded: MERCOSUR in Latin America is one of them, and NAFTA in North America has held discussions on the introduction of features of a customs union. But the transfer of powers and the loss of sovereignty to supranational bodies inherent in the formation of a customs union means that this stage of economic integration has seldom been achieved.

The even greater surrender of national economic sovereignty needed in order to establish common markets makes this form of economic integration rarer than customs unions. The EU was the first example of a common market freely agreed among sovereign nations. Yet, and despite being commonly known as the European Common Market throughout the 1970s and 1980s, it took the EC more than thirty years to become a real common market. Free mobility of goods, services, capital, and labour was only implemented—and still with restrictions and transition periods with regards to certain products and sectors—with the introduction of the Single European Market on the 1 January 1993 (Table 1.1).

But since then the new EU has burnt stages of economic integration much

Table 1.1 The stages of economic integration in the EU

Level of integration	Main features	Period
Free trade area	Free trade among members	From 1958 to the early 1960s
Customs union	Free trade with a common external tariff	in theory from 1958, in reality from the early 1960s until 1993
Common market	Free mobility of factors and assets across member states. No internal invisible trade restrictions	1993–1999
Economic union	Harmonization of economic policy	Early stages in 1993. Partial economic union in 1999
Economic integration	Completely unified economic policy	Not yet achieved

faster than before. As the Single Market was about to be implemented, the member states of the EU were already negotiating in Maastricht further forms of integration leading towards the establishment of an economic union. The agreement to proceed towards Economic and Monetary Union (EMU) was reached in this period and the early stages of harmonization of monetary policies and other economic policies aimed at preparing EU member states for EMU began to be implemented almost at the same time as the common market for certain goods, products, and services was being completed (Table 1.1). The new common currency—the Euro—was adopted by eleven member states of the EU on 1 January 1999. Greece joined two years later. And the process of economic integration—as well as that of political integration—is still under way. Negotiations in order to achieve a greater harmonization of fiscal policies are a sign that complete economic integration may be getting closer.

1.3 Economic integration as a means to achieve competitiveness

What are the reasons for the dramatic increase in momentum of economic integration during the late 1980s and 1990s? Why has a customs union which had experienced relatively little transformation during the first twenty-five years of its existence become first a common market and later an economic union in less than a decade?

There are many reasons that explain the gathering of pace of European economic integration during the last few years of the twentieth century, but all of them are linked to the process of economic globalization. Proponents of globalization underline that since the 1970s a new world economic system has emerged. The main feature of the new global economic system is the high mobility of capital, goods, labour, and, to a lesser extent, services across the world, marking a radical break with the post Second World War past of strong national economies (Gray, 1998; Beck, 2000). Firms and nations around the world compete for capital, customers, and labour in what is regarded to be an increasingly technology-led and volatile market (Dicken, 1998). If firms and nations are to be successful in this increasingly globalized market they have to adapt to the new economic environment and to be able to produce better quality products and services at lower prices. In other words, they have to learn to be competitive.

1.3.1 The limits of European competitiveness

But, were (and are) European firms competitive? Could an economically divided Europe compete and succeed in a globalized world? Across western Europe there was a widespread perception throughout the 1980s and early 1990s that the presence of nationally divided markets was seriously limiting the competitive capacity of European nations and firms in the global market-place. Whereas the US and Japan—the main competitors of the EC in a globalized economy—were large, unified, and relatively cohesive markets, the European market was extremely fragmented. Before the establishment of the Single Market, there where fifteen nationally divided markets within the EU, whose existence generated a series of costs which limited European global competitiveness. Member states, aware of the problem of increasing lack of competitiveness, gave the European Commission the task of solving the structural bottlenecks and of preparing the EC for the creation of a single market. The response from the European Commission to this challenge came in the form of a White Paper entitled *Completing the Internal Market* (1985). The White Paper set the bases for the establishment of a single market and led to the commissioning of a series of reports on different aspects of integration. The best known of these reports is the Cecchini report (1988), which evaluates the costs of having nationally fragmented markets—also known as the costs of the 'non-Europe'—and estimates the possible benefits of the Single Market. According to this report the existence of nationally fragmented markets generated three types of barriers to trade:

a) *Physical barriers*: linked to the presence of intra-EC border stoppages, controls at border checkpoints, red-tape, and the existence of different currencies;

b) *Technical barriers*: related to the use of different national product standards and technical regulations in every member state, to the presence of conflicting business laws, and of protected public procurement markets;

c) *Fiscal barriers*: linked to the lack of fiscal harmonization, ranging from contrasting income and corporate tax rates to differing value-added tax (VAT) rates and excise duties.

The following sub-sections elaborate on each of these types of barrier.

Physical barriers

Until recently intra-EU national boundaries not only delimited the borders between member-states, but also represented a series of barriers to trade and additional costs. The first of these physical costs were the customs related costs. Existing customs controls, border stoppages, as well as the paperwork and red tape associated with them represented a hefty penalty for the free mobility of goods within the EC. Intra-EC trade, and especially the exchange of low value-added and perishable goods, suffered as a result.

The presence of fragmented markets was also linked to high administrative costs and regulatory hassles. Companies willing to engage in trans-border trade had to deal with different national regulations and often with a significant amount of red tape in order to be able to sell their products in other western European countries. For large companies trading large volumes of goods and/or services this implied additional costs. But it was mainly the small and medium-sized (SMEs) companies which suffered the most from these administrative costs, since the costs of engaging in trans-border trade were a higher proportion of their volume of business. In addition, many SMEs lacked the expertise, the time, and adequate human resources to cope with the administrative costs of trade in fragmented markets, a fact that frequently prevented their international expansion.

Together with customs and related administrative costs, nationally fragmented markets brought about protected markets and protectionist procurement (Cecchini, 1988). Until recently countries in Europe had policies for protecting and subsidizing key industries. Fear of foreign dependence in sectors considered essential for the development of the country led to the setting up of the policy of national champions. Every country needed to have at least one public or private industry in every sector deemed to be of 'national strategic interest' and many sectors fell under this broad definition. These generally included petrochemical industries, shipbuilding, the iron and steel industry, car manufacturing, tobacco, telecommunications, air transport, military equipment, and often even chemical industries, information technology, and maritime transport. In some cases, basically in the telecommunications, air transport, and tobacco sectors, this was achieved by the establishment of protected markets and national monopolies. In other sectors national industries were set up and allowed to 'compete' in heavily protected national markets. A third option was to encourage the private sector to develop the industry, although private companies benefited from oligopolistic practices, large subsidies, and protectionist procurement practices by the state. The consequence of these policies of national champions was the emergence of monopolies in telecommunications (BT, France Télécom, Deutsche Telekom, SIP, Telefónica), air transport (British Airways, Lufthansa, Air France, Alitalia, Iberia, Olympic Airways, TAP), and other sectors, and of relatively large public and private companies in many others.

In spite of the fact that many of these companies managed to survive and even to prosper in nationally protected markets, excessive market fragmentation came at a price. The overall consequences of the presence of protected markets and industries were negative to Europe as a whole. Since economic protection meant that many of these companies faced no real external competition and did business in captive markets, there was no pressure for the majority of these firms to develop and/or use state-of-the-art technology or to produce according to international standards, or at internationally competitive prices. In certain sectors, such as shipbuilding and iron and steel, this resulted in underperforming industries, which often relied on subsidies and public contracts to remain in business. In other sectors, such as telecommunications or information technology, the situation contributed to a certain technological backwardness. And in all cases the existence of protected markets led to the excessive fragmentation of sectors in Europe in comparison to its American or Japanese competitors. The differences in the structure of the automobile sector between the US and the EC a couple of decades ago were a paradigmatic example of the effects of fragmented national markets with national champions policies. Although the car markets on both sides of the Atlantic were roughly similar in size, the American market was dominated by two large companies (General Motors and Ford) with a smaller third company (Chrysler) struggling to survive. Such a level of concentration allowed American companies to benefit from economies of scale and to develop larger technology projects. In contrast, the European panorama was much more divided. Each country had one or several national champions: Volkswagen in Germany; Fiat in Italy; Renault, Peugeot, and Citroën in France; Volvo and Saab in Sweden; Rover in Britain; Seat in Spain. If we add the many companies specialized in specific market niches (Daimler-Benz, BMW, and Porsche in

Germany; Alfa Romeo, Lancia, or Ferrari in Italy; Jaguar in Britain) and the numerous truck and van producers at the time, almost every country in Europe—bar the smallest ones—had its own national motor-vehicle industry. And even though excessive fragmentation did not prevent the automobile industry from competing outside European markets (especially in the luxury car sector), this was not the case in other sectors. In the computer hardware industry, for example, the attempts by governments to foster their own national champions ended in almost universal failure. By the mid-1980s many western European countries were trying to promote their own computer companies. Sweden had Ericsson, Germany relied on Siemens, Italy on Olivetti, France tried with Thomson, and even Greece had plans for its own computer industry. Even if all of these companies still exist—Ericsson is a formidable player in the mobile telephones industry, Thomson in the microelectronics sector, and Siemens and Olivetti are powerful industrial conglomerates—none of them is nowadays a major actor in the computer hardware industry.

Policies to promote national champions also resulted in the duplication and excessive fragmentation of public and private R&D efforts. Whereas American research programmes were highly concentrated and enjoyed large funding, European research programmes were conducted on a national basis and often competed against one another. The consequences were research redundancies and a suboptimal outcome of research investment in Europe, especially in comparison to the US or Japan (Emerson et al., 1988).

As a whole, consumers bore most of the costs of the existence of nationally fragmented markets. The existence of physical barriers to trade, red tape, protectionist and national champion policies generally resulted in higher prices for goods and services in the European markets than in larger markets, and fundamentally than in the US. This was especially the case in services, where restrictions to competition were higher. In the telecommunications market, fragmentation and national monopolies meant that European consumers had to pay higher telephone bills than their North American counterparts. Differences within the EC were also important and often related to the different policies adopted in each country. Countries such as Italy and Spain tended to subsidize local calls by increasing the cost of long distance calls, whereas an early liberalization of the telecommunications markets brought the cost of long distance calls in Britain to the lowest levels in Europe. Higher telephone costs than in the US affected not only the consumers' pockets, but also the competitiveness of European companies in a global marketplace, and contributed to a relatively slow European start on the internet. Another market where consumers and companies were penalized by high prices was the air transport market. The control of European skies by national governments and air carriers until the mid-1990s was translated into higher air fares for passengers, as a result of the absence of real competition. Many other sectors, such as the car, home, and health insurance sector, or road and railway transport, had similar problems. In addition, European consumers also had to bear an enhanced cost of commodities and manufacturing products generated by protected industries.

The final physical barrier was the existence of different national currencies, which represented additional costs for the development of economic activity. Most of these costs were transaction costs, that is the cost of exchanging currencies. The transactions costs involved in exchanging currencies were deadweight losses for consumers and firms (De Grauwe, 1997). Apart from direct transaction costs, the existence of different national currencies had other additional costs like the presence of price discrimination between national markets or the higher cost of holding higher international reserves. In addition, the existence of different national currencies had extra costs in the form of higher interest rates and lower FDI for peripheral nations, as a consequence of their exchange rate volatility, their greater market instability, and the greater risk of devaluation (Hitiris, 1998; Darby *et al.* 1999). Finally, the existence of different currencies and the transaction costs of exchanging currencies and having to deal with different regulations and bureaucratic practices contributed to deter consumers and firms from purchasing cheaper goods and services in other countries.

Technical barriers

The second sort of barriers for European consumers and firms were divergent national product standards, different technical regulations, and conflicting business laws. Although originally designed for other purposes, such as to increase health and safety, technical regulations and national product standards became powerful instruments for market protectionism. The implementation of incompatible technical regulations and product standards in a fragmented market led to the establishment of different electricity systems for home appliances, different television systems, different telephone systems, and even to driving on a different side of the road in different European countries. The implementation of these non-tariff barriers not only represented problems for consumers, who could not take their television sets from Italy to the UK, or who had to buy different plugs or adapters for their electric razors when on holiday or moving across countries, but also added considerable costs for European firms which had to adapt their products to the different national standards (Cecchini, 1988). In contrast, American firms could profit from the economies of scale of having to service a large market with homogeneous technical regulations and a single national standard. Once again, SMEs were the prime victims of this sort of non-tariff barriers, since they were more vulnerable to the costs of coping with changing standards across borders and of the duplication of product development related to them than large firms.

Another technical barrier was the existence of protected public-sector procurement and construction markets. In most European countries government supply and construction contracts were restricted to national firms, and, whenever there were no legal restrictions for foreign bidders, technical regulations often discriminated against them. This situation closed large sections of the public sector market to international competition.

Fiscal barriers

The third set of barriers which limited the competitiveness of European firms were of a fiscal nature. The lack of fiscal harmonization within the EC meant different fiscal regimes within the EC for individuals and firms and different rates in indirect taxes, such as VAT. The result of such a variegated panorama was that companies had to cope with and adapt to different fiscal regimes and accounting standards across countries. Subsidiaries of multinational firms often had to duplicate or triplicate their accounting standards in order to cope with the demands of the parent company and the national system of each branch's host country. In addition, as the Cecchini report (1988) underlines, the transnational daily exchange of goods, assets, and know-how between the parent company and the branch or among branches often aroused the suspicion of national authorities trying to prevent tax evasion. This 'fiscal suspicion' limited the flexibility of companies and provoked additional costs in order to respond to national fiscal legislation and the demands of national tax authorities (Cecchini, 1988).

The combination of physical, technical, and fiscal barriers represented an important burden for all those economic actors willing to engage in international trade. The additional costs incurred by companies and individuals doing cross-border deals were a deterrent for many companies, which were thus confined to their national markets. The costs associated with market fragmentation were related both to the size of the actors and the size of the market. In terms of the size of the economic actors, individuals and SMEs stood to lose most from market segmentation, since they had to bear a higher percentage of the costs of engaging in trans-border deals. Large companies were also disadvantaged, especially *vis-à-vis* similar companies trading in the American or Japanese markets. However, thanks to economies of scale, their burden was relatively smaller than that of SMEs.

In terms of the size of markets, firms located in smaller markets were the most vulnerable to fragmented markets. Companies in Ireland, Portugal, or Greece could not rely exclusively on the dynamism of their internal markets and needed to expand internationally if they were to prosper. With national markets that barely exceed 1 per cent of the European market (Table 1.2), their internal markets lacked the scale to allow for long-term expansion, especially in sectors which needed advanced technology or large investments. German, French, or even firms from the integrated market of the Benelux were, in contrast, in a much better position to compete. Their much larger internal markets allowed for greater expansion. However, taken individually, the size of the different European national markets had become too small to compete in a globalized world. Table 1.2 compares the size of national economies in the EU with those of the US and Japan in the year 2000. Although the strength of the US dollar with respect to the Euro in that year led to an overvaluation of the size of the US economy, the Table gives a clear indication of the difference in size between the American and Japanese economy and that of individual EU countries. In 2000 the US economy was 26 per cent larger than those of all the EU member states put together. The size of the Japanese economy was roughly half that of the US and 40 per cent below the size of the total size of the EU economy (Table 1.2). Taken individually, every single economy in the EU was too small to rival that of the US or Japan. The size of the German economy—by far the largest in Europe—was less than one fifth that of the US (Table 1.2) and two and a half times smaller than that of Japan. The UK, the second largest European economy when measured in a common currency, only represented one seventh, and that of France around 13 per cent of that of the US (Table 1.2). Nine of the fifteen EU national economies did not even reach 5 per cent of the size of the US economy (Table 1.2).

In sum, the existence of nationally fragmented markets represented a serious competitive cost for the European economy in terms of its capacity to reach the adequate economies of scale to compete with large integrated markets such as the US or the Japanese market.

1.3.2 The expected benefits of economic integration

If the existence of fragmented markets posed a serious threat for European competitiveness in a globalized economy, many believed—with the European Commission among them—that economic integration offered a solution to the problem. The increasing globalization of the world economy and the simultaneous transformation of developed nations from mass-production to increasingly technology-driven flexible production economies had led to widespread concern about the possible loss of competitiveness of European firms and nations. The basic tenet was that excessive market fragmentation within the European scale was reducing economies of scale and thus obstructing the structural reforms needed to adjust to global challenges. Market integration was thus a response to the recognition of the necessity of greater

Table 1.2 Total GDP in the EU, the US, and Japan, 2000

Country	Total GDP in 2000 (billions of €)	% of the EU economy
Austria	205.5	2.42
Belgium	244.0	2.87
Denmark	174.2	2.05
Finland	131.2	1.54
France	1 399.2	16.47
Germany	2 036.0	23.97
Greece	120.7	1.42
Ireland	101.1	1.19
Italy	1 152.3	13.57
Luxembourg	19.9	0.23
Netherlands	399.1	4.70
Portugal	112.3	1.32
Spain	605.7	7.13
Sweden	248.8	2.93
United Kingdom	1 543.0	18.17
European Union	8 493.0	100.00
United States	10 738.7	126.44
Japan	5 163.2	60.79

Source: EUROSTAT data.

European competitiveness, since integration would have triggered an increase in the size of the European market, a reduction of the costs of trade, a removal of structural bottlenecks, and economic restructuring. Hence from the mid-1980s the EC embarked on a process of economic integration—still under way—which reached its high points in 1993 with the implementation of the European Single Market and in 1999 with the introduction of the Euro, the European single currency.

According to many *ex ante* studies carried out by the European Commission and independent economists, market integration would have led to important cost-saving effects. The Cecchini report (1988: 17) identified three major areas for cost savings resulting from market integration:

a) the 'static trade effect': the benefits reaped from allowing public authorities to buy from the cheapest (i.e. foreign) suppliers;

b) the 'competition effect': the introduction of greater international competition was expected to provoke downward pressure on prices charged by domestic firms in sectors where competition was previously restricted, as a result of the entry of foreign firms in the market;

c) the 'restructuring effect': resulting from the reorganization of industrial sectors and companies under the pressure of the new competitive conditions, which generate economies of scale and greater efficiency.

Other possible benefits of market integration identified by the Cecchini report included the 'savings for private sector buyers who pay less for goods ... whose prices have been reduced by the break-up of restrictive trade practices in the public sector' (1988: 17) and the dynamic effects of greater competition on innovation, investment, and growth. In addition, market integration was expected to generate significant savings for the public sector. These savings included cuts in government subsidies, especially in the support for inefficient firms, and a European-wide rationalization of R&D expenditure.

The combination of all these cost-saving effects was expected to lead to two different kind of benefits: the direct benefits of the eradication of economic frontiers and the indirect benefits resulting from the process of economic restructuring, increases in trade and competition, and greater economies of scale (Tsoukalis, 1993; El-Agraa, 1998). Although, in the short term the direct benefits were expected to outstrip the indirect benefits, in the long run the indirect effects would contribute to the emergence of virtuous cycles of innovation and competition (Tsoukalis, 1993). Together with the microeconomic consequences of the completion of the Single Market, important macroeconomic benefits could also be expected. These benefits would be generated by the opening up of the national public procurement markets and the liberalization of services.

The expected outcomes of the Single Market were thus a lowering of prices as a consequence of greater competition and a greater concentration of resources which would ultimately lead to an increase of consumer purchasing power, a rise in investment, greater job creation, and an improvement in the competitiveness of European firms and companies.

The setting up of the single currency is aimed at bringing additional cost-saving effects, ranging from substantial direct savings derived from the elimination of transactions costs, to indirect benefits related to the better functioning of the internal European markets. The Euro is also likely to generate welfare gains and greater growth from eliminating uncertainty and currency exchanges risks. On the whole the expected benefits of the single currency include positive effects on trade and investment and the possibility of reinforcing Europe's economic role in the world.

Some authors—especially those involved in the early stages of the Single Market—have tried to estimate the potential gains of economic integration in

Europe. The Cecchini report (1988) predicted the gains from the completion of the Single Market to be in the range between 174 to 258 billion €, which, at the time of the report, represented approximately 4 to 7 per cent of the EC's GDP. Emerson *et al.* (1988) calculated gains between 4 and 6 per cent of GDP. Most of these gains would have been accrued as a consequence of the effects of the Single Market on production costs. Additional benefits would come in the form of trade costs, economies of scale, and competition effects (Emerson *et al.*, 1988). Baldwin (1989) was even bolder than Cecchini and Emerson and estimated that the gains from the Single Market could be between three and a half and five times larger, as he considered not just the possible rise in output, but also the long-term effect on growth as a result of increasing the stock of capital. Researchers analysing the possible impact of EMU have been, in contrast, much more reluctant to give estimations of the expected benefits.

1.4 The impact of economic integration

Has European economic integration delivered the benefits predicted by its proponents? Has the EU experienced since 1993 the increases in trade, the more efficient allocation of resources, and the greater growth and welfare gains expected from economic integration? Have European nations and firms become more competitive?

This section of the chapter gives an overview of the recent economic evolution in the areas of trade and foreign direct investment (FDI), economies of scale, productivity, and growth in the EU in order to try to identify if the optimistic predictions of the *ex ante* analyses have been fulfilled.

1.4.1 Trade and FDI

During the 1990s trade has experienced a sizeable increase across the European Union. Exports of goods and services rose from levels of 26.8 per cent of EU GDP in 1988 to 31.73 per cent in 1997 (Table 1.3). Similarly, imports went from representing 26.06 per cent of European GDP in 1988 to 29.25 per cent in 1997.

The 5 point rise in the share of exports as a share of the EU's GDP and the three point expansion in imports represent a greater level of trade creation in absolute terms than in any other developed area of the world. Export expansion in the US in the same period was 3.10 per cent of GDP, whereas in Japan a mere 1.09 per cent (Table 1.3). Import expansion in the US and Japan was 2.2 and 2.15 per cent of GDP respectively. However, if we take into account the relative change in trade creation rather than the expansion in

Table 1.3 Exports of goods and services as a share of GDP

	1988	1991	1994	1997	Change 1988–97	% Change
EU	26.80	26.26	27.79	31.73	4.93	18.40
US	8.99	10.37	10.54	12.09	3.10	34.48
Japan	10.02	10.19	9.27	11.11	1.09	10.88
OECD	17.31	17.89	17.92	21.02	3.71	21.43

Source: EUROSTAT data.

absolute terms, the picture changes. Exports in the US grew at a greater pace than in the EU (Table 3.1) and both the US and Japan experienced greater growth than the EU in imports. As a whole, during the 1990s trade creation in the EU was greater than in other European countries, such as Switzerland, Norway, or Iceland, which did not participate in the process of economic integration. Export growth in the EU—but not import growth—also exceeded that of the countries of central and eastern Europe, with the exception of Hungary. Overall, it can be said that the evolution of European trade in a world context has been rather disappointing, especially in comparison with that of countries like Canada or Mexico which have undergone a much milder process of regional economic integration.

At the national level no clear pattern seems to emerge. Some countries with already open economies at the end of the 1980s, such as Ireland, have experienced a significant increase in trade. Less open countries, like Finland, Sweden, Spain, or Italy have also witnessed considerable trade creation. Yet, not all economies in the EU have benefited equally from the removal of trade barriers. The ratio of exports as a share of GDP has declined in four countries—Germany, Greece, Luxembourg, and Portugal—between 1988 and 1997. Luxembourg, Greece, and Portugal have also seen their share of imports decline. This lack of a clear pattern in the evolution of trade suggests that the supposed greater territorial specialization associated with greater economic integration has not yet happened. European integration has been accompanied by an increase in intra-industry trade. In contrast, the expansion of inter-industry trade has been less important (CEPII, 1997). The relative stability of inter-industry trade has prevented a further concentration of capital intensive industries in core countries to the detriment of the European periphery. In fact, former lagging countries such as Spain and, above all, Ireland have profited from economic integration to expand trade and attract capital-intensive industries. Portugal and Greece have been less successful. However, the level of intra-industry trade suggests that the expected specialization within the EU may be starting to happen within sectors rather than across sectors (CEPII, 1997).

Although often trade and foreign direct investment go hand in hand, economic integration during the 1990s seems to have had an even lower impact on FDI trends than on trade. Net inflows of FDI into EU countries have tended to oscillate more with economic cycles than as a result of reform and economic integration. Table 1.4 reports the FDI net inflows into the EU, the US, and Japan as a percentage of GDP. All other factors being equal, the Single Market does not seem to have led to an increase in the inflows of FDI to the EU. Inflows of FDI reached their peak at the apex of the economic cycle around 1990, just before the implementation of the Single Market, and have since followed a downward trend. When compared to the US, relative the net inflows of FDI into the EU have declined with respect to the period before 1993. FDI represented 1.46 per cent of GDP in the EMU area in 1990 and fell to only 0.83 in 1997. Inflows of FDI into the US have followed an opposite trend rising from 0.86 per cent in 1990 to 1.19 per cent in 1997 (Table 1.4).

Table 1.4 FDI net inflows as a percentage of GDP

Country	1980	1985	1990	1994	1997
Austria	0.30	0.26	0.41	1.08	1.20
Belgium	—	—	—	—	—
Denmark	—	0.19	0.85	3.31	1.70
Finland	0.05	0.21	0.60	1.53	1.78
France	0.49	0.50	1.10	1.19	1.65
Germany	—	—	—	0.09	−0.02
Greece	1.38	1.10	1.21	0.99	0.86*
Ireland	1.43	0.83	1.38	1.55	3.63
Italy	0.13	0.25	0.59	0.21	0.32
Luxembourg	—	—	—	—	—
Netherlands	1.33	1.17	4.35	2.23	2.42
Portugal	0.55	1.16	3.78	1.44	1.68
Spain	0.70	1.19	2.84	1.94	1.04
Sweden	0.20	0.39	0.86	3.16	4.33
United Kingdom	1.88	1.20	3.33	0.90	2.96
EMU area	0.50	0.56	1.46	0.75	0.83
United States	0.62	0.49	0.86	0.66	1.19
Japan	0.03	0.05	0.06	0.02	0.08

* Data from 1996.   Source: World Bank World Development Indicators (2000).

The evolution of FDI has varied enormously across European countries. Only in Austria, Denmark, Finland, Ireland, and Sweden have inflows of FDI experienced a significant increase during the period since the implementation of the Single Market. In the Austrian, Finnish, and Swedish cases, the increase in FDI—as was the case in the previous decade for Portugal and Spain—may be more related to EU membership than to the effects of economic integration. In contrast, in all other EU countries, bar France, net inflows of FDI as a percentage of GDP have declined. The highest declines have occurred in the Netherlands, Portugal, and Spain (Table 1.4).

The 1990s have also brought about a change in FDI. FDI flows among EU member states, which dominated before the completion of the Single Market, have lost some of their previous importance. For the first time in 1996, FDI outflows from the EU to the rest of the world exceeded those within the EU. This may be a sign of the pressures of globalization and of the need to get positions in world markets, but also a symptom of an early waning of the effects of economic integration. Economic recovery and EMU led to a new upturn in FDI in the late 1990s, but it is still early to see if this reversal of trends will be sustained in the long run.

1.4.2 Economies of scale

Another area where economic integration was predicted to have a clear impact is that of economies of scale. *Ex ante* reports frequently highlighted that economic integration was expected to bring about a more efficient concentration of resources, preventing duplication and thus generating economies of scale. European firms were supposed to be the main beneficiaries of these trends.

Competition linked to the Single Market and the establishment of the single currency was supposed to trigger a restructuring effect leading to economies of scale, technology transfers, employment creation, and greater efficiency by European companies. This restructuring effect seems to be taking place. The number of mergers and acquisitions (M&As) in the EU increased by more than two and a half times between 1987 and 1998, from 2775 to 7600 (Table 1.5). The bulk of this increase happened however in anticipation of the Single Market and was partially related to the evolution of the economic cycle. The economic boom of the late 1980s and early 1990s contributed to the wave of mergers and acquisitions which lasted until 1990 (Table 1.5). Since 1990, the total number of mergers and acquisitions in the EU has remained relatively stable, closely following the economic cycle (European Economy, 1999).

However, the stability in the numbers of mergers and acquisitions throughout much of the 1990s hides two profound transformations: the internationalization and the increasing total volume of M&As (European Economy, 1999).

Table 1.5 Total number and percentage of national, European, and international mergers and acquisitions, 1987–1998

	1987	1990	1993	1996	1998
Number	2775	7003	5740	6327	7600
% National	71.6	60.7	63.4	55.7	50.1
% EU	9.6	21.5	15.9	17.4	16.5
% International	18.8	17.8	20.7	26.9	33.4

Source: AMDATA in European Economy (1999).

Whereas in 1987 M&As involving companies from the same European state represented more than 70 per cent of the total, by the end of the 1990s the percentage of national mergers had fallen to slightly above 50 per cent (Table 1.5). The emergence of cross-border M&As has taken place in two stages. The first stage happened during the late 1980s in anticipation of the Single Market and mainly involved companies from two different European member states. The percentage of intra-EU M&As increased from levels of 9.6 per cent in 1987 to 21.5 per cent in 1990. Meanwhile, the percentage of M&As involving a company from outside the EU remained stable and even declined slightly (Table 1.5). The second wave of internationalization—or, in this case, of globalization—of European companies has taken place in the wake of EMU. Whereas the level of European M&As hovered at around 16 per cent of the total between 1993 and 1998, the percentage of M&As involving at least one overseas company almost doubled between 1990 and 1998. In that year, one third of all M&As involved at least one non-EU partner (Table 1.5).

The second feature of the process during the 1990s has been the increasing volume of the deals. The total volume of inward cross-border M&As involving companies in the EU has been multiplied by almost six between 1991 and 1998. An even greater expansion has occurred in EU outward cross-border M&As (Table 1.6). Cross-border M&As picked up pace towards the end of the 1990s, with the volume of inward cross-borders M&As almost doubling between 1997 and 1998 and that of outward M&As almost tripling in the same period (Table 1.6). The spiralling of the process in Europe may be related to the expected economies of scale linked to the launch of the Euro. However, it may also be propelled by the emergence of new global economic actors, resulting from the merger of large transnational companies (TNCs), which increasingly drive other companies to look for partners or acquisitions or to move towards restructuring, in order not to lose their market share and to increase their competitiveness (Kang and Johansson, 2000). Europe has not been isolated from this process. Despite the fact that many of the M&As still involve companies from just one country, such as in the case of the merger of the British chemical firms SmithKline Beecham and Glaxo Wellcome, or the Italian firms Telecom Italia and Olivetti or Pagine Gialle and Tin.it, an increasing number of the largest mergers since the late 1990s have involved firms from different EU member states (Orange and Mannesman, Vodafone and Mannesman, Zeneca and Astra). And European firms are becoming more aggressive in the overseas market, as the deals between Terra and Lycos, or the takeovers of Chrysler by Daimler-Benz and of Amoco by British Petroleum indicate. M&As are becoming so important that they have started to dominate FDI flows in Europe.

Does this mean that European integration has been the driving force behind the increasing concentration of European companies? If we compare cross-border M&A activity in Europe and the US the figures point in other directions. Notwithstanding their recent boom, the growth of M&A activity in the EU has lagged behind that of the US. Growth of cross-border M&As in the US—despite still being lower in volume than in the EU—has clearly

Table 1.6 Volume of cross-border M&As (billion US$)

	Inward				
	1991	1994	1997	1998	Multiplier 1991–8
EU	38.7	58.4	133.6	223.4	5.8
Rest of Europe	4.1	7.4	14.6	17.6	4.3
North America	26.1	62.9	76.3	218.1	8.4
Rest of the World	16.4	67.7	116.5	98.9	6.0
Total	85.3	196.4	341.0	558.0	6.5
	Outward				
	1991	1994	1997	1998	Multiplier 1991–8
EU	50.5	75.3	127.5	330.6	6.5
Rest of Europe	3.4	18.2	42.1	14.4	4.2
North America	15.7	52.0	106.4	175.2	11.2
Rest of the World	15.7	50.9	65.0	37.8	2.4
Total	85.3	196.4	341.0	558.0	6.5

Source: KPMG Corporate Finance in Kang and Johansson (2000).

outstripped that of the EU during the 1990s (Table 1.6). The greater dynamism of North American firms becomes manifest when the regional share of inward and outward cross-border M&As, rather than absolute numbers, are considered (Table 1.7). During the 1990s, North American firms are the only ones that have gained ground both in inward and outward M&As. They increased their share of inward cross-border M&As between 1991 and 1998 by 8.5 per cent and that of outward M&As by 13 per cent. Most of this relative expansion has been at the expense of Japanese and South East Asian firms, countries that until the Asian crisis of 1997–98 were among the most aggressive in the field (Table 1.7). However, European firms have also lost out to North American firms: the EU share of outward M&As remained stable in that period, and that of inward M&As declined by 5.4 points (Table 1.7).

Moreover, the process of economic concentration and rationalization, to which economic integration has contributed, has not sufficed to hoist more

Table 1.7 Volume of cross-border M&As (billion US$)

	Inward				
	1991	1994	1997	1998	Change 1991–8
EU	45.4	29.7	39.2	40.4	−5.4
Rest of Europe	4.8	3.8	4.4	3.1	−1.7
North America	30.6	32.0	22.4	39.1	8.5
Rest of the World	19.2	24.5	34.0	17.8	−1.4
Total	100.0	100.0	100.0	100.0	0.0
	Outward				
	1991	1994	1997	1998	Change 1991–8
EU	59.3	38.4	37.4	59.3	0.0
Rest of Europe	3.9	9.3	12.4	2.5	−1.4
North America	18.4	26.5	31.9	31.4	13.0
Rest of the World	18.4	24.8	18.3	6.8	−11.6
Total	100.0	100.0	100.0	100.0	0.0

Source: KPMG Corporate Finance in Kang and Johansson (2000).

Table 1.8 Location of the world's largest fifty corporations

	United States	Europe	Japan	Other
1960	42	8	0	0
1970	32	14	4	0
1980	23	19	5	3
1990	17	21	10	2
2000	15	16	19	0

Source: Fortune Global 500.

European firms into the group of the world's largest companies. In 2000 the EU had fewer companies among the top fifty in the world than in 1990 (Table 1.8) and only one European company (Daimler-Chrysler) was in the top ten. It seems somewhat ironic that the expansion of the number of European companies among the world's largest fifty occurred fundamentally during the 1960s and 1970s, a period of strongly fragmented national markets, and that it decreased during the peak of integration (Table 1.8).

The economies of scale resulting from the increasing concentration of European firms can thus be attributed more to the process of globalization and to macroeconomic, industry-level, and technology-related factors than to European integration. The Single Market and EMU may be triggering a restructuring of firms and may have fostered the increasing numbers of cross-border M&As that the EU has witnessed during the 1990s, and especially since 1997 (Kang and Johansson, 2000). But then again, the process is not dissimilar to what has been experienced in other parts of the world, and especially in the US.

1.4.3 Productivity

Another area where European integration is supposed to yield benefits is that of labour productivity. Greater competition, the restructuring of firms, and the benefits of greater economies of scale and agglomeration are expected to deliver an increase in labour productivity and make workers in the EU more competitive with respect to their American and Japanese counterparts.

For much of the period since the end of the Second World War, labour productivity in western European countries has been below that of the US and Japan. However, and despite the existence of fragmented national markets, European countries have managed to close the productivity gap with the US during much of the period. Figure 1.1 represents labour productivity growth in the EU, the US, and Japan between 1960 and 2000. Labour productivity growth in the EU during much of the early stages lagged behind that of Japan, but was clearly above that of the US. As a result, labour productivity in the EU converged on that of the US during the 1960s, 1970s, and early 1980s. Productivity convergence is also observed at the national level. Productivity in France outstripped that of the US as early as 1980 (Figure 1.2). Italy and Spain

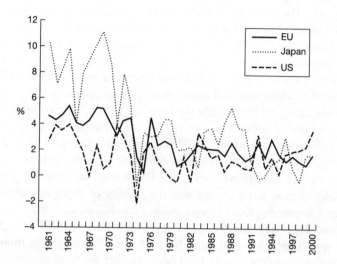

Figure 1.1 Labour productivity growth in the EU, the US, and Japan, 1960–2000
Source: EUROSTAT data.

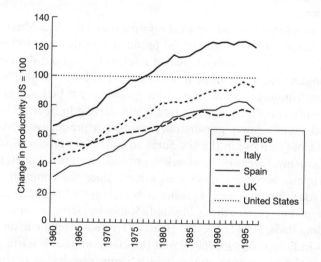

Figure 1.2 Evolution of labour productivity in selected European countries with respect to the US
Source: World Bank World Development Indicators (2000).

also closed the gap significantly. In the Spanish case labour productivity, which was barely more than one quarter of that of the US in 1960, rose to levels above 80 per cent of in the early 1990s. The UK also managed to close the productivity gap, albeit in a rather less spectacular fashion (Figure 1.2).

Labour productivity convergence on US rates came, however, to an end around 1985 (Figures 1.1. and 1.2). Several factors contributed to the halt in convergence. The first one was the increasing technology gap between the US and Europe. The personal computer and the internet revolutions have been led from the US. The US government and large US corporations were able to spend more than their European counterparts on R&D, a factor that contributed to give the US a technological edge with respect to Europe. Fragmented markets, national monopolies or oligopolies, or simply national champions facing relatively little competition within their national markets often prevented the development of new technologies or even access to them in Europe. As a result, the diffusion across Europe of some of the technologies behind recent trends in economic growth, such as computers and the internet, was slower than in the US. A third factor in the productivity slowdown in western Europe was the rigidity of European labour markets (see Chapter 5). Rigid labour market conditions and strict and costly regulations on hiring and firing employees not only resulted in high levels of structural unemployment, but also kept much of the young innovation-prone European talent out of the labour market for long periods of time. The US, in contrast, based their productivity growth during the same period on the capacity to generate and assimilate innovation of a younger labour force.

European integration and national reforms have tried to address some of the inefficiencies at the bottom of the productivity slowdown in Europe. As we will see in Chapter 5, labour market reforms throughout the 1990s have made labour markets in Europe more flexible. The Single Market and EMU are also contributing to solve some of the problems that besieged innovation in Europe prior to the 1990s. The results are starting to be felt. During the 1990s and despite lower growth rates, European productivity levels have remained close to those in the US. Some so-called 'old economy' countries, such as Germany, have performed well in productivity terms. But even in high tech, Europe is becoming more competitive. Since the completion of the Single Market there has been a greater concentration of the R&D effort in a few areas of Europe. Southern England, Southern Germany, and the areas surrounding Paris, Stockholm, and Helsinki are becoming the main technology poles in Europe (Quah, 2001). And this concentration is starting to bear fruit. In mobile communications—which many perceive as the motor of growth in the future—Europe now has the edge. Most mobile technology is European. The largest mobile phone manufacturers are Nokia (Finnish) and

Ericsson (Swedish), whereas the majority of mobile phone microprocessors are manufactured by ARM (a British company) (Hauser, 2001).

Although it is still relatively early to say whether European labour productivity is, once again, going to start growing faster than American productivity, European integration and labour market reforms seem at least to be contributing to allowing Europe to become more competitive in this realm than it was in the 1980s.

1.4.4 Economic Growth

But perhaps the most important question is to try to assess whether European economic integration will allow Europe to keep up with the pace of its competitors and, perhaps, outgrow them. The main objective of European integration is to achieve greater economic competitiveness in order to rival the economic might and dynamism of the US and Japan. The success of this objective should ultimately be reflected in economic growth rates. But, as in the case of trade, economies of scale, and productivity, the empirical evidence is far from clear. In the post-war era, the EU has not been a star performer among the developed economies. As in the case of productivity growth, economic growth in the EU has lagged behind that of Japan during the post-war decades, and, although since the 1960s growth in the EU slightly outstrips that of the US, most of the difference in favour of Europe dates back to the 1960s (Figure 1.3). Growth in the EU has been lower than at least in one of its

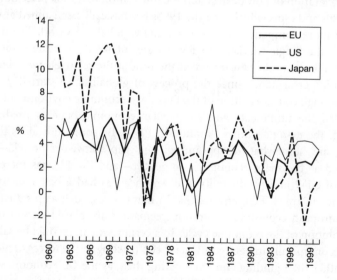

Figure 1.3 Economic growth in the EU, US, and Japan, 1960–2000
Source: EUROSTAT data.

competitors in every decade since the 1960s. The 1960s, 1970s, and 1980s were Japanese decades; the 1990s has been the decade of the US (Figure 1.3). The economic gap in favour of the US has grown since the 1970s (Table 1.9).

And the growth gap between the US and the EU has reached its highest level since the implementation of the Single Market. Between 1993 and 2000 growth in the US outpaced growth in the EU by more than 70 per cent (Table 1.9). This gap is, however, significantly reduced when GDP per capita growth instead of real GDP growth is considered.

If there is one feature that describes European national economic performance since the implementation of the Single Market and during the early stages of EMU, it is its heterogeneity. Some countries have performed extremely well. Growth in Ireland—recently dubbed the 'Celtic Tiger'—has more than doubled that of the US between 1993 and 2000 (Table 1.9). Finland and Luxembourg have also outpaced the US. Yet, the nations that make up the European core have had a dismal relative economic performance during the same period. Growth rates in Germany and Italy have been less than half those of the US. France barely exceeds that threshold and, among the four largest economies in the EU, only growth in Britain has exceeded the EU average (Table 1.9).

1.5 Conclusion

The acceleration of European economic integration that took place during the late 1980s and especially during the 1990s has basically been aimed at making the EU more competitive in an increasingly globalized world. The development of the Single Market and EMU were intended to tackle some of the structural bottlenecks which were at the root of the relatively poor European economic performance since the process of globalization started. However, this thorough transformation of the European economic environment has not produced the immediate and spectacular economic benefits predicted by some of the *ex-ante* studies (Vanhoudt, 1999). By some indicators the early results are somewhat disappointing: the gap between the US—always regarded as the main economic competitor—and the EU has increased in terms of GDP and productivity and America has had a better relative performance in trade, FDI, and M&As. In many areas, such as productivity or FDI, European economic integration seems to have played second fiddle to the evolution of the economic cycle. To a certain extent, it could be said that a more economically integrated EU has been reacting to the forces of globalization rather than guiding and anticipating then, as the US economy seems to have done during much of the 1990s.

It is, nevertheless, too early to conclude that European economic

Table 1.9 Average growth rates in the EU, the US, and Japan, 1960–2000

	Average growth rates per period				
	1960–70	1970–80	1980–90	1990–2000	1993–2000
Austria	4.72	3.64	2.31	2.09	2.03
Belgium	4.91	3.39	2.05	2.08	2.15
Denmark	4.50	2.18	1.58	2.17	2.50
Finland	4.84	3.50	3.09	2.08	3.80
France	5.57	3.31	2.47	1.81	1.95
Germany	4.47	2.74	2.26	1.90	1.48
Greece	8.55	4.71	0.70	2.32	2.43
Ireland	4.21	4.74	3.59	6.62	7.63
Italy	5.72	3.62	2.23	1.49	1.59
Luxembourg	3.56	2.65	4.51	5.56	5.63
Netherlands	5.08	2.98	2.20	2.88	3.06
Portugal	6.48	4.80	3.19	2.55	2.59
Spain	7.36	3.55	3.01	2.44	2.68
Sweden	4.65	1.98	2.02	1.69	2.43
United Kingdom	2.92	1.97	2.69	2.18	2.90
European Union	4.86	3.02	2.42	2.02	2.16
United States	4.25	3.28	3.20	3.21	3.69
Japan	10.17	4.47	4.01	1.27	0.99

Source: EUROSTAT data.

integration is not yielding the expected positive economic effects, first, because the differences in the economic cycle may be at least partially responsible for the observed differences in economic performance between the US and Europe. At the time of the completion of the European Single Market, the US economy was beyond the trough of the economic recession of the early 1990s, whereas most western European economies were only entering it. At the beginning of the twenty-first century, the economies of the EU seem, in contrast, in better shape than the American economy. A second factor to take into account is the time frame. European economic integration may be setting the foundations for a quicker future adaptation by the EU to global economic challenges. There are already some encouraging signs and the real effects of integration will only come to light in the near future. If these effects are broadly positive, the first decade of the twenty-first century may well be a European decade.

2

Cohesion

2.1 Introduction

Have the benefits of economic integration been evenly distributed? Or have some countries and regions benefited more than others? National and regional disparities have always existed in Europe. However, recent economic processes—including the whole process of economic integration—are changing the traditional map of economic disparities. Some nations and regions seem to be making the most of the new economic conditions, whereas other areas are declining. Most dynamic areas include those regions that have found their specific competitive edge or market niche in an increasingly globalized world. These comprise capital regions, many intermediate areas, and some peripheral countries (and most notably Ireland). Declining regions tend to be located in the traditional industrial cores and in many areas of the periphery.

The EU has introduced the objective of economic and social cohesion into its Treaty in order to tackle and prevent the growth of internal disparities within its territory. As a direct consequence of this objective, the EU has reformed and expanded its regional policy and set up a cohesion fund. The question is to what extent these policies have been effective. This chapter addresses the questions of how the process of European integration is affecting the evolution of national and regional disparities within the EU and what is being done to tackle those disparities. Finally, the effectiveness of regional policies is briefly assessed.

2.2 National and regional disparities in the EU

The EU is—together with the US and Japan—one of the three most developed spaces in the world. Its GDP per capita is below that of the US and Japan, but well above any other large area of the world. It is also, after NAFTA, the world's second largest economic space in terms of trade and scores extremely well in a series of development indicators. Economic wealth and development are, however, not evenly distributed across the EU. National and regional economic disparities have always existed and internal contrasts in terms of wealth, levels of development, and socio-economic dynamism are evident.

Until recently a core/periphery structure was clearly discernible. The core included the ten states that in 1985 had levels of GDP per capita above the EU average. Austria, Belgium, Denmark, Finland, France, Germany, the Netherlands, Luxembourg, Sweden, and the UK belonged to this group. Their GDP per capita, measured both in a common currency (the Euro) or—with the exception of the UK—in purchasing power standards (PPS) was above the EU average. Greece, Ireland, Portugal, and Spain, the four countries with the lowest GDP per capita, formed the periphery (Table 2.1). Italy, whose GDP per capita measured in ECUs—the ancestor of the current Euro—was below the EU average, but whose GDP per capita measured in PPS was above it, represented a special case. The north of the country, with GDP per capita levels similar to those of neighbouring Austria and France, could be considered as part of the core. In contrast, the south of Italy shared a similar GDP per capita with Spain or Greece, and, therefore, could be considered as a member of the periphery.

Differences between the core and the periphery were not only manifest in terms of GDP per head, but also in many other economic and social indicators. Countries in the core not only enjoyed higher GDP per capita than the remainder of the EU countries, they also had, as a general rule, higher employment rates, lower unemployment levels, and higher productivity rates than the periphery of Europe (Table 2.1).

Over the last few years the clear-cut core/periphery dichotomy has been somewhat eroded. The relatively poor economic performance of some of the countries of the core—in particular Finland, Germany, and Italy—and the high growth in some areas of the periphery, like Ireland, which in 2000 was the second richest country in the EU after Luxembourg, have contributed to blur the core/periphery pattern (Table 2.1).

Contrasts in GDP per capita, income, employment, and unemployment among countries hide even greater intranational contrasts. In 2001 the GDP per capita measured in PPS of the richest country in the EU, Luxembourg, was 2.7 times higher than that of the poorest country, Greece. In contrast, the GDP per capita of the EU's richest region, Inner London, was 5.8 times higher than that of the poorest region, Ipeiros in Greece. And even stronger contrasts were evident in other areas. Whereas in 1999 regions such as Calabria and Campania in Italy had unemployment rates of 28.7 and 26.8 per cent respectively, unemployment rates in Surrey (UK) or in the Aland Islands (Finland) were a mere 1.5 and 2.1 per cent (Table 2.2).

Table 2.1 National disparities in GDP per capita and unemployment in the EU, 1985–2000

	GDP per capita 1985			GDP per capita 2000		
	€ EU 15 = 100	PPS EU 15 = 100	Unemployment rate 1985 %	€ EU 15 = 100	PPS EU 15 = 100	Unemployment rate 2000 %
European Union	100.0	100.0	10.7	100.0	100.0	8.4
Austria	108.4	108.2	4.4	113.0	111.7	3.3
Belgium	102.3	105.5	8.9	106.2	110.7	8.6
Denmark	140.7	112.5	5.7	145.3	119.0	4.8
Finland	135.2	101.6	14.8	112.9	103.7	9.8
France	117.4	112.0	12.0	102.3	99.0	9.8
Germany	125.9	117.9	9.8	110.4	106.3	8.3
Greece	49.2	60.9	9.6	51.0	67.2	11.2
Ireland	65.9	60.9	10.1	118.9	118.8	4.2
Italy	91.9	101.5	12.3	89.0	98.7	10.5
Luxembourg	128.9	131.3	2.5	200.8	187.9	2.0
Netherlands	109.7	103.4	5.2	111.7	114.0	2.6
Portugal	29.1	55.1	6.7	50.0	75.7	4.0
Spain	53.8	70.5	21.1	68.4	83.0	14.2
Sweden	149.3	113.6	10.4	125.0	104.1	6.4
United Kingdom	100.1	98.4	7.1	115.2	103.1	5.6

Source: EUROSTAT data.

Table 2.2 Regional contrasts in GDP per capita and unemployment

GDP per capita (PPS) (EU 15 = 100)	1998	Unemployment (%)	1999
Inner London (UK)	243.4	Surrey (UK)	1.5
Hamburg (D)	185.5	Aland (SF)	2.1
Luxembourg (L)	175.8	Berks, Bucks, Oxon (UK)	2.1
Brussels (B)	168.8	Utrecht (NI)	2.3
Vienna (A)	162.8	Centro (P)	2.4
Oberbayern (D)	161.2	Luxembourg (L)	2.4
.	.	.	.
.	.	.	.
.	.	.	.
Anatoliki Makedonia (Gr)	55.4	Sardinia (I)	21.9
Peloponnisos (Gr)	52.7	Campania (I)	23.7
Dytiky Ellada (Gr)	52.6	Sicily (I)	24.8
Azores (P)	52.0	Extremadura (E)	24.8
Extremadura (E)	50.2	Andalusia (E)	26.8
Ipeiros (Gr)	41.8	Calabria (I)	28.7

Note:
A   Austria
B   Belgium
D   Germany
E   Spain
Gr   Greece
I   Italy
L   Luxembourg
NL   Netherlands
P   Portugal
SF   Finland
UK   United Kingdom
Source: EUROSTAT data.

Internal economic disparities were evident in almost every single country in the EU, bar Denmark, Luxembourg, and the Netherlands. The most flagrant case was Italy, where the GDP per capita of many regions of the south of the country—also known as the Mezzogiorno—was half that of the north of the country. Trentino-Alto Adige's GDP per capita, which in 1998 was 136.1 per cent of the EU average, more than doubled that of Calabria (60.7), Campania (64), Apulia (65.1), or Sicily (65.2). Regional disparities were also manifest in unemployment rates. Whereas Trentino-Alto Adige or Emilia-Romagna in the north enjoyed unemployment rates of 3.9 and 4.7 per cent respectively in 1999, unemployment in Campania, Calabria, and Sicily, in the

Mezzogiorno, was above 24 per cent. Strong internal disparities were also present in Portugal, France, and Spain. Other countries, such as Britain, Germany, or Sweden—where regional disparities have traditionally been lower— have also witnessed an increasing regional development gap in recent years (Figure 2.1).

The patterns of intranational disparities vary from country to country. In Belgium, Italy, and Portugal there is a north/south divide, with the most prosperous regions located in the north. Spain has a north east/south west divide (the same as France had in the past), whereas in Finland, Sweden, and the UK the richest regions tend to be in the south. Since reunification the

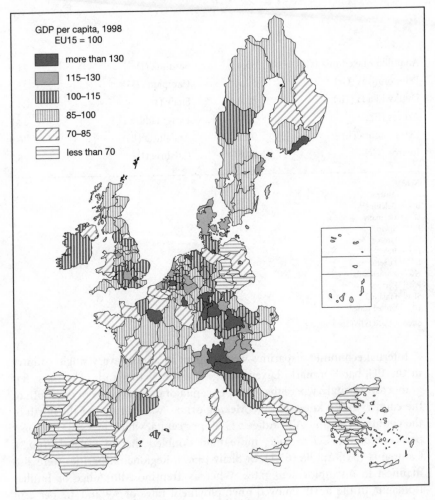

Figure 2.1 Regional GDP per capita in the EU, 1998

south/north divide in Germany has been transformed into a west/east one (Figure 2.1). At a European level the core is now located around the Alps. The highest GDP per capita rates are found between central and southern Germany (Frankfurt, Karlsruhe, Munich, Stuttgart) and northern Italy (Emilia-Romagna, Lombardy). Other high income pockets are found in the large capitals (Brussels, Copenhagen, Helsinki, London, Paris, and Stockholm). The poorest areas in the EU are found in Greece, Portugal, the extreme south of Italy, southwestern Spain, and the *Länder* (regions) of the former East Germany (Figure 2.1). The industrial declining regions of northern France, Wallonia in Belgium, and northern England are becoming peripheries within the core.

2.2.1 Factors behind the existence of territorial disparities

There are multiple factors which contribute to the existence and persistence of national and regional economic disparities in Europe. The first factor is linked to the inherited economic situation of countries and regions in the EU. Differences in levels of GDP per capita not only determine the relative level of development of every country and region, but also reflect long-term differences in other factors such as access to capital or investment which are considered basic elements in fostering economic growth.

The quantity and the quality of the available human resources—also known as human capital—further contribute to the genesis and persistence of economic disparities (Benhabib and Spiegel, 1994). The development potential of an area is related to its endowment in human capital (Chatterji, 1998). Areas with lower levels of GDP and economic growth tend to have a relatively poor endowment of human capital. Their stock of skilled labour—measured generally by the educational attainment or by the average years of education of the labour force—is often below that of neighbouring regions. The skills of the population are however not only related to educational attainment levels. The capacity and will of firms and institutions to provide on-the-job training is another factor influencing economic competitiveness. Lack of resources in lagging countries and regions often results in a lower provision of on-the-job training for workers. But even if, as is increasingly the case, the educational and skills deficit of lagging countries and regions is declining, other human capital related problems are appearing. Perhaps the most important of these new problems is the increasing mismatch between educational supply and labour demand. Future labour market entrants are receiving formal education in fields which have little or no outlets in local labour markets. This problem is not exclusive to peripheral nations and regions, but it is often more acute in lagging areas (Rodríguez-Pose, 1998).

The combination of a relatively poor endowment in human capital with an increasing mismatch between educational supply and labour demand is resulting in an inadequate use of existing human resources in many lagging European regions and nations. The high levels of unemployment, and especially of youth unemployment, in most of the European periphery are a reflection of the inadequacy of existing human resources to fulfil the tasks demanded by a more integrated and competitive economy, on the one hand, and of the incapacity of the local economies to absorb better prepared younger generations, on the other. The result is often increasing frustration and migration of the highly skilled.

Poor accessibility to many areas of the European periphery is another factor behind the existence of disparities in Europe. A good infrastructure endowment has traditionally been considered as one of the preconditions for economic development (Aschauer, 1989). Yet, the gap in accessibility and infrastructure endowment between the European core and its periphery is significant, regardless of the indicators used to measure infrastructure endowment. Keeble, Offord, and Walker (1988) in a study of European regions conducted in the 1980s estimated that some peripheral regions in Europe were seven times less accessible than core regions. More than a decade of heavy investment in infrastructure in peripheral countries and regions through the European Cohesion and Structural Funds have somewhat narrowed the gap, but differences between the core and the periphery remain important.

Poor physical accessibility is frequently associated with poor accessibility to information. Despite recent advances in telecommunications, many peripheral countries and regions in the EU still lag behind in their endowment of 'soft' infrastructure: i.e. modern telecommunications networks. Their access to information, which has become one of the key factors for economic growth in the 'new' or 'information' economy, is deficient and puts these areas at a disadvantage with respect to the core of Europe.

In a world in which technology has become one of the motors of economic development, the capacity to generate and/or adopt innovation is increasingly linked to the economic success of every space (Trajtenberg, 1990). Nations and regions with high investment in basic and applied research by the public and private sectors have a greater development potential. In contrast, the lack of basic and applied research is linked to a low capacity to generate innovation. In the European context, the gap between the core and the periphery in research and development (R&D) expenditure is once again evident. Whereas Finland, France, Germany, Sweden, and the UK spend regularly more than 2 per cent of their GDP in R&D, Greece, Portugal, and Spain do not even reach 1 per cent (Rodríguez-Pose, 2001). The technology and innovation deficit can be somewhat overcome by territories with a high capacity to assimilate innovation generated elsewhere. The early stages of development in Japan and in the Asian Dragons were mainly fuelled by the assimilation of foreign-generated innovation. However, this capacity to assimilate innovation is often linked to a dynamic social structure characterized by a highly skilled population and large participation by the local population in a flexible labour market. The periphery of the EU lags behind the core of Europe both in terms of the skills of the labour force and its use of human resources. With much higher unemployment rates, a relatively low educational attainment of the population, and a more rigid social structure, the capacity of many of the peripheral areas in Europe to generate or to assimilate innovation is well below that of most core areas (Rodríguez-Pose, 1999).

Finally, the sectoral structure of the European periphery does not contribute to its economic dynamism. Whereas core areas in the EU are increasingly specialized in high-value-added service sectors, such as business, financial or real estate and insurance services, many lagging areas still have a swollen primary sector—in many Greek and some Portuguese regions the primary sector still employs more than 30 per cent of the active population—and most employment growth has been recorded in the low-value-added non-market-oriented services.

2.3 European development policies

2.3.1 The need for policy intervention

It has often been argued that territorial differences in factor endowment curtail the development potential of most of the European periphery and, as a consequence, of the whole of the EU. But do differences in factor endowment justify the implementation of an EU-wide development policy? Is European economic integration increasing territorial disparities? And, if so, is a development policy really necessary in order to achieve greater economic dynamism in the periphery and greater economic and social cohesion in the EU? There is no easy and obvious answer to these questions.

The debate within economics on whether development policies are really needed to tackle disparities is inconclusive. Different strands within the field reach different conclusions. For the endogenous growth and the new economic geography approaches, the combination of greater accessibility, higher skills, and a greater capacity to generate and assimilate innovation in core areas is likely to lead to a greater concentration of economic activity in the core and to an increase of economic disparities in the EU (Fujita et al., 1999). From this perspective, European economic integration may thus contribute to accelerating the process of concentration of economic activity and, as a consequence, some sort of development policy is needed in order to counterbalance economic polarization.

In contrast, other economic strands claim that differences in factor endowment are less important for growth, since economic integration is likely to contribute to the channelling of investment and innovation from core regions to areas with lower labour costs and to fostering migration from the periphery to the core. Movements in opposite directions of investment and innovation, on the one hand, and labour, on the other, will ultimately result in economic convergence. Therefore, from this point of view, economic integration will contribute *per se* to the reduction of economic disparities across the EU, making the need for a development policy almost redundant. In addition, neoclassical researchers have found evidence that regional disparities have a tendency to decrease at rates which are close to 2 per cent per annum, regardless of the degree of economic integration (Barro and Sala-i-Martín, 1991; Sala-i-Martín, 1996).

In view of these contrasting economic positions, the decision to set up European development policies to address the existence of economic disparities within the EU has mainly been a political one. The dominating political view in the EU since the 1980s is that economic integration is likely to enhance territorial disparities and therefore a development policy is needed in order to achieve greater economic and social cohesion. As a result, every recent step towards economic integration in the EU has been accompanied by the expansion and strengthening of its development policies. First came the reform of the Structural Funds in 1989 as a response to the Single European Market initiative. It was feared that the Single Market would unleash strong centripetal forces of competition and agglomeration which would ultimately lead to a greater concentration of economic activity in the centre at the expense of the periphery (Krugman and Venables, 1996). With the Maastricht Treaty came the Cohesion Fund, designed to help peripheral countries in the EU prepare for EMU.

2.3.2 The history of the EU development policies

However, the political belief that economic integration in the EU fosters regional disparities is relatively new. It took several decades for European member states and their politicians to reach this conclusion. The early stages of European integration were characterized by the absence of supranational development policies. The 1970s brought about the introduction of the European Regional Development Fund, which represented a first attempt to tackle territorial disparities in western Europe. But, as we will see, its efficiency was circumscribed by a series of problems. Only since the signing of the Single European Act (SEA) was the question of territorial disparities addressed in a more coherent manner. The reform of the Structural Funds which followed the SEA set the foundations of the current European regional policy. In this section we will briefly review the early stages of the European regional policy.

The road towards the establishment of a regional policy

The 1950s and 1960s were characterized by high levels of growth across western Europe. Growth levels of about 6 per cent per year—bar in the UK, which was experiencing the first stages of its economic decline—ensured a period of expanding prosperity. Higher growth in the periphery than in the centre also contributed to temporarily masking the problems of uneven development across European countries and regions. It was as if the free action of market forces and greater growth sufficed to reduce economic disparities. As a consequence, during this period EC member states were more concerned with fuelling economic growth through greater economic integration than with addressing the question of uneven development, which was not regarded as a European-wide problem. The Treaty of Rome reflected this dominating trend of ignoring uneven development. References to economic disparities were limited to the preface and no supranational policy was implemented.

The fact that supranational intervention to curb territorial disparities was ruled out did not mean that development policies were completely absent. Indeed the 1960s were the golden age of development policies at the national level. In view of the persistence of intranational disparities, many European states—including Italy, France, Germany, Great Britain, and Spain—became engaged in different levels of intervention in order to control regional disparities. National development policies adopted different forms and dimensions. There were however some common denominators, such as investment in infrastructure and the provision of incentives to attract investment.

Despite the interest in tackling development problems at the national level, the efforts by the European Commission to achieve some sort of co-ordinated and coherent development policy at the European level were repeatedly shunned by member states. However, by the end of the 1960s the political climate became more favourable towards the adoption of supra-national development policies and in 1969 the Commission took the first steps towards the establishment of a European regional policy. There were several reasons behind this change. First and foremost was the persistence of territorial disparities within Europe. Despite two decades of almost uninterrupted growth the then six member states of the EC still suffered from acute intra- and international spatial disparities. The entry in January 1973 of Denmark, the United Kingdom and, above all, Ireland, exacerbated regional problems. Second, the political wrangling linked to the first expansion of the EC brought the idea of a development policy to the fore. The UK made the creation of a

Regional Fund one of the key issues of the negotiations with the EC. In a Community whose budget was heavily skewed towards the support of Continental agriculture, the UK, with less than 2 per cent of its working population active in the primary sector, considered the establishment of a Regional Fund as a way of recovering some of the payments delivered to the EC budget. Finally, the late 1960s and early 1970s brought about an important change in the western European political scene. The large countries of the EC, which had been governed by Conservative or Christian-Democrat parties during much of the 1950s and 1960s, started shifting to the left. This was the period when the Social-Democrats reached power in Germany and Labour in the UK. It was also the post-de Gaulle era in France and the height of the dialogue between the Christian-Democrats and the Communist Party in Italy. The new governments in these countries were more understanding of intervention than their predecessors.

The early regional policy

In this political climate, the Summit of Heads of State and Government held in Paris on 21 October 1972 took the decision of recognizing the necessity of establishing regional actions and of inviting the Commission to make an inventory of the regional disparities in the expanded Community. As a result of this decision, the European Regional Development Fund (ERDF) was born on 18 March 1975. Its main aim was to correct the principal imbalances within the Community resulting in particular forms of agricultural preponderance, industrial change, and structural unemployment.

The ERDF became the main instrument of the European development policy. Between its foundation and the implementation of the main reform of the European development policy in 1989, the ERDF spent 24.4 billion ECUs in financing 41 051 projects, 80 national programmes of Community interest, 17 Community programmes, and 179 studies. Several features characterize the ERDF during this period. First, its impact on development was more qualitative than quantitative. The Fund was initially established as a subsidiary fund of national regional policies and the budget was allocated through a quota system, independently of the number and quality of the projects presented by each country. The second feature was its constant expansion. Until the reform of the Structural Funds, the ERDF constantly increased its budget and its power of acting independently action from member states. Whereas the funds of the early ERDF were allocated following strict national quotas, little by little the Commission managed to increase its capacity to create a genuinely European development policy. The first step in this direction was the establishment of a 'non-quota' section, amounting to 5 per cent of the total ERDF budget in 1979. The 'non-quota' percentage was intended to finance 'Community' or

'European' investment and, therefore, to liberate the Commission from the rigid corset imposed by the regional policies of the member states. In June 1984 a further expansion of the 'European' dimension of the regional policy was achieved. At the European Summit meeting held in Stuttgart, the quota system was replaced by a system of ranges. Under this system, upper and lower limits were set for every member state over a three-year period. The aim of this reform was to contribute to the correction of the principal regional imbalances within the Community by participating in the development and structural adjustment of regions whose development was lagging behind and in the conversion of declining industrial regions. This amendment presented the Commission with a greater budgetary margin—the sum of the lower margins of the national ranges gave the Commission a discretionary power which amounted to 11.27 per cent of the total ERDF budget—to foster the adoption of development programmes of pan-European interest. The development of programmes (Community programmes or National Programmes of Community Interest) was encouraged to the detriment of purely national development projects, as a result.

In addition, the Commission during this period took significant steps to increase the knowledge and the awareness of the dimensions and evolution of economic disparities in the EC. The publication in December 1980 of the *First Periodic Report on the Social and Economic Situation and Development of the Regions of the Community* (European Commission, 1980a)—the first in a series of Periodic Reports—was a significant step in this direction. In brief, the evolution of the European regional policy until the reform of the Structural Funds was characterized by a continuous quest for a greater degree of independence with respect to national regional policies, despite the constraints imposed on its development by financial limitations and the interests of the member states.

However, the early European regional policy failed to achieve its aim of correcting economic imbalances and to co-ordinate regional policies of member states. Indeed, between the implementation of the ERDF and the reform of the Structural Funds, the gap dividing advanced and backward regions and nations widened. While the gap amongst European regions had been steadily decreasing in the 1950s and 1960s, in the early 1970s the trend was reversed and divergence among regions and nations began to predominate. The paradox is that while regional disparities had decreased during the earlier decades when no European development policy was in place, the arrival of a European regional policy coincided with regional divergence.

The establishment of the ERDF is not to blame for the reversal of the convergence trend in Europe. The early steps of the implementation of the ERDF happened in the midst of the most serious economic crisis western Europe has faced in the post-war period. The dramatic rise of oil prices since the mid-1970s and until the early 1980s contributed to plunging most of Europe into economic recession. Peripheral countries and regions, because of their weaker economic base and their greater dependency on fossil fuels, were worst hit by the crisis.

Although the widening of economic disparities in western Europe during the late 1970s and early 1980s is mainly related to the differential territorial impact of the economic crisis, several factors limited the capacity of the ERDF to curb economic divergence and led some authors, like Croxford, Wise, and Chalkey (1987) or Wise and Croxford (1988), to state that the early regional policy was fundamentally cosmetic with no real impact on regional development trends. These factors can be classified as follows:

1. *The lack of financial resources to establish a 'real' regional policy:* The endowment of the ERDF in 1975 was fairly modest: 257.6 million ECUs, i.e. 4.8 per cent of the budget of the Community. By 1988 it had increased fourteen-fold. This, however, only represented 8.1 per cent of the Community's budget. Taking into account that the total budget of the Community at the time was less than 1 per cent of the European GDP, the amount allocated to solving development problems did not even attain 0.1 per cent of the GDP of the twelve member states. On a regional scale, the modest nature of development funds can be better observed. Regions most favoured by Community projects and programmes were effectively the less developed regions. The amount of capital available was, nevertheless, modest: less than 150 ECUs per capita between 1986 and 1988 in the most favoured region, Basilicata in southern Italy.

2. *The lack of continuity of regional intervention:* Between 1975 and 1989, five different stages of European regional policy can be distinguished. The first four correspond to successive reforms of the original ERDF regulation and philosophy. Thus, the average life of integrated regional actions did not exceed three years.

3. *The excessive extent of the range of operations and investments:* ERDF actions were not confined just to backward territories. The ERDF financed projects and programmes in virtually every single region of the Community.

4. *The absence of a clearly defined structure and of a system of priorities:* As mentioned earlier, in the first fourteen years of its existence, the ERDF financed too many projects, programmes, and studies. The criteria for the selection of a certain programme or project were frequently vague and insufficiently specific. The main guidelines were not implemented as expected and were constantly overridden by the priorities of member states.

5. *The lack of flexibility in the distribution of Funds:* The Commission suffered from a very narrow margin of manoeuvre in order to redistribute funds once allocated.

6. *The primacy of national interest over Community interest:* From the very moment of its establishment, the ERDF often operated as a subsidiary tool of member states' regional policies, instead of serving as the base for the construction of a real 'European' policy. Member states used the Fund as a means of budgetary redistribution rather than to promote spatial development.

7. *Difficulties in the achievement and monitoring of projects:* The monitoring and follow-up of projects tended to degenerate into routine visits with no real evaluation of the level of achievement of goals.

8. *Lack of co-ordination among all actors concerned in regional development:* European interests rarely coincided with those of member states, and the interests of the latter often clashed with regional and local government interests and policies. The criteria for applying the principle of subsidiarity were contentious and unclear, and frequent conflicts of power arose between administrative bodies.

9. *Failure by the Commission to promote the idea of the need for a supranational regional policy:* Most Europeans welcomed the idea of helping less developed regions. For a majority of EC citizens solidarity was, however, limited to their own national boundaries. Only a small percentage agreed to contribute to regional development in other states of the Community (ranging from 48 per cent in the Netherlands, 45 per cent in Germany, and 41 per cent in Italy, to 17 per cent in the UK and 18 per cent in Denmark) (European Commission, 1980*b*: 25).

10. *Lack of co-ordination between regional and sectoral policies.* The aims and territorial effects of the European regional development policies were often at odds with the territorial impact of other European sectoral policies, and, most notably, with the largest European policy, the Common Agricultural Policy (CAP). Whereas most of the expenditure linked to the ERDF was concentrated in peripheral countries, the expenditure associated with the CAP and its main fund the European Agricultural Guidance and Guarantee Fund (EAGGF-Guarantee Section) took place in core countries. This meant that in the late 1980s, EC investment per head in countries such as the Netherlands or Denmark was higher than in Portugal or Spain. Among the peripheral countries of the EC, only Ireland was receiving more funds per capita than the Netherlands.

2.3.3 The reform of the Structural Funds

The persistence of economic imbalances in Europe, together with the inability of the early European regional development policy to tackle disparities, ignited the debate about the need to strengthen and reform the European development policies. Successive enlargements of the EU during the 1980s further contributed to raising awareness about the problem. When Greece joined the EC in 1981 its GDP per capita measured in PPS was just 52 per cent of the EC average. Portugal was at the same level when it joined in 1986, and although Spain fared slightly better—with a GDP per capita of 71 per cent of the EC average—its internal imbalances were strong. This combination of economic and political circumstances created the right climate for a thorough revision of the EC's development policy, and this issue was inserted in the agenda of the discussions leading to the SEA.

Led by the leaders of the peripheral countries, the representatives of the member states adopted the view that the implementation of the Single Market—which was the main objective of the SEA—was likely to enhance, rather than to reduce, territorial disparities within the EC. And further increases in territorial imbalances were deemed to jeopardize the internal stability of the Single Market in the long run and to create tensions among member states (Armstrong and Taylor, 2000). The outcome of these discussions was that the principle of promoting a 'harmonious' economic development and economic and social cohesion was included in the Treaty establishing the European Community (in the former Art. 130a) in the SEA reform of the Treaty. The current Art. 158—which is the modified version of Art. 130a since the Amsterdam reform—states that

in order to promote its overall harmonious development, the Community shall develop and pursue its actions leading to the strengthening of its economic and social cohesion. In particular, the Community shall aim at reducing disparities between the levels of development of the various regions and the backwardness of the least favoured regions or islands, including rural areas. (Treaty establishing the European Community (Amsterdam consolidated version) Art. 158)

And not only did the SEA provide the aim of harmonious economic development and greater economic and social cohesion in the EC, but it also identified the means to achieve this goal. Art. 130b (now Art. 159) states that 'the Community shall also support the achievement of these objectives by the action it takes through the Structural Funds (European Agricultural Guidance and Guarantee Fund (EAGGF), Guidance Section; European Social Fund (ESF); ERDF), the European Investment Bank and the other existing financial instruments' (Treaty establishing the European Community (Amsterdam consolidated version) Art. 159). The European Development Policy was no longer limited to the ERDF. The other Structural Funds, the EAGGF-Guidance Section and the European Social Fund (ESF) were to be co-ordinated with the ERDF in order to set the bases for a reduction of the territorial disparities within the EC.

A profound reform of European development policies followed. This reform—better known as the reform of the Structural Funds—tried to address most of the factors which had limited the effectiveness of the early European regional policy. It was based on the principles of:

a) territorial and financial concentration,

b) programming,

c) partnership, and

d) additionality.

A fifth principle of efficiency was introduced in the 1990s.

Concentration

The main aim behind the principle of concentration was to try to increase the efficiency of European intervention. It was perceived that the earlier European regional policy had spread itself too thin to have any real impact on development. Almost every country and region in the EU was receiving development funds and not enough funding was being channelled to the areas where it was really needed. Concentrating the intervention in those regions with the most serious development problems was conceived as a way of increasing the effectiveness of the European regional development policy. Five objectives were originally established in order to determine which regions received which funds and the level of funding for different groups of regions. The number of objectives has changed over the years. A sixth objective was added to the original five after the 1995 enlargement. A revision of the principle of concentration in 1999 led to a reduction of the number of objectives to three for the period 2000–6. The three objectives are the following:

- *Objective 1: Promoting the development and structural adjustment of regions whose development is lagging behind*: This objective is aimed at the promotion of development and structural adjustment in lagging regions (defined as those whose per capita GDP is less than 75 per cent of the EU average and the sparsely populated northern areas of Sweden and Finland). All the Structural Funds are involved in this objective which for the period 2000–6 affects 22.2 per cent of the EU population. The whole of Greece and Portugal bar the Lisbon area, the former East Germany with the exception of East Berlin, nine regions in Spain, six in southern Italy, parts of Ireland, Austria, parts of northern Finland and Sweden, the French Overseas

Territories, and an increasing number of British regions are included in Objective 1. 69.7 per cent of all the Structural Funds have been allocated to Objective 1 regions (European Commission, 2000). Formerly lagging regions whose GDP is now above 75 per cent of the EU average are also eligible for what is known as Objective 1 transitional assistance. The objective of this transitional assistance is to 'avoid an abrupt cessation of Community funding and consolidate the achievements of earlier structural assistance' (European Commission, 2000: 11).

- *Objective 2: Supporting the economic and social conversion of areas facing structural difficulties:* This objective is intended for the development of regions affected by industrial decline and of rural areas. Urban areas with a high long-term unemployment rate or high poverty levels, and areas dependent on fisheries are also included in Objective 2. The main measures under this objective are to improve the opportunities for the creation and development of production activities and the promotion of new enterprises.

- *Objective 3: Adapting and modernizing policies and systems of education, training, and employment:* This non-territorial objective seeks to support active labour market policies to reduce unemployment and to improve access to the labour market. The enhancement of employment opportunities through education programmes and on-the-job learning, and the promotion of equal opportunities for men and women are further targets of this objective. The actions within this objective are to be implemented outside the Objective 1 regions (European Commission, 2000).

In addition to the Objectives, through which the bulk of the development funds are channelled, the EU has set up a series of Community Initiatives. Community Initiatives give the European Commission greater leeway in establishing European-wide development objectives. The number of Community Initiatives, which flourished in the early 1990s, has been reduced in recent years. Community Initiatives for the period 2000–6 cover the fields of cross-border and transnational co-operation (Interreg); economic and social regeneration of cities (Urban); rural development via integrated programmes (Leader); and combating discrimination and inequalities in access to the labour market (Equal). They represent approximately 5 per cent of the Structural Funds budget.

Programming

The reform of the Structural Funds also introduced the principle of programming. In contrast to the situation before the reform, when the Community mainly financed individual development projects, the principle of programming implies that each project should be included within a development plan. There is now much greater emphasis on the design and implementation of coherent development strategies through the multi-annual programming of assistance. As a result, medium-term (five or six years) strategic planning has been introduced. The programming of assistance usually adopts the following stages. First, development plans are drawn up by the member states and presented to the European Commission. In the case of Objective 1, the Commission examines the plans submitted by each member state and, based on the plan and in consultation with the member states, adopts a Community Support Framework (CSF), which is supplemented by operations programmes (Ops). These are the actual guidelines for the implementation of the programmes. In the cases of Objectives 2 and 3 the Commission adopts what is known as single programming documents (SPDs).

Partnership

Involving as many actors as possible in the process of design, implementation, and monitoring of economic development strategies usually renders development policies more efficient. The principle of partnership introduced after the reform of the Structural Funds aims precisely at this, achieving a close co-operation between the European Commission and the national, regional, and local institutions concerned with economic development. The co-operation is not just limited to regional or local authorities, but often involves other economic and social partners designated by the member state (European Commission, 2000). The principle of partnership thus contributes to generating a constant dialogue between the Commission, member states, regional and local governments, and other social and economic actors. The dialogue normally reaches its climax during the preparatory stage of the development plans.

Additionality

The principle of additionality was introduced in order to prevent member states from cutting their national development policy and thus making European development policies a mere substitute for the national development effort. Under this principle, member states have to maintain their public expenditure in development action at least at the same level as in the previous programming period.

Efficiency

Given the problems experienced in the follow-up of projects prior to the reform of the Structural Funds, the principle of efficiency has been designed to guarantee the correct management and to monitor the effectiveness of the implementation of European development actions. Under the efficiency principle, member states, in the first place, and the Commission are responsible for the implementation and monitoring, and for the effectiveness of the measures taken. The Council Regulation of 21 June 1999 laying down general provisions on the Structural Funds establishes a series of responsibilities for member states which basically affect the authority responsible for the managing of programmes and projects and the Monitoring Committees. The European Commission is also required to liaise with the managing authority and with the member states.

A thorough process of evaluation of development programmes has been set in place. *Ex-ante*, mid-term, and *ex-post* evaluations are performed, with the member state having primary responsibility for the two former, and the European Commission for the latter. There are also a series of additional controls and provisions to guarantee the diffusion and publicity of the actions undertaken.

2.3.4 The Cohesion Fund

The political belief that that EMU was likely to further enhance the concentration of economic activity in core areas led the Maastricht summit to set up a new Cohesion Fund benefiting the poorest members of the EU. Article 161 of the Treaty (formerly Art. 130d) establishes that 'a Cohesion Fund . . . shall provide a financial contribution to projects in the fields of environment and trans-European networks in the area of transport infrastructure' (Treaty establishing the European Community (Amsterdam consolidated version) Art. 161). The original objective of the Fund, introduced in 1993, was to alleviate the burdens which transition to EMU would impose on the least prosperous member states.

As stated in the treaty, the Cohesion Fund has been used to finance projects aimed at improving the environment and developing transport infrastructure in those member states whose per capita GNP was less than 90 per cent of the EU average at the time of the signing of the Maastricht Treaty (Greece, Ireland, Portugal, and Spain). Special emphasis is placed on the financing of trans-European transport networks. More than 60 per cent of the Fund is allocated to Spain, with more than 15 per cent going to Greece and Portugal, and between 2 and 6 per cent allocated to Ireland.

2.4 The efficiency of European development policies after the reform of the Structural Funds

The reform of the Structural Funds and the introduction of the Cohesion Fund have represented a huge boost in the European effort to achieve economic and social cohesion. From being a non-existent section of the European budget in the 1960s, and representing a relatively minor policy area throughout the 1970s and most of the 1980s, development policies have now become, just behind the CAP, the second most important European policy in budgetary terms. The expenditure on development progammes and projects has jumped from levels of around 5 per cent of the EU budget in the 1970s to about 15 per cent in 1990, and to more than a third in the year 2000. For the period 2000–6, €213 billion have been allocated for the development of structural measures and €18 billion to the Cohesion Fund. In addition €47 billion have been set aside to support the development of central and eastern European applicants to join the EU. This effort represents an annual expenditure of around 0.4 per cent of the EU total GDP in development strategies, which is basically concentrated in trying to achieve the development of lagging areas.

Has this effort paid off? Has the reform and considerable expansion of the EU's development policies succeeded in achieving greater economic and social cohesion and in offsetting the apparently pernicious territorial effects of greater economic integration? These are not easy questions to answer. Economic growth and the evolution of economic disparities are affected by numerous factors. The economic cycle, the comparative advantages of each territory, closeness to markets, or the sectoral production structure are among the factors which determine the evolution of regional disparities in any given period. Development policies and the measures associated with them are just an additional factor influencing the evolution of regional disparities. It is therefore difficult to analyse to what extent any reduction or increase in the economic gap between the core and the periphery of the EU is the direct result of the impact of development policies. This has to be borne in mind when the evolution of territorial economic disparities in western Europe is presented in the following pages.

At first sight, it could be claimed that the reform of the Stuctural Funds and the introduction of the Cohesion Fund have been a success, since the four member states which have been the main beneficiaries of these development funds have been able to close the economic gap with respect to the European average. As seen in Figure 2.2, in the period before the reform of the Structural Funds the catch-up of the countries in the periphery of the EU had been relatively small. Two of the Cohesion countries, Greece and Spain, had experienced no convergence towards EU GDP per capita levels between the mid-1970s and the reform of the Structural Funds. Their GDP per capita rates in 1988—58.2 and 73.8 per cent of the EU average respectively—were lower than in 1977. Portugal and Ireland had experienced very slow convergence (Figure 2.2). Since the reform of the Structural Funds the situation has changed radically. There has been a relatively strong catch-up in all four Cohesion economies. Ireland represents the most spectacular case. With rates of real growth throughout much of the 1990s in excess of 8 per cent per annum, Ireland's GDP per capita in 2001 (measured in PPS) was, as mentioned earlier, second only to that of Luxembourg. This represented an increase of 54 percentage points—from 65.9 to 118.8 per cent with respect to the EU average—in the eleven years between 1989 and 2000. Portugal's convergence has also been significant, and although the catch-up in Greece and Spain has been less spectacular, both countries were at the turn of the century closer to the EU average than in the mid-1980s.

National convergence has also been fuelled by the relatively poor economic performance of some of the most developed economies in the EU. Economic growth in France, Germany, Sweden, and, to a lesser extent, Italy has been well below the EU average since the late 1980s (see Table 2.1). This is, however, far from being a universal trend. The smaller countries of the core have outperformed their larger counterparts. Austria, Belgium, Denmark, Finland, the Netherlands, and, above all, Luxembourg—all of which had GDP per capita levels above to the EU average in the mid-1980s—have diverged and grown above the European average.

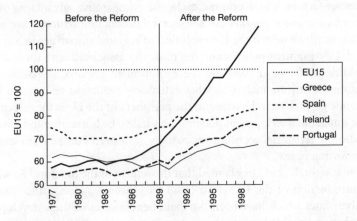

Figure 2.2 Evolution of GDP per capita measured in PPS in the four Cohesion countries, 1977–2000

Source: EUROSTAT data.

The catch-up by countries in the European periphery since the reform of the Structural Funds has led some authors (e.g. European Commission, 1994; Leonardi, 1995) to claim that regional intervention in the EU has been a success. Strategies to achieve greater economic and social cohesion have borne fruit and, as a consequence, territorial disparities in the EU are dwindling. The picture is unfortunately not as simple. A look at recent regional economic development trends within the EU as a whole and within individual countries reveals a much more complex and nuanced picture. Figure 2.3 depicts the growth of GDP per capita in the regions of the EU and in those of Italy, Spain, and the UK between 1977 or the nearest year for which data is available (in the case of the EU) or 1980 (in Italy, Spain, and the UK) and 1998. The vertical axis in every individual graph represents regional growth with respect to the EU or the national average during the period of analysis. The horizontal axis represents the initial GDP per capita in each region. On both axes the European or national average is equal to 100. The general growth trend across regions is illustrated by the linear regression line. Each territorial unit in Figure 2.3 is divided into three graphs which stand for three different stages of European integration: 1977–86, indicating the height of the customs union; 1986–93, denoting the transition between the signature of the SEA and the establishment of the Single Market; and 1993–8, representing the Single Market and the preparation for EMU. The choice of the three countries is related to different levels of involvement of EU development policies in them: high, in the case of the main beneficiary, Spain; medium, in the case of Italy; and relatively low in the case of the UK.

As indicated by the negative slope in every graph referring to the whole of the EU, the last few decades have been characterized by a reduction of regional disparities. Overall, growth in the poorer regions has outstripped that in the richer regions since the late 1970s, regardless of the level of economic integration. There was moderate regional convergence in the last stages of the customs union, and there has been moderate convergence since the Single Market was implemented (Figure 2.3). There is, however, no sign at the regional level of the rapid catch-up that seems evident at the national level. The reform of the Structural Funds and the introduction of the Cohesion Fund do not seem to have led to greater growth in the regions that are the main recipients of the EU development policies and, as a consequence, there is no increase in regional convergence during the early stages of the Single Market, with respect to the previous stages of regional integration. In fact, when regional growth trends within individual countries are analysed, the picture that emerges is quite different. As regional integration progresses, intranational regional divergence seems to be increasingly becoming the norm, rather than the exception. In the three countries included in Figure 2.3, the advent of the Single Market and the preparations for EMU seem to mark the transition

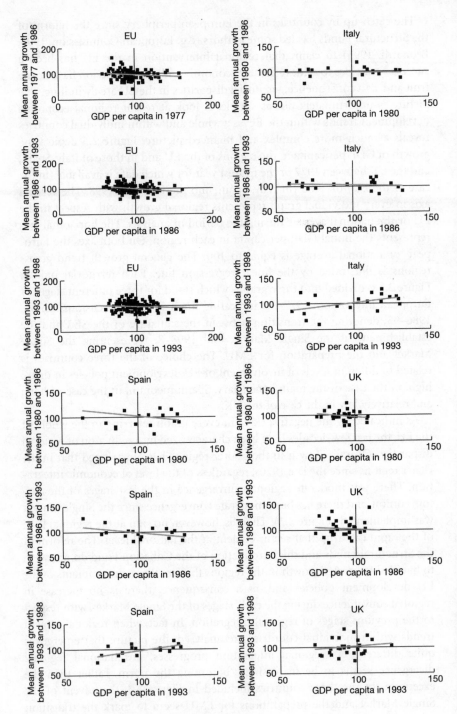

Figure 2.3 Regional growth trends in the EU, Italy, Spain, and the UK

Source: Own elaboration with EUROSTAT data.

from regional stability or slow convergence, to slow regional divergence. The early stages of the Single Market have been characterized by higher growth in the richer than in the poorer regions of these three countries, regardless of the level of intervention. This is the case in the UK, whose regions until 1998 had received relatively little support from the Structural Funds, as well as in Italy, whose southern regions have enjoyed Objective 1 status during the period of analysis, and Spain, the main recipient of Structural and Cohesion Funds.

The complex nature of recent regional growth trends is corroborated by Figure 2.4, which maps GDP per capita growth in the EU between 1985 and 1998. It highlights how the highest rates of growth in Greece, Portugal, and Spain have not taken place in the less developed regions, but often in the more advanced areas. Spain is a clear example of this trend. The highest rates of economic growth between 1985 and 1998 have taken place in the two most advanced regions, Madrid and Catalonia. These two regions have concentrated more than two thirds of all foreign direct investment coming into the country since Spain joined the EU, a large percentage of the company headquarters, the most advanced R&D facilities, and most of the advanced business, real estate, and financial services (Rodríguez-Pose, 1998). In contrast many of the regions which have enjoyed Objective 1 status throughout the period have not fared as well. This is the case of many regions that traditionally had a strong reliance on agriculture. Galicia in the north west, Castile-León, Castile-La Mancha, and Estremadura in the centre, and Andalusia in the south have all grown at rates below the Spanish average. Old industrial regions have also not performed well. Asturias, another Objective 1 region in the northern Spanish rim, has witnessed the lowest rate of growth in Spain (Figure 2.4).

The situation is similar in Portugal, where growth in the relatively prosperous areas of Lisbon and the Tagus Valley and the north of the country has outstripped that of the centre. In Greece, the fastest growth has been concentrated in the tourist regions of the islands of the Aegean and Crete. Outside these dynamic areas, growth patterns are similar to those witnessed in Portugal or Spain: whereas Athens and its region have enjoyed a relatively good economic performance, the Peloponnese, central Greece, and parts of Thrace have fallen behind (Figure 2.4). In Ireland the greatest economic dynamism has been concentrated in and around Dublin.

Assisted regions in other countries of the EU have also not performed particularly well. During the 1990s growth in the Objective 1 regions of the south of Italy was lower than in the north of the country. This is especially the case of the regions facing the Thyrrenian Sea. Calabria, Campania, and the islands of Sardinia and Sicily have been amongst the least dynamic regions in Italy during the late 1980s and throughout the 1990s. The southern regions

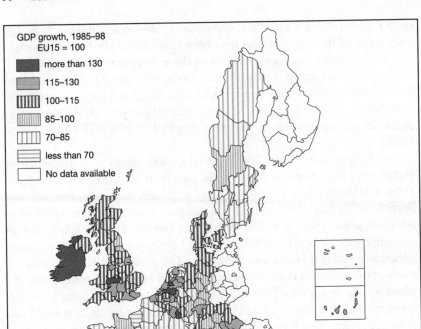

Figure 2.4 Evolution of regional GDP per capita in the EU, 1985–1998

facing the Adriatic Sea—Abruzzo, Molise, and Apulia—have shown greater dynamism, but their growth rates have been well below that of the north east of Italy (Figure 2.4).

The tendency towards greater economic polarization within countries is not exclusive to the member states which have received the bulk of European structural funding. There has been a concentration of economic activity in core areas and large capital regions across Europe. Brussels, Copenhagen, Helsinki, London, Paris, and Stockholm have benefited from it. Berlin has also become one of the most dynamic cities in Europe since German reunification. Increasing regional polarization within countries of the EU has resulted in a decline in regional convergence (Armstrong, 1995; De la Fuente and Vives, 1995; Neven and Gouyette, 1995; López-Bazo *et al.*, 1999).

Hence, since the implementation of the reform of the Structural Funds there has been a mixture of national convergence and regional divergence. Inequalities across states have fallen by 25 per cent, whereas regional inequalities within states have risen by 10 per cent. As a result, regional income inequalities in western Europe occur nowadays within rather than across member states (Puga, 2000).

Another factor which casts doubts on the capacity of the Structural and Cohesion Funds to achieve greater economic and social cohesion has been the fact that over time there has been little change in the member states benefiting from the Cohesion Fund or in the regions which qualify for Objective 1 status under the Structural Funds. Despite national convergence across western Europe throughout the 1980s and 1990s, the four original cohesion countries—Greece, Ireland, Portugal, and Spain—are still supported by this Fund. Ireland is likely to come out in the near future, but Greece, Portugal, and Spain have GNP per capita rates still well below the support criterion. The permanence is also striking when Objective 1 regions are considered. Despite the cutting back of the areas eligible for assistance in the period 2000–6 in order to free up funds for enlargement (Armstrong and Taylor, 2000), the map of Objective 1 regions has not changed much since the reform. Most of the regions which met the criteria to become Objective 1 in the period 1989–93 are still Objective 1 regions in the period 2000–6. This is the case the whole of Greece or of the whole of Portugal, bar the region of Lisbon and the Tagus Valley. Nine out of the original ten Spanish, and six out of the original eight Italian regions still qualify as Objective 1, as do all the regions in the former East Germany, with the exception of East Berlin. In Ireland only the eastern and southern parts of the country have come out of Objective 1. Lack of change in the number of assisted regions further highlights the fact, to the extent that peripheral countries have converged since the reform of the Structural Funds and the implementation of the Single Market, convergence has been mainly linked to the performance of their core areas, rather than of the regions with the greatest degree of assistance.

If anything, the number of Objective 1 regions has tended to increase rather than decrease. Regions such as Burgenland in Austria, South Yorkshire, West Wales and the Valleys, Cornwall, and Merseyside in the UK, and the central and northern areas of Sweden have joined the ranks of the Objective 1 regions in recent years.

Analysis of the evolution of unemployment—a key indicator in the selection of Objective 2 regions—also highlights that the objective of economic and social cohesion is still far from being achieved. As Overman and Puga

(1999) underline, the late 1980s and early 1990s have been characterised by a greater polarization of regional unemployment rates. The number of regions with high and low unemployment rates is growing at the expense of those with levels of unemployment close to the EU average. This polarization has a strong geographical component too. The areas with high unemployment often coincide with Objective 1 regions. High unemployment rates are found in most of Spain, southern Italy, northern France, and Corsica. Low unemployment levels, in contrast, coincide with the dynamic areas of the core, such as the south east of England, northern Italy, southern Germany, and the Netherlands.

2.5 Conclusion

Aware of the huge economic disparities within its territory and of their implications for further economic integration, the EC began to take steps in the 1970s to try to spur economic development in lagging areas and, hence, reduce economic imbalances. The belief that further economic integration, such as the completion of the Internal Market or Economic and Monetary Union, could generate greater inequality provided a further political and economic incentive for the design and implementation of European-wide development strategies. The aim was to achieve greater economic and social cohesion which, in addition to the general aim of territorial solidarity, would contribute to prepare lagging regions to withstand greater competition in a more integrated market.

Development policies have thus grown with economic integration. After an initial period of mild and rather haphazard intervention, the preparation for the Single Market brought about the reform of the Structural Funds, and in preparation for EMU, the Cohesion Fund. All these changes and reforms have contributed to transforming European development policies from a minor and rather disorganized policy in the 1970s and early 1980s to the second largest policy in the EU, just behind the CAP.

Achieving economic and social cohesion is, however, proving more elusive than expected. Despite some national convergence in GDP per capita, the 1990s have seen an increasing divergence within countries and the significant persistence of regional disparities. The map of the EU, in terms of regional disparities, still looks much like that of the early 1980s and—with a few individual exceptions—relatively little change has been achieved. Regional policy has also been unable to curb an increasing unemployment polarization within Europe.

The persistence of economic disparities and the polarization in unemployment rates cannot be blamed on the supposed inefficacy of European development policies. As mentioned earlier, economic intervention is only one—and perhaps not the most important—of the possible factors influencing growth and it may still be too early to conduct a proper assessment of the efficacy of the European development strategies. There are however voices which are starting to question whether this sort of intervention is likely ultimately to generate greater cohesion across Europe, or whether, as it has been claimed of previous development policies developed at national level, it may not lead to a greater dependency of lagging areas on transfers from the core (Puga, 2000; Rodríguez-Pose, 2000; Vanhoudt *et al.*, 2000). Beyond the short-term positive impact of infrastructure investment, many of the regions benefiting from the greatest level of intervention are now more open than ever to competition, but still lack the necessary internal economic and human resources to compete on level terms. Under these conditions, greater economic and social cohesion may remain for long extremely difficult to achieve.

II
SOCIETY

3

Ageing

3.1 Introduction

In comparison to the rest of the world, the EU is ageing. A higher life expectancy, together with a steep fall in fertility rates, linked to the changing structure of the family and in gender roles, are keeping the size of the population of the EU stable and leading to the formation of inverted demographic pyramids. In many western European states more than 15 per cent of the population is now over 65, and in some regions this percentage is approaching one quarter. And the ageing problem is likely to become extremely serious once the baby boomers move beyond their age of fertility. This process is already jeopardizing the sustainability of European welfare systems and may limit the economic potential of western Europe as a whole. Most EU countries have set policies in motion aimed at curbing the ageing trend.

This chapter addresses the problem of ageing and what it means for the future development of the EU by looking first at recent demographic transformations in the EU, with special emphasis on the ageing of the European population. The factors behind the process of ageing are analysed in Section 3.3. Section 3.4 presents the policies aimed at tackling demographic change and their social and economic implications.

3.2 Demographic change in the EU

3.2.1 The slowdown in population growth

The EU is still the most populous area in the developed world. With 375 million inhabitants in the fifteen member states in 2000, it had 97 million inhabitants more than the US and 258 million more than Japan. However, the relative weight of the EU's population within the developed world has been declining steadily. The US has been catching up rapidly. If in 1960 the population of the US represented only 57 per cent of that of the EU, by 2000 the ratio had risen to 74 per cent. The catching up by Japan has been much slower, with its population creeping from 30 per cent in 1960 to 31 per cent of that of the EU in 2000.

The EU has had relatively low rates of population growth during the whole of the second half of the twentieth century. Between 1960 and 1997 the population of the EU never rose by more than 1 per cent in a single year (Figure 3.1). By contrast, in the same period, the population of the US rose by more than 1 per cent in eighteen years and that of Japan in eight years. And population growth in the EU has been falling. In 1974 it rose by less than half a percentage point for the first time since the end of the war and has remained below that threshold ever since (Figure 3.1). Japan's population growth only fell below that threshold in 1987 and the US population growth has remained at levels of around 1 per cent per annum. The slowdown in population growth has meant that the western European population is stabilizing slowly. It took the EU only eight years to add 20 new million inhabitants to its population in the 1960s; the next similar increase was achieved twelve years later; and it has taken an additional eighteen years to add 20 million more. The report on *Replacement Migration* by the United Nations Population Division (2000) has predicted that the population of the EU will reach its peak around 2005, before starting to decline at increasing speed. According to the medium variant of this report, the EU will have 331.3 million people in 2050, that is 44 million people less than in 2000 (a loss of almost 11 per cent) and 18 million less than the predicted population of the US in that year. The UN estimates that twelve out of the current fifteen EU member states will lose population, with the populations of Italy, Spain, and Greece falling by more than 20 per cent. Only the Irish population will expand. In France and Luxembourg it will remain more or less stable.

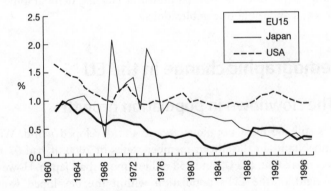

Figure 3.1 Population growth in the EU, the US, and Japan, 1960–1997

Source: World Bank World Development Indicators (2000).

3.2.2 The decline in birth and fertility rates

The root of the changes in population trends in Europe has to be searched for in what Van de Kaa (1987) has called the second demographic transition. The first demographic transition was fuelled by medical advances that led to a rapid fall in mortality and, as a consequence, to a period of high population growth. The second demographic transition is more complex and more related to changes in human attitudes than to technical progress. The number of marriages is dropping, and when marriages occur, they tend to happen later in life. There is mounting marriage instability, leading to rising divorce rates, and throughout the western world there has been an important increase in cohabitation and extra-nuptial fertility. Nowhere have these transformations been more profound than in western Europe and, and as a consequence, no other space in the world has experienced the decline in birth and fertility rates that has accompanied the second demographic transition in the EU.

Figure 3.2 depicts the evolution of birth and death rates in selected European countries, the US, and Japan. Similar characteristics can be appreciated across all countries. One of these is the stability of mortality rates. Mortality in western Europe, the US, and Japan remained relatively stable during the last four decades of the twentieth century. The annual death rate fluctuated around ten per thousand, with Japan—which had the lowest death rates in the developed world—being the only exception (Figure 3.2).

Birth rates, on the contrary, underwent a steep decline throughout the EU, as well as in the US and Japan, from their post-war peaks of the 1960s. In the EU, the decline has led to a stabilization of crude birth rates at eleven births per thousand inhabitants in the 1990s. Japan's birth rate started to decline later than that of the EU, but has stabilized earlier. The US birth rate also suffered an initial decline, but since the mid-1970s has hovered at levels of fifteen births per thousand inhabitants per year (Figure 3.2.).

The timing and the slope of the decline in crude birth rates allow us to distinguish between different demographic patterns. Three distinct types seem to emerge from Figure 3.2:

a) **'Population growth'**: Countries belonging to the 'population growth' group suffered an early fall in birth rates, but births have subsequently stabilized and remain above the number of deaths. As a result countries in this group, such as France or the Netherlands, have experienced natural population growth during the 1990s (Figure 3.2). The only other EU country which belongs in this group is Ireland, although its birth rate started to fall later than that of France or the Netherlands. The US demographic pattern also fits into this group. The higher birth rates of the US determine

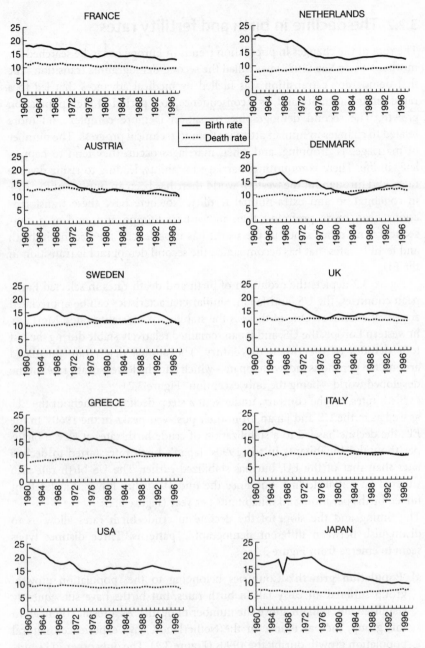

Figure 3.2 Evolution of birth and death rates in selected European countries, the US, and Japan, 1960–1997

Source: World Bank World Development Indicators (2000).

that its population dynamism is closer to that of Ireland, than to that of France or the Netherlands.

b) **'Early zero growth'**: The four countries (Austria, Denmark, Sweden, and the UK) represented in the middle of the Figure 3.2 are examples of 'early zero growth'. As in the case of the countries included in the 'positive growth' group, 'early zero growth' countries underwent a reduction in birth rates during the 1960s and 1970s. But, in contrast to what happened to the previous group, birth rates continued to fall until zero or negative population growth rates were achieved. Negative and zero population growth triggered a reaction, reflected in a rebound of birth rates, more marked in Sweden or the UK, than in Austria or Denmark (Figure 3.2). The rise of birth rates was however short-lived. Since the 1990s 'early zero growth' countries have witnessed a renewed decline in birth rates and natural population growth has remained close to zero. The natural demographic patterns of Belgium, Germany, and, to a lesser extent, Finland, can be also be included in this group.

c) **'Late zero growth'**: Birth rates in 'late zero growth' countries began to fall later than in the other two groups. The main drop in births did not take place until the mid-1970s in Italy and the early 1980s in Greece (Figure 3.2). Zero natural growth rates have only been achieved in the late 1980s and early 1990s and no rebound in birth rates has been observed. Spain and Portugal, as well as Japan (Figure 3.2), also follow this demographic pattern, although, in the case of Japan, lower death rates mean that zero natural population growth rates have not yet been reached.

National demographic patterns hide important intranational differences. Whereas death rates tend to be fairly homogeneous across European regions, significant regional disparities are observed in birth rates. Figure 3.3 maps regional crude birth rates in the EU in 1997. The map highlights that demographic patterns are far from homogeneous in many EU countries. One such case is Italy, where extremely low birth rates in the north west and centre of the country contrast with relatively high rates in the southern regions of Campania and Sicily. However, demographic patterns do not exactly reproduce the economic north/south divide of the country (see Chapter 2). Southern regions, such as Sardinia, Abruzzo, and Molise, had similar birth rates to the centre of the country, and Trentino-Alto Adige in the north stood out because of its high birth rate. An east/west division is visible in Germany. Every single region in the former East Germany had birth rates below levels of nine per thousand. None of the regions in West Germany had such low birth rates. There were, however, contrasts between higher rates of birth in the south and the north of the country and lower rates in

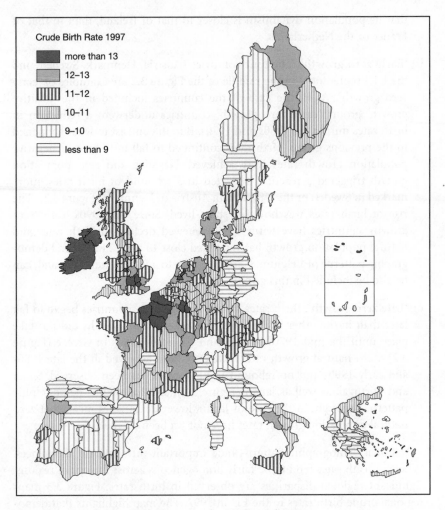

Figure 3.3 Regional crude birth rate in the EU (in ‰), 1997

the centre. In the UK, the greatest demographic dynamism was concentrated in London and the Home Counties. The south west had lower birth rates. France, the Netherlands, Portugal, and Spain also harboured significant internal contrasts.

A factor worth mentioning is that the traditional division between low birth rates in the core and high birth rates in the periphery of Europe has completely disappeared. To a certain extent it has almost been reversed. Of the former periphery, only Ireland, Northern Ireland, and the Portuguese region of the Azores were among the regions with the highest birth rates. Most other peripheral areas, such as the whole of Greece, about half of the Italian Mezzo-giorno, the whole of Spain, and parts of Portugal had the some of the lowest birth rates in Europe. A relatively high birth rate in the EU is becoming a metropolitan phenomenon. Large urban areas, such as the capital cities—with the exceptions of Athens, Berlin, and Vienna—have higher birth rates than their respective national average. The difference is particularly strong in the cases of Brussels, London, and Paris. Factors such as the concentration of hospitals in large cities partly explain this phenomenon. But more than this factor, the explanation of higher birth rates in large urban centres than else-where in the EU is related to an increasing concentration of young adults in these regions.

Low birth rates are just one external sign of a more worrying phenomenon for the long-term growth of the European population: declining fertility. Women in western Europe are deciding to have fewer children than ever before and fewer children than in any other space in the world. Total fertility rates in the EU are below those of any other society, bar Japan and eastern Europe (Coleman, 1996b). Total fertility rates (TFR)—which is a measure-ment of the number of babies a woman would produce if she experienced current age-specific fertility rates throughout her lifetime—in the EU in 1997 ranged between 1.91 babies per woman in Ireland and 1.15 in Spain. This was in clear contrast with TFRs of more than 6 in Sub-Saharan Africa, or even with those of Northern Africa (almost 5) and Latin America (more than 3). Among the developed countries, all EU member states had lower fertility rates than the US (TFR, 1.99), and only Finland and Ireland were above the TFR of Australia (1.80).

Fertility has been declining in western Europe since the mid-1960s. In 1970 ten out of the fifteen states of the EU had TFRs above the replacement rate (TFR 2.1) (Table 3.1). Ireland's fertility (TFR of 3.93 in 1970) was even close to that of many developing countries. And of the five countries below the replacement rate (Denmark, Finland, Germany, Luxembourg, and Sweden), none was below levels of 1.8. Fertility rates fell in central and northern Europe during the 1970s, originating a core/periphery divide in fertility. By 1980 only the four Cohesion countries (Greece, Ireland, Portugal, and Spain) were still above the replacement rate. The TFR of Germany was below 1.5 and the other EU countries—bar France, the UK, and the four Cohesion countries—were at levels between 1.5 and 1.7. Ten years later, only Ireland and Sweden were above the replacement rate. This was a decade of rapid fertility decline in the periphery of the EU. TFRs in Greece, Portugal, and Spain fell from above the replacement rate in 1980 to below 1.5 in 1990. Italy had the lowest TFR with 1.26 and only Austria and Germany had fertility rates that could be compared with those of the four Mediterranean countries. The fall in the number of babies has continued throughout the 1990s. In 1997 not only none of the EU member states had a TFR above the replacement rate, but six countries had rates below 1.5 (Table 3.1). Spain's low fertility rate (TFR 1.15) was above only these of Bulgaria and Latvia in the world. As in the case of crude birth rates, fertility decline in the periphery means that there is no longer a centre/periphery dichotomy. The pattern has been reversed, with lower TFRs in the southern periphery and higher in the Scandinavian countries.

The dimension of the drop in fertility comes to light when the rates of change in TFRs are taken into account (Table 3.1). The only country in the EU where fertility has not fallen between 1970 and 1997 is Finland. Fertility in the two other Scandinavian countries in the EU (Denmark and Sweden) and Luxembourg has declined only moderately. Everywhere else in the EU the drop in fertility has been strong, with the European periphery experiencing the greatest fall. Ireland, Italy, and Spain had TFRs in 1997 which were less than half their level in 1970. Portugal and Greece had seen their rates almost

Table 3.1 Total fertility rates in EU member states, the US, and Japan, 1970–1997

Country name	1970	1980	1990	1995	1997	Fertility in 1997 as a % of 1970
Austria	2.29	1.62	1.45	1.40	1.37	59.83
Belgium	2.20	1.67	1.62	1.57	1.60	72.73
Denmark	1.95	1.55	1.67	1.79	1.75	89.74
Finland	1.83	1.63	1.78	1.81	1.85	101.20
France	2.48	1.95	1.78	1.66	1.71	68.84
Germany	2.03	1.44	1.45	1.25	1.35	66.50
Greece	2.34	2.23	1.40	1.32	1.30	55.63
Ireland	3.93	3.23	2.12	1.87	1.91	48.60
Italy	2.42	1.64	1.26	1.17	1.20	49.48
Luxembourg	1.98	1.50	1.62	1.68	1.71	86.36
Netherlands	2.57	1.60	1.62	1.53	1.53	59.49
Portugal	2.76	2.19	1.43	1.45	1.44	52.19
Spain	2.84	2.22	1.33	1.19	1.15	40.55
Sweden	1.94	1.68	2.13	1.74	1.74	89.74
United Kingdom	2.44	1.89	1.83	1.71	1.70	69.76
Japan	2.13	1.75	1.54	1.42	1.39	65.11
United States	2.48	1.84	2.08	2.06	1.99	80.24

Source: World Bank World Development Indicators (2000).

halve, and in the remaining countries fertility was between three fifths and two thirds of its 1970 level (Table 3.1).

The analysis of the evolution of TFRs highlights the existence of a rapid convergence across western Europe. The five countries represented in Figure 3.4 follow similar downward trends from different peaks in the mid-1960s. In the cases of France, Germany, and Sweden, the greatest decline occurred during the late 1960s and 1970s. In Ireland and Spain the fall in fertility started in the late 1970s. Fertility rates in France and Germany follow parallel trajectories. The convergence in TFRs was only broken by Sweden in the late 1980s, when a combination of family policies and an economic boom resulted in a rise in its TFR. It was at this time that some demographers (eg. Coleman, 1996b) started to talk about divergence in fertility. The divergence was however short-lived. The economic recession of the early 1990s brought the upward trend in Swedish fertility to an end, with fertility rates in Sweden going back to their 1982 levels (Figure 3.4).

3.2.3 The ageing of the European population

The decline in birth and fertility rates has not only stabilized western Europe's population growth, it is also profoundly altering its age structure. On the one hand, thirty years of falling birth rates have made the younger population cohorts smaller than older ones. In 1998 the largest population cohort measured in five-year groups was that of those aged between 30 and 34. With 30.5 million inhabitants in that age group, the size of the cohort was 50 per cent

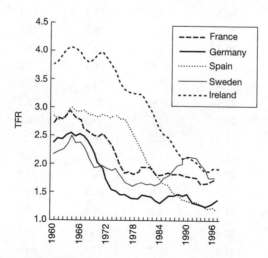

Figure 3.4 Evolution of total fertility rates in selected European countries, 1960–1997
Source: World Bank World Development Indicators (2000).

larger than the cohort of those between 0 and 4. Indeed the cohort of those aged between 55 and 59 was larger than that of those under 5. On the other hand, nutrition and health improvements, together with better and healthier life-styles are expanding the life expectancy of the European population. Europeans live longer and reach old age in a better physical condition than a generation ago. Women in every country in the EU, with the exception of Denmark, Ireland, and Luxembourg, can now expect to live at least until the age of 80. In Denmark, Ireland, and Luxembourg female life expectancy is also close to 80. Male life expectancy is lower, but only in Portugal is it below 72. Overall, in 1997 all countries in the EU had a life expectancy at birth of above 75 (Table 3.2). The life expectancy of European citizens was similar to that of other developed economies and it had increased between 1970 and 1997 at rates which varied from only 2.8 per cent in Denmark to 11.2 per cent in Portugal.

The combination of falling birth and fertility rates and rising life

Table 3.2 Life expectancy at birth in the EU, the US, and Japan, 1970–1997

	1970	1980	1990	1997	Change 1970–97 (in %)
Austria	70.3	72.7	75.7	77.3	10.0
Belgium	71.2	73.2	76.0	76.8	7.9
Denmark	73.3	74.3	74.7	75.3	2.8
Finland	70.3	73.2	75.1	76.9	9.4
France	72.0	74.3	76.8	78.1	8.4
Germany	70.5	72.6	75.1	76.7	8.8
Greece	71.8	74.4	76.9	77.7	8.2
Ireland	71.1	72.7	74.6	75.9	6.8
Italy	71.9	73.9	77.1	78.2	8.8
Luxembourg	70.3	72.7	75.2	76.5	8.7
Netherlands	73.5	75.7	76.9	77.5	5.4
Portugal	67.4	71.4	73.7	75.0	11.2
Spain	72.3	75.5	76.7	77.9	7.7
Sweden	74.5	75.9	77.5	79.1	6.2
United Kingdom	71.7	73.8	75.6	77.1	7.6
United States	70.8	73.7	75.2	76.1	7.5
Japan	71.9	76.0	78.8	80.0	11.2

Source: World Bank World Development Indicators (2000).

expectancy is ageing the population of the EU both in absolute and relative terms. In absolute terms, the number of people over 70 in the EU in 1998 (41.5 million) had increased by 40 per cent with respect to 1980. In relative terms, the percentage of the population aged 65 and above had risen considerably between 1960 and 1997 in all European countries, bar Ireland (Table 3.3). In Greece, Finland, and Portugal the percentage of the population aged 65 and above doubled between 1960 and 1997 (Table 3.3). Italy and Spain were not far behind.

There has been considerable convergence among EU member states since 1960. In this year two groups of countries could be distinguished: the countries with more than 10 per cent of their population aged 65 and above in central and northern Europe (Austria, Belgium, Denmark, France, Germany, Ireland, Luxembourg, Sweden, and the UK) and those with lower percentages of elderly population in southern Europe, Finland, and the Netherlands.

Table 3.3 Population aged 65 and above (% of total) in the EU, the US, and Japan, 1960–1997

	1960	1970	1980	1997	Change 1960–97 (in %)	Change 1980–97 (in %)
Austria	12.0	14.1	15.4	14.8	23.3	−3.5
Belgium	12.0	13.4	14.3	16.0	34.1	12.0
Denmark	10.6	12.3	14.4	14.7	39.2	2.2
Finland	7.2	9.2	12.0	14.4	99.2	20.0
France	11.6	12.9	14.0	15.4	31.9	10.0
Germany	11.5	13.7	15.6	15.5	34.5	−0.7
Greece	8.2	11.1	13.2	16.6	100.9	26.0
Ireland	11.2	11.3	10.7	11.3	1.0	5.2
Italy	9.3	10.9	13.2	16.6	78.2	26.1
Luxembourg	10.8	12.0	13.5	13.9	28.6	3.4
Netherlands	9.0	10.2	11.5	13.4	49.0	16.5
Portugal	8.0	9.2	10.5	16.1	101.2	53.6
Spain	8.2	9.8	10.7	15.9	93.9	49.1
Sweden	12.0	13.7	16.3	17.3	44.4	6.1
United Kingdom	11.7	12.9	15.1	15.8	35.0	4.7
United States	9.2	9.8	11.2	12.3	34.1	9.9
Japan	5.7	7.1	9.0	15.5	169.8	71.1

Source: World Bank World Development Indicators (2000).

Finland, with only 7.2 per cent, had the lowest proportion of elderly population (Table 3.3). Higher levels of ageing in the peripheral countries have
evened out differences among EU member states. In 1997 the great majority
of the member states had between 14 and 17 per cent of their population
above the age of 64. The highest rates of elderly population were found in
Sweden, followed by Italy, Greece, Portugal, and Belgium. Ireland was the only
exception, with a proportion of elderly population two thirds the European
average. Among the other developed economies, only Japan had a worse ageing problem than the EU. Although in 1997 the proportion of its population
above the age of 64 was slightly lower than the EU average, its rate of ageing
throughout the period, and especially during the 1980s and 1990s, was higher
than in any European country. In the US, as well as in Australia or Canada,
ageing was much less of a problem. The percentage of the population aged 65
and above in these countries was closer to that of Ireland than to the European
average.

The ageing process seems to have peaked in the 1980s in some European
countries. Since then, Austria and Germany have seen a small relative decline
in their elderly population, due to the incorporation into the ranks of the
elderly of the depleted war generations. In Denmark, Ireland, Luxembourg,
Sweden, and the UK the proportion of elderly population has remained
relatively stable. In contrast, the Mediterranean countries have seen the percentage of those aged 65 and above swell since 1980 (Table 3.3). Population
projections by the United Nations Population Division (2000) predict that the
process of ageing in the EU is far from over. According to the medium variant
in these projections, the elderly population in the EU is going to increase from
61.6 million people in 2000 to 95.6 million in 2050. This increase of 55 per
cent will be reflected in changes in the population structure. The percentage of
the elderly population will jump from 16.4 to 28.9 per cent (Table 3.4).
According to this projection, of the four largest EU countries, only the UK is
predicted to have less than one quarter of the population over the age of 64. In
Italy, the proportion will be greater than one third. And the number of adults
per senior citizen will decline dramatically from levels of around four today to
slightly more than two in France, Germany, and the UK and one and a half in
Italy in 2050 (Table 3.4). The US will not be spared from the ageing process,
although by 2050 its proportion of elderly population will be roughly similar
to that of some European regions in 2000.

At a regional level the panorama is even more complex. Ageing is becoming
a key issue in numerous southern European regions. Four regions in the
centre of Italy (Emilia-Romagna, Liguria, Tuscany, and Umbria), the French
Limousin, the Portuguese Alentejo, and the northern islands of the Aegean in
Greece already face a serious ageing problem. More than 21 per cent of their
respective populations are above the age of 64. One fifth of the population of

Table 3.4 Predicted evolution of the total and elderly population in selected European countries, the EU, and the US, 2000–2050

	Total population		Pop. Change	Elderly population (65+)		% Elderly		Support ratio (15–64/65+)	
	2000	2050	2000–5	2000	2050	2000	2050	2000	2050
France	59.08	59.88	1.35	9.41	15.26	15.93	25.48	4.10	2.26
Germany	82.22	73.30	−10.85	13.44	20.79	16.35	28.36	4.17	2.05
Italy	57.30	41.20	−28.10	10.41	14.37	18.17	34.88	3.72	1.52
UK	58.83	56.68	−3.65	9.43	14.11	16.03	24.89	4.06	2.37
EU	375.28	331.31	−11.72	61.60	95.60	16.41	28.86	4.08	1.96
USA	278.35	349.32	25.50	34.83	75.90	12.51	21.73	5.28	2.82

Note: Population in millions.   *Source*: Own elaboration with United Nations Population Division data. Medium variant.

many other regions in Italy, Greece, northern Spain, southern and central France, the south west of England, and central Sweden is made of senior citizens (Figure 3.5).

Population ageing is so widespread across the EU that only a handful of European regions have proportions of elderly population that can be compared with the US rate. These are either former peripheral regions (Ireland, Northern Ireland, the north of Portugal, and Campania in Italy), capital regions (London and Paris), or completely new territories regained from the sea (the province of Flevoland in the Netherlands).

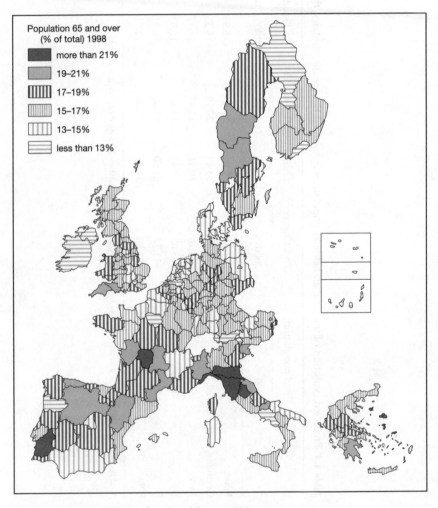

Figure 3.5 Regional share of senior citizens, 1998

3.3 The factors behind ageing

As we have seen, the combination of falling birth and fertility rates and the increase in life expectancy is profoundly altering the demographic structure of the EU. But what are the causes behind rising life expectancy and falling fertility rates? How can the ageing process be explained?

As we have seen, ageing has two sides: higher life expectancy and low fertility. It is easier to explain the causes behind higher life expectancy than to outline the reasons of falling fertility in Europe. I will start with the former before addressing the latter. Higher life expectancy is closely associated with the advancement of medicine and health. The eradication—or near eradication—of many infectious and contagious diseases, the advancement in the treatment of degenerative diseases, and nutritional and health improvements have contributed to lengthening the life of western European citizens and to keeping mortality rates close to their natural level. Social factors, like the relative wealth of European societies, which allow for the development and implementation of medical advances, or the reduction in the number of hours worked during life, also contribute to raising the number of European citizens that reach old age.

Explaining why European women are postponing having babies and, when they do, deciding to have fewer children than their mothers and grandmothers is more difficult to assess. Technical progress explanations do not provide the answer. Advances in and greater availability of contraceptive methods have facilitated the reduction in fertility. The generalization of the contraceptive pill and of the use of other female contraceptive methods has given women greater control over family planning. Although some claim that the generalization of the contraceptive pill is the main factor behind declines in fertility (Murphy, 1993), the more general view is that other factors play a greater role. Contraceptive measures have been adopted in Europe for centuries and cannot be regarded as the sole or the main factor behind the decline in fertility in Europe. They tend to be considered more as a tool in family planning than as one of the causes of the decline.

Most explanations of the reduction in fertility in Europe are of a socioeconomic nature. The economic approach, first developed by Gary Becker (1981), takes into account the pecuniary and time costs of having children. When children were regarded as an important economic asset for the future of the family and there was a high probability of not reaching adulthood, having children was considered a need in order to safeguard the future of the family. Once infant mortality rates have been reduced to a minimum and children are no longer be perceived as sources of future family support, as is the case in all

European societies, the cost of having children increases. And this cost is not just valued in terms of the material and emotional support a child needs until she or he leaves the family home, but also of the opportunity costs of child-bearing. These opportunity costs are greater in societies with a high female participation in the labour market. Having and raising children represents for many women a period out of the labour market and, in some cases, even excludes them permanently from it. Despite the fact that increasingly more and more women are taking full-time jobs after maternity, many women still stop working altogether after their have they first child and many only return to the labour market as part-time workers or when the child or children are of school age. This situation was sustainable for most families during the years of the post-war social compromise, when the generally accepted social roles were that of the male breadwinner and of the mother in charge of the children (Esping-Andersen, 1999). Several factors have radically changed this panorama.

First comes the decline in job stability across western Europe. As described in Chapter 5, the period since the mid-1970s has been one of rising unemployment and rising precariousness in the labour force. Real wages have declined in many sectors and a single salary often does not suffice to support a normal family. Moreover, relying on just one salary in a world in which job stability is becoming something of the past entails significant risks. Therefore and in contrast to previous decades, female work is increasingly an economic necessity for families.

The second set of factors is related to what is known as the sociological approach. Sociological explanations of postponing and/or reducing child-bearing look into the rising educational attainment of women and their greater participation in the labour force as the two key factors. In most west-ern European countries the educational gap between men and women has been drastically reduced over the last few decades. In some countries women even outnumber men in university education. Access to education has given recent generations of women greater possibilities in the labour market than their mothers ever had. Female employment, in general, and the number of mothers in paid jobs, in particular, has increased dramatically (Ermisch, 1996). Between 1970 and 1997 the proportion of women employed has risen by more than 40 per cent in the Netherlands, Portugal, Denmark, Ireland, and the UK. Lower increases have been achieved in most countries and only in Finland, Italy, and Spain has the rise in female employment been below 10 per cent (Table 3.5).

It has been argued that female employment status is the main determinant of the presence and number of children and, consequently, of the decline in fertility in western Europe. Working women tend to have fewer children and have those children later in life than women who do not work. Kalwij (2000)

Table 3.5 Evolution of female employment in the EU, 1970–1997

	Female emp. 1970 (%)	Female emp. 1997 (%)	Male emp. 1997 (%)	Increase in female emp. 1970–97	Female as a % of male emp. (1997)
Austria	38.4	46.2	65.6	20.3	70.4
Belgium	30.5	36.3	56.4	19.0	64.4
Denmark	36.1	55.2	68.8	52.9	80.2
Finland	43.7	46.6	56.1	6.6	83.1
France	36.2	41.2	56.3	13.8	73.2
Germany	38.6	43.1	61.5	11.7	70.1
Greece	25.7	30.8	59.0	19.8	52.2
Ireland	26.2	38.3	61.5	46.2	62.3
Italy	28.5	28.9	55.8	1.4	51.8
Luxembourg	26.7	36.8	63.5	37.8	58.0
Netherlands	25.9	46.8	68.4	80.7	68.4
Portugal	25.4	45.7	63.2	79.9	72.3
Spain	24.4	26.4	52.1	8.2	50.7
Sweden	35.8	49.2	57.3	37.4	85.9
United Kingdom	35.6	50.0	64.9	40.4	77.0
EU	—	39.9	59.5	—	67.1

Source: World Bank World Development Indicators (2000).

even indicates that female employment is a much more important factor than the expansion of female education when adopting family planning decisions. In his analysis of birth patterns in Dutch households, he finds that after controlling for female employment status, the educational attainment of both the woman and the man in the households are found to have little effect on the presence and number of children.

Overall, greater access to education and the greater participation of women in the labour force have brought about changes in the attitude of women and families towards child-rearing. With younger women as qualified as men and earning in many cases as much as their partners, traditional family roles are changing. Mem are becoming more involved in child-rearing (Joshi, 1998). Yet, this sort of attitude is still far from widespread across Europe. Throughout western European societies childcare still has a much greater impact on a woman's time than on a man's. Hence the opportunity cost of having a child is greater for women and increases as women's wages rise (Ermisch, 1996). As a consequence, women with higher relative wages tend to postpone first births and to reduce the number of children they have (Heckman and Walker, 1990). If these factors are added to the greater job market instability, to high male unemployment, and mounting lone parenthood and divorce rates, the prospects for change in fertility rates in western Europe look bleak.

The predominant demographic theories that explain low fertility by a combination of economic and social factors, which include greater female education and labour participation, and the opportunity costs of having children, are to a certain extent contradicted by empirical evidence in Europe. The argument that female employment reduces fertility is challenged by the fact that the lowest fertility rates in the EU are found in Spain and Italy, precisely the two countries with the lowest female employment levels (Table 3.5). In contrast, Denmark, the UK, Sweden, the Netherlands, and Finland, the countries with the highest rates of female employment, had relatively high fertility rates within the EU context. Explanations linked to the level of education and the rising opportunity costs as women's wages rise could explain high teenage pregnancy rates in the UK. But the UK is an exception in this field. Teenage pregnancy rates are low in most other EU countries and the tendency everywhere in Europe is to move towards later maternity (Coleman, 1996b). Child-bearing by women in their thirties is increasingly common, precisely at a time when the opportunity costs for women tend to be higher.

In view of these discrepancies between theoretical explanations and empirical evidence in the EU, other factors must be taken into account in order to explain differences in fertility rates and ageing trends in western Europe. One of these factors is the impact of family policies, which is analysed in the next section.

3.4 Policies aimed at tackling demographic change

Policies aimed at tackling demographic change in western Europe have two aspects. The first aspect is made up of family policies, whose main aim is to address some of the factors responsible for low fertility. The other aspect is social policies for the aged.

3.4.1 Family policies

Many European governments have not remained idle in the face of the declining fertility and the progressive ageing of their populations and have adopted a range of pro-natalist family policies aimed at encouraging women and families to have more children and thus to limit the effects of ageing. The adoption of pro-natalist family policies is nothing new. They were first implemented in the inter-war period in Sweden, France, and Belgium in order to try to redress falling birth rates. But the dimension and the scale of current family policies in the EU are unprecedented (Gauthier, 1999). European countries have implemented a host of 'family friendly policies', which in many cases include child benefit packages, public childcare measures, maternity and parental leave, and other public support measures for working mothers.

Family policies aimed at promoting fertility vary widely across the EU. Some countries have put into practice comprehensive sets of measures that go beyond the narrow realm of family policy, whereas others have adopted more piecemeal policies. The greatest effort to promote fertility has taken place in Sweden, whose fertility policy has not only included a generous child benefit package and equally generous public childcare provision and maternity and parental leave, but also a 'whole raft of measures, including a series of equal opportunities agreements, to make employment and family life compatible' (Hantrais, 1997: 366). The other Scandinavian countries, Denmark and Finland, have been less bold in their approach than Sweden. They have adopted child support packages as well as measures to promote greater gender equality, but the resources devoted to family and related policies have fallen short of the Swedish model. In Denmark, female part-time work has been encouraged. Despite these internal differences, Scandinavian countries on the whole can be considered to be at the forefront of the effort to make child-rearing and female work compatible.

France also stands out in the EU for its family-friendly policy. French family policies have been designed in order to enable economically active women to continue raising children. These pro-natalist measures have been targeted at achieving a horizontal and vertical redistribution of resources to families with children, with specific emphasis on the promotion of families with three children (Hantrais, 2000). Belgium and Luxembourg have adopted family policies that follow closely the French model.

Generous family policies are also the norm in Austria and Germany. However, in the Austrian and German model the bulk of resources have been devoted to support mothers who stay at home to look after children (Hantrais, 1997). This has led some researchers to define German family policy as a breadwinner regime (Gustafsson et al., 1996). The UK's family policy, in contrast, has been dominated by means-testing and the aim of tackling child poverty. Low-income mothers and families have benefited the most from support measures.

The Netherlands, Ireland, and the Mediterranean countries have, in contrast, been less prone to try to foster child births through family policies. The reluctance to intervene in family affairs in these countries has different origins. In some countries (basically Ireland) the Catholic Church still has a tight grip on family matters. In others—chiefly Italy and Spain, but also Ireland—the family is regarded as a private institution and therefore best left to individual decisions. Past experiences of pro-natalist policies linked to dictatorships have also made Italy and Spain—as was earlier the case with Germany—somewhat wary of meddling in the realm of the family. A further expectation for the paucity of family benefits is the cost of this sort of policy for countries that, with the exception of the Netherlands and, until recently, Ireland, had fewer public resources to spend. The unwillingness to intervene in family affairs does not mean that child support packages are absent or that other family-friendly measures, such as maternity or parental leave, do not exist. However, these measures have been conspicuously less generous than in the rest of the EU. The relatively low provision of child support measures in the Netherlands has been somewhat compensated by labour market conditions which favour female part-time work (Crouch, 1999).

Has the adoption of family policies across the EU contributed to curbing declining fertility? Are family policies likely to provide a remedy for the ageing process in western Europe? It is always difficult to assess the impact of any public policy. Many factors beyond the control of policy-makers may affect the outcome of specific measures. Family policy is no exception. There have been strong claims that different family policy regimes in Europe have had little influence on the evolution of fertility rates. Gauthier (1996) argues that in light of recent changes in family structure and of the entry of women into the labour force, the impact of traditional family policies on increasing fertility and reducing the ageing of the population has been weak. Hoem (1993) maintains that changes in fertility and birth rates are more the result of economic circumstances and social factors and that the role of policy in such changes is at best limited. Others, in contrast, claim that family policies matter. Pinelli (1995), for example, suggests that policies and institutions contribute to bringing together the economic needs of working women and child-bearing and rearing.

The evidence on the evolution of fertility rates in western European countries is inconclusive on this matter. Some evidence supports the argument that family policy is effective. The paucity of family policies in the Mediterranean countries may have contributed to depressing their TFRs. The meagre support for mothers and families in Greece, Italy, and Spain is doing little to encourage women from these countries to have more babies or to have them earlier. Higher fertility in the states which have devoted more resources to family policies, such as Sweden, Finland, Denmark, France, or the UK, may be a sign that a well-targeted and structured policy—even if incapable of reversing the fertility trends—may prevent its free fall. Some have seen in the sudden rise of the Swedish TFR during the late 1980s a further sign of the positive effect the combination of family policies with measures aimed at achieving equality in the labour market may have on child-bearing decisions (Pinelli, 1995). In addition, it has been claimed that different family policy regimes lead women to adopt different child-bearing behaviours. This has been argued by Hantrais (1997) in the cases of France and the UK, two countries with similar fertility trajectories. The more universal French approach to family policy is encouraging more working women to have children and keeping the number of women who remain childless low. In contrast, the British means-tested approach to family policy is contributing to a greater proportion of mothers staying at home to look after their offspring or entering part-time work (Hantrais, 1997: 373). This tendency is more marked amongst mothers with low levels of educational attainment (Gustafsson *et al.*, 1996).

Other pieces of evidence, however, point in a different direction. One is the fact that, despite having similar family policy regimes, fertility in Portugal has remained higher during the 1990s than in Greece or Spain. These different trajectories can neither be explained by the adoption of different policies, nor by the timing of the fertility decline, since the three countries followed similar paths until the late 1980s. Another piece of evidence that works against the possible impact of family policies has been the drop of fertility in Sweden. The sudden fertility rise of the late 1980s came to an end in the early 1990s and by 1995 the TFR in Sweden was already below that of Denmark or Finland, despite relatively lower efforts by the latter on family policies (Coleman, 1996b). The fact that the decline in fertility coincided with a profound economic recession in Sweden reinforces the arguments of those who like Hoem (1993) hold that the evolution of TFRs is more closely related to economic and cultural factors than to policy changes.

In sum, although there is little doubt that family policies play some role in child-bearing decisions and their timing, there is less evidence to support the claim that they encourage women and families to have more children. Different forms of family policies seem to have an influence on factors like the age of having children or on the form of reincorporation (or lack of it) of women into the labour force after childbirth. Yet countries that have put more resources into family-friendly policies have not, on the whole, seen their fertility rates hoisted well above those that have made a lower effort or almost no effort at all in this realm.

3.4.2 Social policies for old age

Social policies for old age are the other side of the ageing process across Europe. An ageing population (and a population that lives much longer) is putting services that cater for and/or are targeted at the elderly under increasing strain. This basically affects pensions, health services, and long-term care costs. As in the EU these sorts of services are generally performed by the public sector, the cost of ageing falls directly on the state.

Social policies for old age have quickly become one of the most—if not the most—important areas of public policy in financial terms. Old age expenditure alone was 10.9 per cent of the European GDP in 1997 (Table 3.6). Few EU states departed from this mean. The exceptions were Italy and Sweden, at the top end, and Luxembourg, Portugal, and, above all, Ireland, at the bottom end. High old age expenditure in Sweden was related to its generous pension scheme, whereas in Italy it resulted from the large number of pensioners below the age of 65. Low old age expenditure in Ireland, Luxembourg, and Portugal is based on their greater demographic dynamism and younger populations.

Cuts in public expenditure, in general, and in social and welfare services, in particular, have not affected the size of old age expenditure as a percentage of

Table 3.6 Old age expenditure as a percentage of GDP and social expenditure in the EU

	Old age expenditure as a percentage of GDP			Old age expenditure as a percentage of social expenditure		
	1997	1993	1980	1997	1993	1980
EU 15	10.9	10.7	—	38.3	36.8	—
Austria	10.6	10.5	9.0	36.8	36.4	34.0
Belgium	8.5	8.5	6.8	30.1	29.0	—
Denmark	11.6	10.7	—	38.2	33.5	—
Finland	8.5	9.5	6.1	29.1	27.5	30.9
France	11.0	10.5	8.1	35.6	33.9	—
Germany	11.5	11.1	10.8	38.4	38.3	40.5
Greece	9.8	9.0	—	41.4	40.5	—
Ireland	3.2	4.3	4.7	18.1	20.8	—
Italy	13.4	12.8	8.3	51.6	49.0	—
Luxembourg	7.1	7.1	8.0	28.6	29.0	—
Netherlands	9.3	10.2	7.5	30.8	30.3	—
Portugal	7.0	6.1	—	31.0	29.0	—
Spain	8.7	8.4	6.2	40.8	35.2	35.3
Sweden	12.3	13.0	—	36.6	33.8	—
United Kingdom	10.1	10.2	—	36.3	34.5	—

Source: EUROSTAT data.

GDP. Between its peak, in 1993, and 1997, social expenditure in the EU fell from levels of 29.1 per cent of GDP to 28.3 per cent. Old age expenditure, in contrast, has managed to increase slightly its share of GDP from 10.7 to 10.9 per cent. The highest relative growth has taken place in Denmark, France, Germany, Italy, Portugal, and Spain (Table 3.6). If compared with the situation in 1980, of all the countries for which long time series of data are available, old age expenditure has gone down in relative terms only in Ireland and Luxembourg. The demographic dynamism of these two countries is once again the main factor behind the freeze in expenditure. In all other countries the relative increase in old age expenditure has been significant: 7 per cent in Germany (which in 1980 already had levels of expenditure close to the 1997 EU average), more than a sixth in Austria, a quarter in Belgium and the Netherlands, more than a third in Finland, France, and Spain, and a staggering 61 per cent in Italy (Table 3.6).

Old age expenditure in the EU represented almost two quarters of all social expenditure in 1997 (Table 3.6). The highest percentages were found in three of the countries with the lowest fertility rates: Italy (more than half), Greece, and Spain. Once again, Ireland had by far the lowest old age expenditure in relative terms.

An elderly population living longer than ever before is also more likely to require health care than a young population. This results in growing pressure on health services across Europe and a need to reform many of them in order to adapt to the specific health needs of the elderly. The cost of sickness and health care in the last years of the twentieth century was around 7 per cent of European GDP and an increasing share of health expenditure was devoted to the needs of the elderly. Other social costs resulting from an ageing population are linked to the rising institutionalization of the elderly in residential care, nursing homes, and to the welfare costs of caring for the elderly in the home. But not all costs of an ageing population fall on the public sector. Across Europe many of the elderly in need of care are still catered for by their families, a factor that has knock-on effects on women's work and family economies.

3.5 Conclusion

The ageing process in the EU poses a serious challenge for the future of European societies. An increasingly aged society tends to be a more conservative and risk-averse society than a society in which young people predominate; it is less open to innovation and foreign influences and, therefore, less mobile and less able to compete. Population ageing also represents a challenge for public and private finances across the EU. On the one hand, rising pension, health, and long-term care costs are pushing national public finances to the brink of bankruptcy, unless the ageing trend is redressed or public finances are reformed. On the other, more money needs to be spent in order to try to encourage women and couples to have more children.

The EU seems to be going in this direction. As we have seen, the UN Population Division (1999) predicts that by 2050 the EU will have one person over the age of 65 per two adults. If this prediction were to be correct, the EU will be by far the most aged society in the world, and some of the above-mentioned problems may appear. National executives are increasingly aware of this situation and are starting to adopt measures. In some cases the measures are directly targeted at stemming the process of ageing. Family policies have become more aggressive in many EU countries since low fertility rates became common (Gauthier, 1999). Replacement migration, as suggested by the UN Population Division (2000), may play a greater role in curbing the ageing process in the future. In other cases, the policy measures and reforms are aimed more at reducing the current and future economic costs of ageing. Measures to make early retirement more difficult or to encourage workers to opt for private pensions go in this direction. Plans to raise the retirement age are also under consideration in certain countries.

The vision of the ageing process presented in this chapter may be, however, a rather reductionist one. The chapter basically assumes the prevailing vision of an ageing society more as a financial burden than as an asset. This vision may not necessarily be what lies ahead. People are reaching the age of retirement in much better health than hitherto, and medical and health care advances are making sure that many senior citizens still have long productive years in front of them. Today's senior citizens are also more open to innovations and new trends than their predecessors of earlier generations. Hence the future in a society with a larger percentage of over 65s may be much less gloomy than most of the current literature predicts. But even in the best-case scenario, an increasingly aged society would certainly have different needs from our current society and this would imply thorough structural reforms in western Europe.

4

Migration and xenophobia

4.1 Introduction

While the EU ages, many neighbouring countries to the east and south have young and dynamic populations who find few outlets in their local labour markets. The combination of these factors has led to the development of large migration flows towards western Europe. As we have seen in Chapter 3, some claim that massive long-term migration is the main solution for the ageing problem, as well as a way of easing the social and economic pressure on the countries of origin of the migrants. The Single European Market sanctioned the principle of free movement of EU citizens within the member states. Yet, the panorama changes radically as far as migration into the EU is concerned. European and national immigration laws tend to discourage immigration from outside the EU, a factor which has led to the flourishing of a clandestine trade in foreigners wishing to work in what King, Lazaridis, and Tsardanidis (1999) have called the new European 'Eldorado'. The increasing presence of migrants on west European streets, together with the existence in some European countries of a large 'non-white' population, is also creating additional internal problems. Xenophobia, the fear and hatred of the 'other', is growing across western Europe and is sometimes reflected in the growth of racist attitudes and in the emergence of racist right-wing parties.

In this chapter I will present how migration flows within and towards the EU have changed in the last few decades and the problems being generated by new migration flows. In order to achieve this I will first briefly review the different conceptions of migration and its forms. Section 4.3 will focus on the migration trends in and towards Western Europe since the end of the Second World War. Section 4.4 deals with the emergence of a new form of migration in the 1990s. Finally, Section 4.5 presents the problems related to the assimilation of migration in the EU, with special attention paid to legislation on migration and to the growth of xenophobia and racism and the emergence of racist parties.

4.2 Migration and its forms

In its simplest form, migration refers to the movement or displacement of a person or a number of persons from one place to another. There are numerous forms of migration. One classification refers to the number of people involved. Migration can be individual, when only one person moves; group migration when it involves a group of people; or mass migration when large groups of people move. Another classification makes reference to the origin and destination of the migrants. Migration can be regional, when it occurs within the limits of a region; inter-regional, when it is confined within national borders, or international, when migrants move from one country to another. Migration can also be temporary, when migrants move on a seasonal basis or for a determined period of time, or permanent. A fourth classification distinguishes between legal and illegal migration. Legal migration is conducted within the framework of the law, with migrants obtaining work and residence permits in their country of destination. Illegal migration is clandestine, increasingly in the hands of mafias and racketeers, with immigrants living in poor conditions and under the risk of expulsion or deportation if caught by the authorities (Budapest Group, 1999).

But perhaps the most important classification refers to the motives of migrants. Migration can be triggered by economic or other reasons. Economic migration takes place when people move from one place to another in search of jobs and/or a better life. Whether it involves nineteenth and early twentieth century Europeans going to America, Italians, Turks, and other Mediterranean people looking for jobs in the cities of Germany or France in the 1950s and 1960s, Mexicans and other Latin Americans crossing the Rio Grande into the US, or present-day Eastern Europeans and Sub-Saharan Africans moving into the EU, economic migration has become the most common form of migration towards developed countries since the end of the Second World War. Economic migration can adopt two forms:

a) Migrant-initiated: When migrants, on their own initiative, decide to set off for another country in search of better working and living conditions for themselves and, very often, their families. This migration is completely voluntary and migrants are not forced or coerced to leave their places of origin. It is the most common form of economic migration.

b) Employer-initiated: When employers, faced with a shortage of local labour, decide to recruit labour from other areas. International employer-initiated labour migration is frequently managed by the state, which often tends to organize the recruitment of workers abroad. Employer-initiated migration was common throughout the 1950s and 1960s, but its importance has waned in recent times.

The evolution of economic migration is closely related to economic cycles. During the early stages of economic expansion, unemployment tends to fall and immigration rises rapidly. Emigration falls as immigration expands. At the peak of the cycle unemployment and emigration are reduced to a minimum, as immigration peaks. The start of economic recession brings about a reduction in the number of immigrants and a rise in unemployment. As economic conditions worsen, net emigration replaces immigration, with the trough in the economic cycle being characterized by high emigration and unemployment (Fielding, 1993: 11).

The other side of the coin of economic migration is migration provoked by non-economic causes. Although the array of non-economic causes which may force individuals to migrate is almost boundless, the main factors behind non-economic migration tend to be natural disaster, war, and political and/or social persecution. Migrants displaced by non-economic factors are distinguished in the eyes of the public from normal economic migrants, and normally referred to, depending on their status, as refugees or asylum seekers.

Natural disaster tends to strike unexpectedly and provokes sudden spurts of mass migration. Earthquakes, volcanic eruptions, floods, and serious droughts are the most frequent causes of this sort of movement. Natural disaster migration tends to be temporary, with refugees returning to their places of origin once the conditions that triggered the migration recede, although in some extreme cases—such as the destruction of the majority of the island of Montserrat by a volcanic eruption—natural disasters may force permanent migration. The relatively benign natural conditions and the level of development of the EU have made the possibility of migration as a result of natural disaster within Europe relatively remote. However, the EU is becoming an increasing target for migrants fleeing natural disasters elsewhere in the world.

War provokes the displacement of large groups of people leaving conflict areas. Migration as a result of war has been common in Europe in the past, and was one of the main factors in the large displacements of refugees during the first half of the twentieth century. During the second half of the twentieth century, migration as a result of war became rare in Europe. The collapse of the Iron Curtain and the successive conflicts in the former Yugoslavia have, however, produced new flows of refugees in Europe during the 1990s.

A third cause of non-economic migration is political and/or social persecution. This occurs when individuals are forced to migrate for fear of their lives or personal security. Political and social persecution may take different forms. Opposition to autocratic regimes and dictatorships and being of a different race or religion are the most common reasons for persecution. People fleeing persecution are often given a different status to most other migrants and classified as political refugees or asylum seekers. The main difference between the two categories is that the granting of asylum to refugees is generally co-ordinated by international organizations within the framework of government programmes, whereas asylum seekers apply for asylum on arrival at the host country. All countries in western Europe have asylum laws, although the generosity of different asylum regimes varies widely from country to country. Migration motivated by political and/or social persecution was common in Europe in the inter-war period and during the Cold War. Nazi Germany or communist regimes of eastern Europe became an important source of refugees claiming political asylum. After a certain lull coinciding with the final stages and the collapse of communism in eastern Europe, the number of asylum seekers has been growing significantly in the EU in the last few years of the twentieth century.

Economic and other forms of migration are not mutually exclusive and classifying any individual as an economic or any other form of migrant could be misleading. Many factors shape any individual decision to migrate and often a series of economic, political, and social reasons play a role in this decision.

4.3 Mass migration in post-war Europe

Mass migration is by no means a new phenomenon in western Europe. The movement of peoples into, within, and out of western Europe can be traced back to the dawn of history. In modern times mass migration out of Europe predominated. America, Australasia, and South Africa were the main destinations of millions of Europeans. The outward movement peaked at the beginning of the twentieth century, when an average of more than a million Europeans were leaving Europe annually for America.

The second half of the twentieth century saw a reversal of this trend. Mass migration out of western Europe was replaced by migrations within and into western Europe. The end of the Second World War brought about a profound resettlement of population. The redesigning of European borders at the end of the war and the flow of war refugees back to their places of origin put an estimated 25 million people on the move (Kosinski, 1970). The flow of people was mainly from east to west. It involved approximately 12 million ethnic Germans expelled from former German territories in East Prussia, Pommerania, and Silesia, which became parts of Poland and the Soviet Union, and from their former homes in Czechoslovakia, Hungary, Romania, and the Soviet Union. Around 4 million ethnic Germans initially settled in East

Germany, but the bulk of the migration of ethnic Germans (around 8 million people) was into West Germany. The movement was not just in one direction. 10.5 million displaced persons, which included prisoners of war, camp survivors, and people who had worked as slave labour—but also ordinary people—left Germany. The redesigning of Europe's borders also generated movements of ethnic Poles, Russians, Finns, Hungarians, Italians, and Turks (King, 1993b).

The establishment of communist regimes in countries occupied by the Soviet army triggered a renewed flow of migrants from east to west. The main movement was from East into West Germany. Between the creation of the German Democratic Republic and the erection of the Berlin Wall in 1961—which completely sealed East German borders—approximately 3.8 million East Germans fled to West Germany. Poles, Czechs, and Hungarians also moved to the West in the early stages of communism, although in far lower numbers.

During the 1950s, the war-caused and political east–west flow started being substituted by an economic south–north migration. The post-war decades were a period of huge economic expansion in western and central European countries. Between 1960 and 1974 real GDP in the then EC increased by 90 per cent and industrial output by 103 per cent. The economic and industrial expansion in the EC created a great demand for jobs, especially in low-skilled and poorly paid sectors which the local workforce increasingly rejected. The flow was started in the 1950s by Italian workers moving to Germany, Switzerland, and France. Spaniards, Portuguese, and Greeks followed. The third wave was basically made up of Turks and Yugoslavs, with a final wave of workers from the Maghreb and the Third World (King, 1993b). The flow of migrants was not exclusively south–north. Finns constituted the main foreign group in the Swedish market and the UK labour force benefited from the contribution of hundreds of thousands of Irish.

Migration in the 1950s and 1960s was often employer-initiated and state-managed. Employers in countries with expanding job markets looked to the south for cheap and amenable labour, which was increasingly difficult to recruit at home. National consulates in the countries of origin of the migrants and national ministries played an important role in the early stages of recruitment, as brokers between migrants and firms. Once a sizeable community of migrants had been established in the host country, voluntary migration took over. Migrants from specific places in southern Italy, western Spain, Portugal, or any other source country targeted specific destinations in France, Germany, or any host country, where they had or were likely to find relatives, friends, or people from the same area.

The flow of migrants into the host countries was far from homogeneous. The countries of origins of immigrants varied widely from one host country to another. Germany, the main host country in the post-war decades, had received successive waves of East Germans, Italians, Yugoslavs, and Turks (King, 1993b). France had a large inflow of Portuguese and Algerians, with lesser numbers of Spaniards, Italians, and Moroccans. Turks and people from the ex-colonies in the Caribbean and Indonesia formed the majority of immigrants in the Netherlands. Italians and Moroccans dominated in Belgium and the Portuguese in Luxembourg. Finns outnumbered any other nationality among migrants to Sweden, and the Irish and West Indians and people from the Indian Subcontinent made up the bulk of the immigrants in the UK.

The dimension of the south–north economic migration of the 1950s, 1960s, and early 1970s was phenomenal. By the mid-1970s almost 5 per cent of the population of the Netherlands was foreign. Immigrants made up between 5 and 10 per cent of the population of France, Germany, and Sweden. The proportion rose to 10 per cent in Belgium, 15 per cent in Switzerland, and almost 25 per cent in Luxembourg. Around 15 per cent of the population of Paris was foreign born and, for a period, it was considered, after Lisbon, the second Portuguese city in the world. There were around 1.2 million Turks and 600 000 Italians in Germany, almost 900 000 Portuguese and 800 000 Algerians in France, and Italians numbered 450 000 and 300 000 in Switzerland and Belgium respectively (SOPEMI, 1977).

Not only did the origin of migrants vary from one country to another. The sectors in which they worked also varied. In West Germany most migrant workers found jobs in manufacturing, around 15 per cent went into construction, and smaller numbers into low-skilled services. In France around 30 per cent were employed in construction. A lower proportion found jobs mainly as health workers and in manufacturing. In the UK there was less concentration. Different migrant groups were employed in different sectors. Public services were the main initial destination for West Indians, whereas South Asians found jobs in competitively weak manufacturing sectors, such as textiles (SOPEMI, various years).

There were also differences in the formal rights of immigrants. In Germany, Austria, and Switzerland immigrants were legally entitled to stay as long as their contract lasted. The German conception of migrants as *Gastarbeiters* (or guest workers) implied high levels of job security but little else. Once the contract finished or if unemployed *Gastarbeiters* found their possibilities of remaining in Germany limited. Immigration legislation in Switzerland was even stricter. The rigid legal framework in these countries meant that the possibilities of permanent settlement or of obtaining citizenship were extremely reduced, if not impossible. In countries which received a considerable inflow of immigrants from colonies or former colonies (the UK, France, and the Netherlands) the rights of immigrants were generally more developed. Immigrants sometimes came with British, French, or Dutch passports. In other cases they could apply for permanent residence or citizenship after a period living in the country (Rasmussen, 1997).

The post-war immigration flow ended—or, at least, changed—with the economic crisis of the 1970s. Growing unemployment in western Europe (see Chapter 5) meant that from 1974 onwards, the years when population outflows exceeded inflows became frequent in Austria, Belgium, France, Germany, and Switzerland. Employers stopped recruiting migrant workers and between 1974 and 1980 the stock of migrant workers in the main seven European host countries fell by 1 million or 22 per cent of the stock (SOPEMI, various years). *Gastarbeiters* and other migrant workers were encouraged to return to their countries of origin. However this return migration was neither universal, nor did it affect all groups of immigrants in the same way. Countries in the south of the EU and the former Yugoslavia benefited most from the return of migrants. Economic and political improvements in home countries contributed to bolster return migration to Greece, Italy, Portugal, or Spain. The biggest absolute falls in foreign workers took place among the Italian, the Spanish, and the Yugoslav communities living abroad. In relative terms, the greatest decline occurred among the Greeks and the Spaniards (SOPEMI, various years). The number of Italians and Spaniards in France halved between the beginning of the crisis and the late 1980s. The number of Greek workers declined in Germany, Sweden, and Switzerland during the same period. And Ireland managed to pull back a proportion of its citizens living in the UK and elsewhere in Europe. In contrast, although migration from countries outside the EU momentarily lost pace, return migration was much less evident than in the case of the countries of the EU periphery. A recovery of the flows since the late 1970s and family reunification contributed to increase the size of these communities in EU countries. The number of Turkish workers increased by 80 and 40 per cent in the Netherlands and Germany respectively between the mid-1970s and 1990. The number of Moroccans living in the Netherlands more than doubled. It grew by more than 70 per cent in Belgium and France in the same period. And the number of Algerians—the largest foreign group in France in the late 1970s—also expanded (SOPEMI, various years).

Despite these changes, the 1980s were a period of relatively low migration across Europe. High unemployment in many European countries and tighter immigration laws cut immigration flows.

4.4 The renewal of migration in the 1990s

The 1990s and the early twenty-first century have witnessed a revival of migration flows within and towards the EU. The economic bonanza of the second half of the 1990s and the reduction of unemployment rates associated with it and with the introduction of flexibility in many European labour markets (see Chapter 5), together with the implementation of the principle of free movement of people in the Single Market, have contributed to the rise in mobility. The proportion of foreigners and foreign-born population has increased in all of the EU since the mid-1980s, with the exception of France (as a consequence of the high numbers of naturalizations) (SOPEMI, 1999). In 1997 there were 18.6 million foreigners living in EU countries (bar Greece for which no statistics are available), 40 per cent of them in Germany alone (Table 4.1). This represented an increase of more than 5 million people—or almost 40 per cent—since 1987. The greatest absolute increase has taken place in Germany, with a growth of more than 3 million over ten years. In relative terms, the greatest growth of foreigners has taken place in Finland, Austria, and Italy (Table 4.1). With respect to the total population of the country, the highest percentages of foreign population were found in Austria, Belgium, Germany, and, above all, Luxembourg, where foreigners made up more than a third of the total population.

Although recent inward migration flows have taken the percentage of foreign population living in EU countries from levels of around 3.6 per cent in the mid-1980s to around 5 per cent in 1997, the proportion of foreigners living in the EU is still rather small in comparison to that of the US, where in the mid-1990s more than 9 per cent of the population was foreign-born, and of traditional migration countries such as Australia and Canada (Table 4.1).

The increase in foreign population in the EU has been the result of migration flows during the 1990s that differ in many ways from those of the 1950s, 1960s, and early 1970s. First, the traditional south–north division between sources and destinations of migrants within the EU has been completely slashed. Finland, Greece, Ireland, Italy, Portugal, and Spain are no longer sources of emigrants, but have positive migration balances. In some cases, such as Italy, the change happened as early as 1972 (Montanari and Cortese, 1993a). Intra-EU migration is no longer south–north. It occurs in both directions. Ireland's booming economy has attracted large numbers of skilled workers from elsewhere in the EU. Similar flows of qualified individuals have been described in Spain and Portugal, where sun-belt type communities of northern European pensioners are mushrooming. In addition, the 1990s have made all these countries the targets of mass migration from the south and the

Table 4.1 Foreign or foreign-born population, 1987 and 1997

	Foreign population in thousands		% of total population	
	1987	1997	1987	1997
Austria	326	733	4.3	9.1
Belgium	863	903	8.7	8.9
Denmark	136	250	2.7	4.7
Finland	18	81	0.4	1.6
France	3 714	3 597	6.8	6.3
Germany	4 241	7 366	6.9	9.0
Ireland	77	114	2.2	3.1
Italy	572	1 341	1.0	2.2
Luxembourg	103	148	26.8	34.9
Netherlands	592	678	4.0	4.4
Portugal	95	175	1.0	1.8
Spain	335	610	0.9	1.5
Sweden	401	522	4.8	6.0
UK	1 839	2 066	3.2	3.6
EU	13 312	18 584	3.6	4.9
Australia*	3 247	3 908	20.8	21.1
Canada*	3 908	4 971	15.4	17.4
US*	14 080	24 600	6.2	9.3

Notes: * Data for Australia, Canada, and the US refer to foreign-born population in 1986 and 1996.
Source: SOPEMI, 1999.

east. This means that the socio-economic division between north and south has moved south and is now located along the Mediterranean, which increasingly fulfils the same function as the Rio Grande between the US and Mexico: the division between the developed and the developing worlds (Montanari and Cortese, 1993*b*). The former Iron Curtain also marks a similar divide to the East.

Second, and in contrast to common practices in the US, Canada, or Australia, employer-initiated migration and government involvement in managing migration in the EU has almost become a thing of the past. Although there have been recent attempts by governments to resolve specific skills shortages in the labour market by these methods—most notably the attempt

by the German government in the year 2000 to recruit computer program-
mers in India—European employers and governments are now more
reluctant to meddle in migration. Tighter immigration legislation for the
former and political opposition for the latter are barriers which have led to
the decline in these practices. Migration is thus now almost exclusively
migrant-initiated.

Another factor which distinguishes migration at the end of the twentieth
century and beginning of the twenty-first century from earlier waves is the
increase in clandestine and illegal immigration. The completion of the Single
Market and the implementation of the free movement of people within EU
borders has been paralleled by a tightening of national and European immigration laws *vis-à-vis* the rest of the world. The result of more restrictive laws
has been an increase in the number of people who decide to come and stay in
the EU illegally. This process has led to the flourishing of mafias and other
organized crime syndicates trying to smuggle immigrants into Europe. The
consequence is that many of the new immigrants from developing countries
are deprived of the most basic rights.

Finally, the most important factor is the greater diversification of immigrant groups (Salt, 1992). The traditional immigration of masses of unskilled
labour into the EU in the earlier wave has been substituted by a more complex
migration pattern, in which migrants can be divided into three groups:

a) the highly qualified: the highly qualified migrants are generally citizens
   from other EU states, who take advantage of the free movement of people
   within the EU, or even workers from other developed countries (e.g. the
   US, Japan, or Australia), who benefit from the greater mobility of skills in a
   globalized world;

b) low-skilled economic migrants and clandestines: economic migrants from
   developing countries form the majority, often forced to enter the EU
   illegally as a result of more restrictive immigration legislation;

c) refugees and asylum seekers: political migrants mainly from developing
   countries escaping wars and political persecution.

4.4.1 Migration of the highly qualified

The migration of highly qualified individuals in the EU has boomed during
the 1990s. The numbers of foreigners working in areas such as finance, banks,
insurance, and multinational companies in general has expanded enormously
during the last years of the twentieth century. The main beneficiaries of
these migration flows have been the financial centres of the Continent.
French, Italians, Germans, Dutch, Spanish, and Swedes make up a significant

proportion of all those working in the City of London. Banks and insurance companies in Frankfurt are staffed by non-German Europeans. And similar trends are evident in Paris, Berlin, Madrid, Copenhagen, or Stockholm. Multinational companies, especially those close to large urban centres and airport hubs, are increasingly recruiting foreigners. The multinationals located around Schiphol airport in the Netherlands are truly becoming multinationals according to their staff profile. The same is happening in those companies located in the London–Bristol corridor, or on the outskirts of Paris. But the benefits of a pool of highly qualified and highly mobile European workers is expanding to other traditionally less open sectors. Milan's fashion industry is increasingly recruiting on a European, if not global, basis. Universities and research centres in the UK, Ireland, the Netherlands, and Scandinavia have seen a notable increase in the numbers of French, German, Italian, Spanish teachers and researchers. The notoriously rigid university and public research systems of the latter countries pushed many of their teachers and researchers abroad. However, the tide is also shifting in the other direction. The slight opening up of university systems in countries like France, Germany, or Spain is starting to encourage researcher mobility towards these countries. And even the last national bastion in the labour market, public service, is being opened *de facto* in certain EU countries, and most notably the UK.

The spark that triggered the increase in mobility of highly skilled EU nationals has been the establishment of the Single Market. The implementation of the principle of free mobility of people has simplified cross-border migration across the EU. Although cultural and linguistic barriers remain, no longer are work or residence permits needed for EU nationals to work in another EU country. However, the simplification of the bureaucracy of cross-border migration plays only a relatively minor part among the factors which have led to an increase in the movement of highly qualified workers. The mutual recognition of qualifications established in the Maastricht Treaty has further simplified mobility for people holding university degrees. Although the recognition of degrees is still a long bureaucratic process in certain countries, especially in the public sector, in other countries with more flexible labour markets or in the private sector the recognition of qualifications is almost automatic. In addition, freedom of movement in the EU has come at a time when younger generations are better prepared and better travelled than ever before. The number of young Europeans who not only have university degrees, but who also speak foreign languages or who have studied abroad, is much larger than among previous generations.

The simplification of the bureaucratic aspects of mobility and the preparation and willingness to move of younger generations of Europeans have been combined with the processes of globalization and European integration. The globalizing of the world economy and the greater competition linked to it and to the process of European integration are pushing companies to restructure in order to survive and become more competitive. As mentioned in Chapter 1, this process has really taken off in the last five years of the twentieth century. And this restructuring in order to remain competitive is forcing companies—and increasingly universities, research centres, and public sectors—to secure the best staff, regardless of national origin. Recruiting is therefore no longer local or national, but increasingly European and global in nature. Companies announce their vacancies in several countries or on the web and expect to get applications from different parts of the world. Young and highly qualified Europeans are taking advantage of these opportunities. This has led to a radical change in the profile of the European migrant. In contrast to the low-skilled worker from the south of Europe, Ireland, or Finland of the 1960s and early 1990s, the European migrant of the 1990s and early twenty-first century is a highly qualified young professional. No country is benefiting more from this change in the profile of migrants than the UK, where in 1990 33 per cent of the EU (non-Eire) male nationals were professionals and managers (Salt and Ford, 1993).

The change in migration trends does not stop, however, within European borders. Having learned from the success of the US in attracting highly qualified migrants and of their impact on the US economy, European countries are adopting more permissive policies towards qualified migrants from outside the EU. These include a *de facto* more permissive use of work permits for the highly qualified, which has led to an influx of Americans and Japanese in financial services (Salt and Ford, 1993), and measures to link foreign investment to a leaner work permit legislation in several EU member states.

4.4.2 Migration of the low-skilled and the problem of the clandestines

The greater mobility of the highly qualified during the 1990s and early twenty-first century may be qualitatively important, but it is tiny in comparison to the flows among the low-skilled. Migration at the lower end of the scale has increased radically since the beginning of the 1990s and has been dominated by people from outside the EU. As mentioned earlier, the traditional division of the south of Europe as the source and the north as the destination of low-skilled migrants has disappeared. The whole of the EU is now the target of large flows of immigrants escaping poverty to the east and south of the EU's borders.

In contrast to the mobility of the highly qualified, the low skilled and the skilled blue-collar western Europeans have remained relatively immobile in this period of change. The mobility of these groups, who filled the ranks of the previous wave of European migrants, has been impaired by several factors. First is the sectoral shift of the European economy. Manufacturing employment has steeply declined in many European countries since the 1970s and there are fewer vacancies in these areas. Most of the vacancies in the EU now occur in the specialized service sector jobs or in the low value-added service jobs. The former require highly qualified skills; the pay in the latter is often so low that European workers cannot or do not want to compete for those jobs with immigrants from outside the EU. The persistence of unemployment in some sectors of the European economy and in some areas of the EU is an additional factor discouraging the mobility of relatively low-skilled western European workers. Many of the areas where most of the new jobs are being created still have relatively high levels of unemployment. The emergence of a dual economy in large European urban agglomerations has meant that, whereas cities like London, Paris, Frankfurt, Berlin, or Madrid are creating a large number of jobs at the top end of the scale, unemployment at the lower end remains high (Rodríguez-Pose, 1998). Hence the chances for the low-skilled of finding suitable jobs—or better jobs than at home—are slim. Finally, cultural barriers to mobility are still much higher for the low-skilled than for the highly qualified. Although in countries like the Netherlands or in Scandinavia, the linguistic barriers to European mobility (especially in the case of knowledge of English) have all but disappeared, in the remaining European countries the personal cost of moving to another country remains high.

Although immigration from outside the EU was already common in the earlier waves of economic migration, with a large number of Turkish workers settling in Germany, Algerians and other North Africans in France, West Indians and South Asians in the UK, and Surinamese and Indonesians in the Netherlands, only in the 1990s has the phenomenon of low-skilled migration from outside the EU acquired a truly global dimension. Not only is western Europe receiving more immigration from outside the EU than in the 1980s, but the regions of origin of the migrants are increasingly diversified (SOPEMI, 1999).

The first massive flow of migrants of the 1990s coincided with the fall of the Berlin Wall and took an east–west direction. A first wave of Poles, Czechs, and Hungarians into Germany and Austria or of Baltic people into Scandinavia immediately after the fall of the Wall, was followed by other waves of former-Yugoslavs, Albanians, Romanians, Bulgarians, Ukrainians, and Russians into western Europe. In the second half of the 1990s Poles still made up the majority of immigrants coming into Germany, but the number of former-Yugoslavs, Romanians, and Albanians settling in the EU had crept up spectacularly (SOPEMI, 1999). The consequence of this mass migration from the East are the relatively large Polish communities not only in Germany or France, but also in traditionally unlikely destinations for mass migration such as Greece, Italy, Ireland, Spain, or Portugal. Greece and large European cities have large numbers of Albanians and groups of Romanians are increasingly visible in many western European countries.

The second half of the 1990s saw a decline in migration from the East. Although the east–west flow continues, its numbers—at least the official numbers—have declined, especially in Germany (SOPEMI, 1999). The economic and political improvements in certain major countries of origin (see Chapter 6)—and fundamentally in Poland—have contributed to stemming the flow. East–west migration is being replaced by south–north flows. The Mediterranean has become the 'European Rio Grande': a division between poverty to the south and east and the promise of a new 'Eldorado' to the north. The whole of the EU is acting increasinly as a magnet for migrants from all over the Third World. Large numbers of northern and Sub-Saharan Africans, Latin Americans, people from the Middle East, Central and South East Asians and Chinese are knocking on European doors. In many ways and for many people, the EU has become as attractive a destination as the US. And sometimes a closer and easier destination to get in. The new wave of south–north migration is not dissimilar from that experienced by the US for decades. However, the Mediterranean is a longer and more difficult border to police than the Rio Grande or the deserts of Arizona. The fact that it is a sea, rather than a land, border also implies greater risks for migrants who face a dangerous and unfortunately occasionally fatal crossing.

Part of this northward migration by people from outside the EU is legal. The number of migrants from outside the EU has grown exponentially during the 1990s. Legal migration is, however, probably only the tip of the iceberg. A large proportion of those coming into the EU to work do so illegally. Many enter the EU through its eastern terrestrial border, after having made sometimes long trips from parts of eastern Europe or, increasingly, Asia. Others make perilous sea crossings from the Turkish coast to the Greek islands or the Greek mainland, or from North Africa to southern Spain or the Italian islands of Sicily and Lampedusa. Given the illegal nature of this migration, it is difficult to assess its volume. However, The International Centre for Migration Policy Development estimates that in the last years of the twentieth century between 400 000 and 500 000 migrants were smuggled into the EU annually.

Most migrants become illegal by simply staying after their visa has expired (Salt, 1989). However, as in the case of the illegal migration into the US, the tightening of border controls in the EU is pushing more and more immigrants into the hands of mafioso-style gangs and crime syndicates. Many of the illegal immigrants coming into the EU are asked to pay large sums of money to the gangs that make the border crossings. Since many do not have the money, they become indebted to the gangs and work illegally on arrival in order to repay their debts. In these sorts of jobs they have no rights and often get paid only a fraction of the minimum wage. Many women are forced into prostitution. The border or the Mediterranean crossings are conducted in appalling conditions. Large numbers of clandestines are hidden in trucks or crammed in boats. The consequences are often tragic. The death of 54 Chinese men and women starved of oxygen in a Dutch truck while trying to enter the UK in 2000 is unfortunately not an isolated case. The constant stream of bodies of clandestines washed up by the sea onto Spanish beaches is another testimony to the dimensions of the problem.

Once in the EU, legal unskilled migrants frequently find jobs in low value-added services, for example, as cleaners or waiters, or in marginal activities. Men also find jobs in the construction industry and in labour-intensive agriculture (SOPEMI, 1999). Many clandestines also work in these sectors, but their lack of rights make them an easy prey for exploiters (Budapest Group, 1999). Despite a tightening of controls over employers of illegal labour since the beginning of the 1990s in the great majority of EU countries, the constant inflow of migrants desperate to find any sort of jobs has guaranteed the persistence of exploitation. Finally, many clandestine immigrants are forced to participate in informal activities. These vary from working as street sellers to criminal activities.

4.4.3 Refugees and asylum seekers

Western Europe has witnessed an expansion of refugees and asylum seekers since the end of the 1980s. The causes behind the increase of asylum seekers are related to the proliferation of civil wars and ethnic and nationalist conflict in Europe, Africa, and other parts of the globe since the end of the Cold War. The devastation caused by war and the risk of political persecution by many regimes in the developing world have pushed many people to look for shelter in the EU. Others, however, claim that many refugees and asylum seekers are in reality economic migrants lured by Europe's prosperity.

The flow of asylum seekers towards the EU has multiplied in the 1990s. The collapse of communist regimes in Eastern Europe, the break-up of Yugoslavia and the Bosnian war, together with increasing regional conflict outside Europe generated large numbers of asylum applications in the early 1990s. Germany was the main destination of asylum seekers throughout the 1990s. Asylum applications exceeded 100 000 every single year between 1988 and 1997, reaching more than 400 000 in 1992 (Table 4.2). The post-war German policy, which guaranteed asylum seekers full welfare support during the lengthy period of consideration of their application, was a key factor in making Germany the top European destination. The introduction of tougher legislation on asylum on 1 July 1993 cut the total number of applications by more than

70 per cent in just two years. In relative terms, Sweden and Austria were receiving even more asylum claims than Germany (SOPEMI, 1999).

Towards the end of the 1990s the flow of asylum seekers had changed. The UK, which in 2000 received more than 100 000 applications, is replacing Germany as the main destination (Table 4.2). Belgium, Ireland, and the Netherlands have taken over from Sweden and Austria as the countries with the largest contingents of asylum seekers as a percentage of their populations.

Changes in the destination of the flow of asylum seekers are closely related to changes in asylum legislation in the host countries. Restrictive measures, such as the extension of a visa requirement to a large number of countries or the limitation of the right of asylum to nationals of countries which have not signed the United Nations Convention on Refugees and on Human Rights, have curbed asylum applications in most EU countries in the second half of the 1990s (SOPEMI, 1999). The UK is the main exception. The introduction of a restrictive legislative framework in 1996 only momentarily stemmed the flow. Between 1998 and 2000 the number of applications soared again in the EU. The growing numbers of asylum seekers in the EU are related to the renewal of conflict in the Balkans. Ethnic cleansing and war in Kosovo were a major factor in the increase. Albanians and Kurds also make up a large proportion of all asylum seekers (SOPEMI, 1999).

Higher numbers of asylum seekers in the late 1990s have not meant that the number of applications granted has risen dramatically. Despite the introduction of new legislative frameworks which have speeded up the process, the granting of asylum is still a lengthy affair in most EU member states. Tougher legislation has contributed to a decline in applications but also to an increase in the proportion of applications granted. Still the number of those refused asylum clearly exceeds those who are allowed to stay legally. In many countries the proportion of rejections exceeds 90 per cent. The prospect of expulsion or

Table 4.2 Number of asylum applications in selected EU countries, 1985–1999

	1985	1988	1992	1996	1999
Belgium	5 387	4 510	17 675	12 433	35 778
France	28 925	34 352	28 872	17 405	30 830
Germany	73 832	103 076	438 191	117 333	95 113
Netherlands	5 644	7 486	20 346	22 857	39 286
Sweden	14 500	19 595	84 018	5 774	11 771
UK	6 200	5 740	32 300	29 640	70 410
EU	159 180	210 740	672 380	227 800	352 380

Source: EUROSTAT data.

deportation if rejected has led many asylum seekers to join the ranks of the clandestines, contributing to the increasing problem of illegal immigration.

4.5 The European response to migration

4.5.1 The new migration wave and immigration policy in the EU

What has been the reply by EU member states to the migration wave of the late twentieth century? What has been the attitude adopted by different countries towards the new forms of immigration? Two basic positions have been adopted depending on the national origin of migrants. On the one hand, the adoption of free mobility of labour within the framework of the Single Market has opened up European borders to EU citizens. On the other, EU countries have increasingly passed and implemented harsher legislation and policing in order to restrict the entrance of migrants from outside the EU. This has led to the creation of a strong mobility divide between the privileged EU citizens and the citizens of the rest of the world.

The implementation of the Single Market on 1 January 1993 marked the fall of barriers to personal mobility within the EU for EU citizens. Although the principle of free mobility of labour was already included in the Treaty of Rome (now in Art. 39 of the Treaty), free mobility only began to be implemented thoroughly and effectively from the onset of the Single Market. From that date onwards EU citizens have been able to move and reside freely—and perhaps more importantly with little administrative hassle—within the territory of the member states. EU citizens can thus now move without worrying about residence or work permits or additional red tape. The requirements to reside in one state are the same as for the nationals of that state.

Measures included in the Maastricht Social Chapter to guarantee social security provision and the mutual recognition of social security payments and benefits, as well as the provision of normal medical services for all short-term visitors, have further promoted the mobility of Europeans, as have the removal of physical border controls in the Schengen area or the award of the right to vote to non-national EU citizens in local and European elections.

In contrast to the opening of borders to EU nationals, European attitudes towards the mobility of non-EU citizens have been much more restrictive. Immigration policies for non-EU nationals have traditionally been the realm of national governments. Until recently each European national government laid its own rules and set its own immigration quotas. But despite national independence on immigration matters, immigration policies across western Europe have tended to follow similar paths since the second half of the 1970s. The economic crisis of the 1970s and growing popular hostility towards migration—which in certain EU countries was reflected in the emergence of xenophobic and racist attitudes—contributed to a convergence of national migration policies across Europe. This convergence was characterized first and foremost by a reduction of the number of migrants allowed into the country and in some cases even by closing national borders to migration. This latter attitude was adopted by Germany as early as November 1973 and was later followed by France. A second feature in the convergence of migration policies was the widespread adoption of measures—which often included financial help—to encourage return migration. A final feature was the tightening of legislation everywhere in order to first make immigration more difficult and then to discourage and/or prevent family reunification, which, by the end of the 1970s, was already leading to a rise in the number of foreigners living in the economic core of Europe. France and Germany started requiring a period of residence before allowing the families of foreign workers to reside in the country. In some cases the allocation of work permits to direct relatives of foreign workers was restricted (Rasmussen, 1997: 91).

The convergence in migration policies across western Europe in the 1970s happened without a co-ordination of efforts by national governments. Different national governments and politicians reacted similarly to the twin challenges of the late 1970s: economic crisis and the increasing unease of the population with the presence of large contingents of foreigners. National legislations evolved in a similar direction. Tough migration policies were adopted across western Europe. Asylum laws were tightened and measures were adopted in order to make it more difficult to obtain asylum, especially in Austria and Germany (del Fabbro, 1995; Wakolbinger, 1995). In countries like Britain and France relatively liberal laws on accession to citizenship were changed (Ubbiali, 1995).

The similarity of the problems faced by European states soon brought representatives from different countries together in order to discuss and tackle the 'migration problem' from a supranational perspective. The first attempts to exchange information on and to co-ordinate migration policies took the form of ad hoc groups, such as the Trevi Group, the Ad Hoc Group on Immigration, or the Police Working Group on Terrorism. These groups were set up outside the formal framework of the European Communities, made up of officials from the national ministries of the interior and justice. These committees played an important role in raising the awareness and the profile of migration issues and of the need to co-ordinate migration policies among European states (Bigo, 1994; den Boer and Wallace, 2000).

The greatest development in this direction came in 1985 with the creation of the Schengen Group, which led to the Schengen Agreement. In this Agreement the Benelux countries, France, and Germany abolished their own internal borders controls, while establishing a common visa policy and a database containing a registry of all those individuals unwanted in any of the countries in the Schengen area. Little by little other EU countries joined the Schengen Agreement and only Ireland and the UK have remained outside. The Schengen Agreement was turned into a Convention in 1990. The transformation of the Schengen Agreement into a Convention marks a turning point in European migration policy, since it heralds a much wider Europeanization than hitherto of migration policies. And this Europeanization came in the form of a strong restriction on the mobility of non-EU citizens within the countries since refusal of entry in one member of the Schengen Convention implies refusal of entry in all Schengen countries, without any guarantee of freedom of movement between countries once in the Schengen area (Rasmussen, 1997: 162–4). The Schengen Convention also marks the 'securitization' of migration policy in the European space, as it connects migration and asylum matters to terrorism, transnational crime, and border controls (Huysmans, 2000: 756).

The introduction of the 'third pillar' for developing co-operation in justice and home affairs (JHA) in the 1992 reform of the Treaty of the European Union was an additional sign of the Europeanization and 'securitization' of migration policies. Yet, until this point, migration policies were developed through intergovernmental co-operation and, this, according to Kostakopoulou (2000: 498), led to the establishment of an institutional framework which lacked coherence, consistency, and democratic accountability and which resulted in policies that were little more than an extension of past national restrictive policies.

The most important step towards overcoming intergovernmental co-operation was taken in the 1997 Amsterdam summit, when many of the areas of co-operation in JHA (immigration and asylum, external border controls, visas, and the rights of third country nationals, among others) were incorporated into the Treaty of the European Union. In addition, most of the clauses of the Schengen Convention were also introduced into the Treaty, in the form of a 'Protocol on Integrating the Schengen *Acquis*'. Such a change represented the end of intergovernmentalism as the method of dealing with migration matters in the EU, but it has not completely meant the end of state power on issues of migration. The Amsterdam reform

offers states the opportunity to expand the logic of control and law enforcement which underpinned the intergovernmental framework of co-operation, and to construct new forms of power which not only increase their regulatory capacity within a geographically contained structure, but also enable them to impose their security agenda beyond the confines of the Union, (Kostakopoulou, 2000: 514)

The Europeanization of migration policy did not imply a reform of the restrictive national migration regimes that had been imposed in western Europe since the 1970s. If anything, it has come to reinforce the restrictive nature of migration policy in the EU by creating what some now call the emergence of a 'Fortress Europe' (Rasmussen, 1997), that is a Europe in which the homogenization of external borders has meant tougher border controls, tighter legislation on immigration and asylum, and greater police co-ordination and the creation of the Europol, the embryo of a future European-wide police.

4.5.2 Xenophobia and the emergence of a 'Fortress Europe'

Why has there been a tightening of European laws towards immigration and asylum seekers? Why has the Europeanization of migration laws led to the emergence of a 'Fortress Europe'?

It has been claimed that the tightening of European legislation on migration is the result of increasing demands by the population. Europe has witnessed since the late 1970s and throughout the 1980s and 1990s an increase in xenophobic and racist attitudes which have contributed to spread a negative image of immigrants. Eurobarometer polls carried out on the issue have come to confirm the negative perception of migrants and migration by the general population. Figure 4.1 shows the response of EU nationals to a survey conducted by Eurobarometer in October–November 1997, the European Year against Racism, on the issue of the number of foreigners living in their country. Only one in ten of the citizens of the EU believed that there were not many foreigners living in their country. Forty per cent thought that there were a lot and 45 per cent thought that there were too many. National differences were striking. In a clear change from a much more tolerant attitude before the country became a centre of inward migration (Triandafyllidou and Mikrakis, 1995), Greece came out as the most xenophobic country in the EU. Seventy-one per cent of Greeks thought that there were too many foreigners living in their country (Figure 4.1). In Belgium, Italy, Germany, and Austria more than 50 per cent of the population thought the same. If those who think that there are a lot of foreigners living in their country are added to those who think there are too many, the two categories make a two thirds majority in every single country in the EU, with the exception of Finland (Figure 4.1).

Xenophobia seems thus to be rife across the EU, regardless of factors such as whether the host country has been a traditional destination for immigrants (Belgium, Germany, or France) or has only recently become a country of immigration (Greece, Italy). Xenophobic attitudes are found to be more

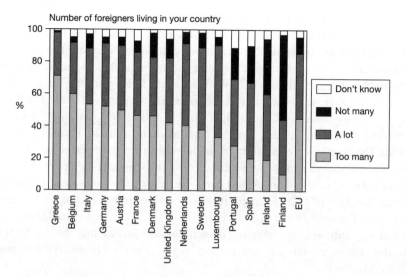

Number of foreigners living in your country

Figure 4.1 Attitudes towards foreigners in the EU

Source: Eurobarometer 48.

widespread among pensioners, house persons, and those with the least education. They are least ingrained in young people, managers, and those with the highest levels of education (Eurobarometer 48, 1997).

Xenophobic attitudes have provided a breeding ground for the emergence of xenophobic and racist parties. Most of these parties have appeared in those countries where the negative perception of foreigners is more entrenched among the population. Six of the seven countries identified in the Eurobarometer survey as more hostile towards foreigners have witnessed in recent years the emergence or the revival of parties that have openly played the xenophobic or racist card. Jean-Marie Le Pen's Front National in France is the xenophobic party that has endured the longest electoral success, regularly commanding—despite ups and downs—more than 10 per cent of the national vote in parliamentary, European, and in the first round of French presidential elections (Ubbiali, 1995). The Freedom Party in Austria was transformed from 1986 onwards—under the leadership of Jörg Haider—from a relatively mainstream liberal party into a populist and xenophobic party (Wakolbinger, 1995: 15). This change of direction contributed to raise the profile of the party in the eyes of the Austrian electorate. Its electoral support in national elections jumped from less than 10 per cent in the 1980s to around 25 per cent during most of the 1990s and even led it to became a member of the ruling coalition. In Italy, the populist and secessionist Northern League irrupted onto the political scene in the early 1990s. With the increase in immigration into Italy, its early anti-southern populist discourse has been transformed into one with a distinct xenophobic touch. The League has also been hoisted to government in coalition with Forza Italia and the Alleanza Nazionale (another party with a strong nationalist and xenophobic past) in the right-wing governments of Silvio Berlusconi. In Belgium the Vlaams Blok commands more than a quarter of the votes in some parts of Flanders with an openly xenophobic and racist discourse (Cools, 1995), and in Germany extreme right-wing parties, like the Nationaldemokratische Partei Deutschlands, the Deutsche Volksunion, or the Republikaner, have performed well in certain regional elections (del Fabbro, 1995). In Denmark, the Progress Party, founded originally as a tax protest party, has resorted to widespread prejudice about Muslims in order to revive its electoral fortunes (Mouritsen, 1995: 53). Greece is the only country in this group that has so far been spared from this tendency, although the absence of xenophobic parties may be connected to the relative novelty of immigration in the country (Triandafyllidou and Mikrakis, 1995).

In the remaining European countries the emergence of xenophobic or racist parties has been contained. The lower hostility of their populations towards immigrants may be a factor in this development (see Figure 4.1). However, in some cases the anti-immigration rhetoric of the extreme right-wing parties has been to some extent adopted by mainstream conservative or right-wing parties. The most blatant example is the British Conservative party between 1997 and 2001, which resorted to issues such as illegal migration and 'bogus' asylum seekers in a failed attempt to win greater electoral support. The backing of the European population for tougher migration laws has led other mainstream right-wing parties to radicalize their position on the issue and to borrow some of the rhetoric of xenophobic parties in order to curb the flow of votes to the extreme right. This is the case of the RPR and the UDF in France, Forza Italia in Italy, New Democracy in Greece, and, to a lesser extent, the Christian Democrats in Germany and the Popular Party in Spain.

Tougher migration controls at the national and European level, popular hostility against foreigners, and the xenophobic discourse of populist right-wing parties in Europe are creating a self-reinforcing vicious circle leading to the 'demonization' of immigrants. The European collective imagination is increasingly associating immigration with criminality, unemployment, and hoards of welfare claimants (Doty, 1996). Immigrants are, in addition, often portrayed as 'a threat to national culture'. They are represented as 'others', aliens to the national group and, therefore, to be excluded from the host society (Triandafyllidou, 2000). The vision of immigrants as hard-working individuals who contribute to economic development and to increasing the cultural vitality, so common in countries like the US in the past, is much less prominent in western Europe (Martiniello, 1995). Restrictive European-wide immigration laws are doing nothing to rectify the negative image of migration. On the contrary, they may be contributing to it by 'securitizing' migration (Huysmans, 2000). Current European legislation depicts immigration as a security issue, as a cost to European societies, and as something that should be restricted. In brief, the image of immigration into Europe is that of a burden or a problem, rather than of an asset (Favell and Tambini, 1995).

The negative portrayal of immigration in the law and elsewhere has also fostered racist and negative reactions to immigrants (Huysmans, 2000: 766) and contributed to an increase in the acts of violence against immigrants and racial minorities. Attacks on refugee hostels or individual immigrants were common in Germany until the German courts decided to adopt a less lenient position with the perpetrators of such acts. And even tougher court action has not sufficed to eradicate attacks on foreigners. In other countries sporadic acts of violence against immigrants and asylum seekers have become increasingly common, and, in the cases of countries with a long tradition of immigration like Britain or France, the climate against immigration is sparking racial tensions between radical right-wing groups and the children and grandchildren of former immigrants, as a string of race riots in northern England in 2001 shows.

4.6 Conclusion

As in the 1950s and 1960s, western Europe is experiencing a new wave of mass migration. The migrants are however no longer predominantly western European: migration within the EU has been basically limited to highly educated workers. The bulk of migrants are made up of people from outside the EU. Traditional sources of migrants, such as North Africa or Turkey, still provide a certain percentage of those coming into western Europe. But the origins of the immigrants have become more diversified than in the earlier migration wave and basically cover the whole world.

The renewal of migration is making western Europe more diverse and cosmopolitan. Yet the reaction of European citizens to this increase in diversity has been, on the whole, one of rejection. A majority of EU citizens perceive the flow of migrants as a threat to their identity, culture, employment, and security, rather than as an asset. This negative perception has fuelled—and, to a certain extent, has been fuelled by—a reaction by national and European institutions. EU countries have passed restrictive migration and asylum laws with the aim of stemming the flow of foreigners. There has been greater co-ordination of national migration policies and, since the

Amsterdam Reform of the Treaty of the European Union, the majority of migration issues fall within the realm of European policies. The Europeanization of migration policies has, nonetheless, not represented a change in direction. If anything, it has led to harsher legislation and greater enforcement of restrictive migration measures. Hostility towards migration has also provided a breeding ground for the emergence of right-wing xenophobic and racist parties across the European political spectrum.

This European-wide reaction against migration is not succeeding in creating a 'Fortress Europe'—a Europe almost closed to migrants—but it is driving many migrants, desperate to flee poverty in their countries of origin, underground. The sealing of European borders is also contributing to a flourishing of racketeers and criminal gangs specializing in smuggling illegal immigrants into the EU. And, as a whole, ethnic and religious relations have become more tense.

There is no easy solution to the problem of migration. On the one hand, Europe needs migrants to redress the ageing problem. New migrants can also contribute enormously to future economic growth and cultural development in the EU. On the other hand, the EU wants to avoid some of the problems linked to the short-term arrival of large numbers of foreigners. Reconciling both objectives is difficult, but it may prove even more demanding if the current negative image of migration is not improved.

5
Unemployment and social polarization

5.1 Introduction

The post-war economic boom brought about nearly full employment and a developed welfare system across most of western Europe. This golden age of industrialism—or the Fordist period, as it is also known—is associated with an unprecedented period of economic prosperity and to a dramatic reduction of poverty. Class divisions, although still important, reached their lowest level during the post-war decades. The middle class was thriving and a developed welfare system in most western European countries provided a safety net for families, the elderly, and the unemployed. The processes of socio-economic restructuring, globalization, and European integration have provoked a radical shift in this panorama. Some of the changes have been positive, especially on the gender side, with a much greater incorporation of women to the labour market. However, many European countries have witnessed a significant rise in the levels of structural unemployment over the last two decades and the welfare system is facing mounting challenges. There has also been a recent shift towards greater social polarization and social exclusion. Some countries, such as the UK, have tried to tackle long-term high rates of unemployment by liberalizing their labour market. They seem to have been successful at reducing unemployment, but at the cost of an increasing underclass of precarious and underpaid workers, many of them women, migrants, and from ethnic minorities. Other countries have been more reluctant to follow this route, but have suffered longer from high unemployment levels. In any case, the demise of the post-war prosperity has resulted in a widening of the gap between those with a stable job and those in precarious employment or unemployed, giving way to the development of long-term socially excluded strata and to the emergence of new social classes: the so-called 'A-team' and 'B-team' in Denmark, the 'two-thirds society' in Germany, the 'two-speed society' in France and the new 'underclass' in the UK (Esping-Andersen, 1999: 10).

This chapter looks at these changes in the EU. It first studies employment change in the light of the processes of globalization and European integration. The third section of the chapter examines the roots of high unemployment followed by the measures that have been adopted to tackle unemployment across the EU. Section 5.4 describes the emergence of new forms of employment in the post-industrial society and its effect of social polarization. The final section deals with the challenges these changes are imposing on European welfare states.

5.2 Employment change in the post-industrial age

There is widespread agreement among social scientists that European and other developed societies have undergone a profound change in recent years. The industrial system of mass production developed since the beginning of the twentieth century reached its climax between the early 1960s and early 1970s and has since been in decline as a result of a combination of techno-logical challenges and economic integration processes, which can be described under the general term of globalization. The demise of the mass production system is giving way to the rise of a post-industrial society in which employment and employment conditions are radically different from the previous period (Boyer, 2000).

The mass production era had engendered across western Europe a social system based on three pillars: full employment, prosperity, and social citizenship (Esping-Andersen, 1999). Unprecedented levels of prosperity which lasted for almost three decades, coupled with full (male) employment, fostered the emergence of a large middle class fundamentally constituted of skilled blue-collar industrial workers and rising numbers of white-collar service employees (Goldthorpe, 1992). The rights associated with social citizenship further contributed to social stability. Workers enjoyed considerable work stability within the framework of a heavily regulated labour market. Furthermore, the industrial middle class was protected by the large social mesh provided by distinct national versions of the welfare state (Esping-Andersen, 1990).

The shift in the system of production and the process of socio-economic restructuring, which began during the early 1970s, have shaken the foundations of the established economic, social, and political orders. The most significant transformation has been the rise of unemployment across most of western Europe. It is notoriously difficult to measure unemployment rates.

National statistical institutes usually measure the number of unemployed in two different ways: either as the number of people looking for a job and those not looking but willing to accept a job if offered one, or as those registered as unemployed and willing to claim unemployment benefits. In most cases the difference between both measures of unemployment is significant. In a few cases it can be extreme: in Spain, during periods of the 1990s the gap between both measurements was more than 1 million people in a labour market made up of around 12 million individuals.

Bearing in mind the problems related to the accurate measurement of unemployment, since the beginning of the industrial crisis unemployment has risen in the whole of western Europe. Whereas in the early 1970s all current members states of the EU—with the only exceptions of Ireland and Italy—had unemployment rates below 5 per cent, since the first oil crisis of the mid-1970s the panorama has radically changed. Unemployment rates began to creep up consistently from 1975 reaching rates of 10 per cent or higher in many western European countries during the 1980s. In countries such as Ireland and Finland unemployment rates hovered around 20 per cent in the 1980s and 1990s respectively, and Spain endured rates above 20 per cent during much of the period between 1984 and 1998 (Figure 5.1). Women have suffered the most as a result of the crisis. Since the 1970s female unemployment has been several points above male unemployment across the EU, bar Scandinavia (Figure 5.1).

By the mid-1990s all the large western European countries, with the exception of the UK, had unemployment rates which were around 10 per cent or above of the total active population. The economic recovery of the late 1990s has contributed to bringing unemployment rates down. But, in comparison with other economies around the world, West European labour markets have been less proficient at creating jobs.

Few countries in the EU have managed to avoid high unemployment. Luxembourg is probably the only genuine exception. The Netherlands and the UK have performed notably better than their neighbours during the 1990s, probably thanks to their more flexible labour markets. But this does not mean that these to countries have been spared the problem in the near past. Unemployment in the Netherlands peaked at 12 per cent of the labour force in the early 1980s and has been below that level ever since. The number of jobless in the UK has followed economic cycles more closely than anywhere else in western Europe and reached 11 per cent of the labour force in the mid-1980s and then again in the early 1990s.

When subnational unemployment rates are considered, important intranational differences are also unveiled. Figure 5.2 maps regional unemployment rates in the EU in 1999. The highest unemployment rates tend to be concentrated in many peripheral areas and in those areas undergoing strong

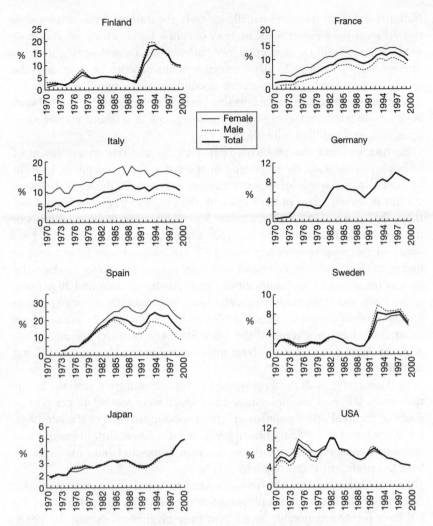

Figure 5.1 Evolution of unemployment rates in selected European countries, Japan, and the US, 1970–2000

Sources: World Bank World Development Indicators (2000) and EUROSTAT.

processes of industrial restructuring. Unemployment rates above 16 per cent in the south of Italy, southern and western Spain, and the former East Germany can be included in the former category, the high rates of northern France, Wallonia in Belgium, and the old industrial havens of West Germany or northern England in the latter. Many inner city areas also suffer from relatively high unemployment rates. Low unemployment rates, by contrast,

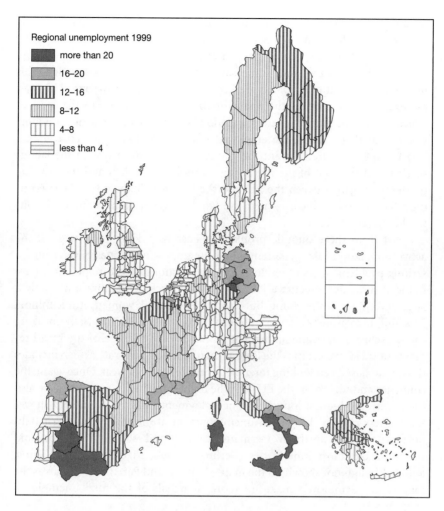

Figure 5.2 Regional unemployment rates in the EU, 1999

tend to be found in the peripheries of large urban regions and in many intermediate regions, such as those in the south of Germany, Austria, and northeastern and central Italy.

Several reasons contribute to making mounting unemployment one of the main economic and social problems for the EU. First and foremost, having a large percentage of the willing-to-work population idle represents a waste for the European economy. And, given the rigidity of European labour markets, the occurrence of unemployment is higher among the younger and better prepared generations. Youth unemployment has consistently remained several points above overall unemployment rates in Europe. In parts of Italy and Spain youth unemployment rates have even exceeded 40 per cent of the population under 25. Since the younger generations have enjoyed more widespread access to—and, some say, a better system of—education, this means that the better prepared are kept out of the labour market. This was, for example, the case in the Spain of the early 1990s, where the level of education of the unemployed population, measured in years of schooling, was higher than that of the employed population (Rodríguez-Pose, 1998). The European failure to grant the younger generations access to the labour market is at the root of the increasing technological deficit and the growing productivity gap between the EU and the US (see Chapter 1), whose economy has massively incorporated the younger generations into the labour market in recent years.

Apart from the economic problem of keeping a large percentage of the active population idle, persistently high unemployment rates have created a serious problem of social exclusion. Large sections of the population have found it difficult to secure a job. The socially excluded embrace not only a large percentage of the young, but also the less-skilled, women, ethnic minorities and, increasingly, a large section of those over 50. Territorially speaking social exclusion and unemployment go hand in hand. One of the measurements of social exclusion is the long-term unemployment rate, which includes those who have been looking for a job for more than one year. Once again, the countries and regions in the EU with the highest unemployment rates are also those with the highest long-term unemployment rates. As Figure 5.3 shows, the highest rates of long-term unemployment are found in southern Italy, northern Spain, northern Germany, central and southern Greece, and Belgium, and most inner cities (Berlin, Brussels, Madrid, Rome, Vienna, and—although not shown on the map—London and Paris). In these areas the long-term unemployed make up more than half of the total unemployed (Figure 5.3).

Long-term unemployment tends to be less of a problem in countries with more flexible (the UK and the Netherlands) or more regulated (Scandinavia) labour markets. Long-term unemployment also has a lower incidence in relatively dynamic areas, with the exception of the inner cities. Regions in northeastern and central Italy and in southern Germany—among the most dynamic spaces in the EU in the late twentieth century—have long-term unemployment rates which are well below their respective national average (Figure 5.3). In northeastern and central Italy the long-term unemployed represented less than one third of the unemployed.

If we add that long-term unemployment is not only positively associated with the total unemployment rate, but also negatively associated with the active population, the EU not only has a problem of social exclusion but of

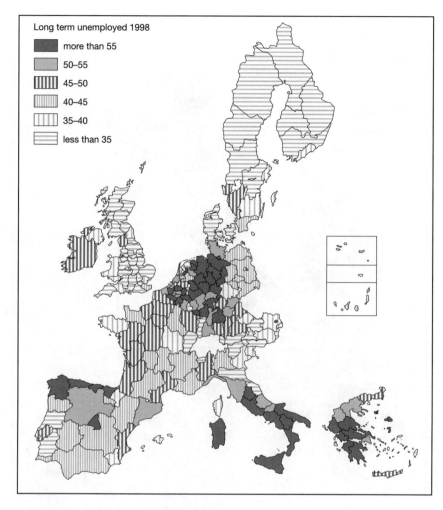

Figure 5.3 Long-term unemployed as a percentage of the total unemployed, 1998

territorial exclusion as well. The highest rates of long-term unemployment
and of total unemployment occur precisely in those countries and regions
with the lowest employment share. The poorest regions in Spain and the
south of Italy had employment rates which in 1998 were below 40 per cent of
the total working-age population. Elsewhere in the EU similar low rates of
participation in the labour force could only be found in the industrial declining region of Hainault (Belgium). Other regions in Belgium, the north of
France, and Italy, were not far behind (Figure 5.4).

In contrast, local labour markets included more than three fifths of the total

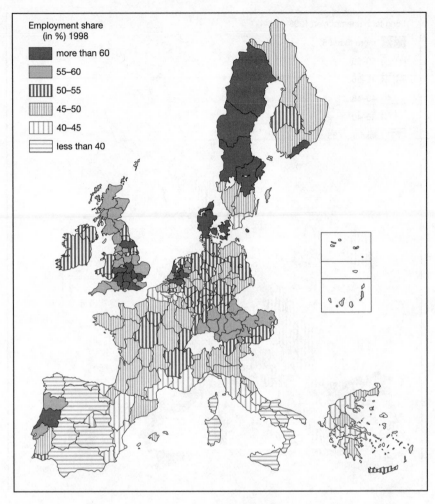

Figure 5.4 Regional employment as a share of the total population, 1998

working-age population in many of the regions with the lowest unemploy-
ment and long-term unemployment rates. These were concentrated in
Denmark, central and northern Sweden, the Netherlands, and the south of
England (Figure 5.4).

The combination of social and territorial exclusion represents a
considerable financial problem for many of the countries in western Europe
and for the EU as a whole. Unemployment benefits have expanded with
unemployment since the 1970s. In 1997, unemployment support represented
7.2 per cent of European social expenditure. Although this was relatively

little in comparison to expenditure on old age pensions and sickness and disability benefits—which between them represented more than three quarters of total social expenditure (see Chapter 3)—no other type of social expenditure has grown at a similar rate since the early 1980s. There are no data available for the whole of the EU for the period starting in 1980. However, data for selected EU member states highlight the increasing importance of unemployment benefits in government budgets. Table 5.1 represents unemployment expenditure as a percentage of total social expenditure and shows the evolution of unemployment expenditure in selected European countries in three years: 1997, the last year for which social expenditure data were available at the time of writing; 1993, the year of the highest unemployment across the EU; and 1980, the first year for which social expenditure data were available.

The data show the increasing scale of unemployment expenditure. In three of the four countries for which data have been available since 1980, unemployment expenditure as a share of total social expenditure doubled between 1980 and 1997. In Finland it trebled. Spain is the exception: unemployment expenditure as a share of social expenditure has not increased, but has remained high since the beginning of the 1980s. Unemployment expenditure in Spain reached its peak in 1993, when it represented 21.1 per cent of total social expenditure (Table 5.1). Despite the reduction in

Table 5.1 Unemployment expenditure as a percentage of total social expenditure and the evolution of unemployment expenditure in selected European countries

	Unemployment expenditure as a percentage of total social expenditure			Evolution of unemployment expenditure at constant prices, 1990 = 100		
	1997	1993	1980	1997	1993	1980
EU12	7.2	9.1	—	135.8	158.1	—
Austria	5.3	5.4	2.0	149.1	140.2	34.7
Finland	13.0	15.6	4.3	274.1	314.1	40.5
France	7.5	8.8	—	115.1	124.6	59.6
Germany	8.7	10.2	3.7	224.1	240.2	53.3
Ireland	15.0	16.2	—	157.4	141.9	47.0
Italy	1.8	2.2	—	127.2	149.2	79.0
Netherlands	10.5	8.8	—	140.7	117.3	58.0
Spain	13.8	21.1	15.4	96.5	150.4	55.7

Source: EUROSTAT data.

unemployment rates during the second half of the 1990s, unemployment expenditure has remained high across the EU, still accounting for more than 5 per cent of total social expenditure in every member state, bar Portugal, the UK, and Italy. In some countries, however, higher levels of unemployment support were disguised under other social categories, such as old age expenditure in Italy, where only approximately a quarter of those aged between 55 and 64 are employed (Barro and Grilli, 1994), or disability benefits in the Netherlands (Van Dijk and Folmer, 1999).

When the evolution of unemployment expenditure in constant terms is analysed, the expansion of the financial burden of unemployment in EU states becomes even clearer. France, Italy, the Netherlands, and Spain have doubled their unemployment expenditure since 1980. Unemployment expenditure in Ireland has experienced a threefold increase; in Austria and Germany, it has been multiplied by four, and, in Finland, by six. Sudden increases in unemployment have a dramatic effect on public finances. In the three years between 1990 and 1993, most EU countries suffered a rise of expenditure on unemployment of at least 40 per cent. In Germany, reunification and the crisis of the early 1990s made it rise by 140 per cent, and in Finland, whose unemployment rate more than trebled after the economic and political collapse of the Soviet Union (see Figure 5.1), unemployment support expenditure rose by 214 per cent in only three years (Table 5.1).

Persistently high unemployment is also affecting the competitiveness of the EU in world markets. High unemployment, far from being a world-wide phenomenon, seems to be fundamentally a European problem. Unemployment in the US has remained below that of the EU since the late 1970s. American unemployment rates have closely followed economic cycles, peaking in 1975, 1983, and 1992. However, US unemployment has never exceeded 10 per cent in the post-war era (Figure 5.1) and the US economy has been creating jobs and incorporating young talent into the labour market at a much faster rate than European economies. In Japan, unemployment, although rising slowly since the early 1970s, cannot really be considered a problem. Despite enduring its worst recession in the post-war period, unemployment rates only went above 3 per cent of the labour force in 1995, a rate only comparable to that of the best European performers. Moreover, in contrast to Europe, both in the US and Japan there is no significant difference between male and female unemployment rates (Figure 5.1).

In sum, persistently high unemployment rates in the EU in the last two decades of the twentieth century have become an important economic, social, and financial problem not only for most EU member states individually, but also as a key barrier in the process of European integration.

5.3 **The roots of persistently high unemployment**

What are the reasons behind the persistence of high unemployment in the EU? Why have western European countries endured much higher unemployment rates than the US or Japan? There is no single factor, but a constellation of factors that explain the persistence of high unemployment in western Europe.

Many of the explanations of high unemployment in Europe point towards the regulatory framework. Western European economies tend to be much more regulated than the North American economies, Australia, New Zealand, or even Japan. Hence, a combination of high labour taxation, strong trade unions, high minimum wages, and lofty social benefits may be the cause of the unemployment differential between the EU and the rest of the developed world.

The level of taxation of labour is generally brandished—especially by employers' representatives in Europe—as the most important factor behind the higher rates of unemployment in the EU. Taxes on labour tend to be much higher in western Europe than in Japan or the US. Burda and Wyplosz (1993) highlight the significant differences in taxation across the developed world. The overall marginal tax rate was higher than 60 per cent in all EU member states, bar Belgium and the UK. Even in these two countries the overall marginal tax rate was higher than 50 per cent. In Japan and the US it was 23 and 40 per cent respectively. The average employer tax rates were particularly high in Belgium, France, Italy, and Sweden, whereas the average employee tax rate exceeded 30 per cent in Finland, Italy, and Sweden. High employment taxes and contributions have also made the cost of hiring and firing employees much higher on average in the EU than in the US.

These numbers point towards the existence of a strong relationship between the taxation of labour and unemployment: the higher the taxation of labour, the higher the unemployment rate. This relationship is however far from perfect. Some of the Scandinavian countries (especially Denmark and Sweden), whose overall marginal tax rates have been similar to—if not higher—than those found elsewhere in the EU, have tended to have lower than average unemployment rates. In contrast, Spain, whose taxation of labour has been marginally lower than that of the EU during the last decades of the twentieth century, has endured the highest unemployment rate. In light of this, it can be claimed that the taxation of labour only has an indirect effect on unemployment rates, since the effect of taxation would tend to have a greater influence on wages than on the genesis of unemployment.

The power of European trade unions has been considered another factor behind high unemployment rates. Union membership is much higher in Europe than in the US or Japan. In Scandinavia union membership is almost universal. Around three quarters of the Danish and Finnish workforce is unionized, and the percentage is even higher in Sweden. In the rest of the EU union membership varies widely. Whereas many European countries have rates of union membership which hover around 50 per cent of the workforce, in countries such as France, Greece, Portugal, and Spain, trade union membership is below a quarter (Ebbinghaus and Visser, 1999, 2000). The evolution of trade union membership in the late twentieth century also varies widely across the EU. Many of the heavily unionized nations have seen union membership remain relatively stable or even increase. There have been increases in membership in Scandinavia and in Belgium. In contrast, trade unions in the less unionized countries have generally witnessed a fall in membership. The decline in trade union membership has been most spectacular in France, where trade unions lost 50 per cent of their members during the 1980s alone. The size of Spanish trade unions dwindled considerably in the late 1980s and early 1990s. Union membership in the UK was also dented during the Thatcherite years. British unions however fared better than their French counterparts.

The power of European trade unions stems however not only from their number of affiliates, but also from their participation in centralized collective bargaining. Collective bargaining tends to be much more centralized in western Europe than in other developed countries. This means that unions actually represent a larger share of the workforce than what their membership may suggest at labour and wage negotiations. This does not make much difference in countries where trade union membership is almost universal. However, in countries such as France and Spain, where trade union membership is relatively small, the degree of centralization in collective bargaining gives unions a much greater coverage than their membership would suggest (Ebbinghaus and Visser, 2000). In France and Spain, for example, 82 and 70 per cent of their respective employed population was covered by collective bargaining, a similar percentage to countries with a much more unionized workforce, such as Italy, the Netherlands, or even Sweden.

In contrast, trade unions are much less powerful in North America or Japan. Trade union membership in the US, although higher than in France, is much lower than in most EU member states. Moreover the degree of centralization of collective bargaining in the US or Japan is also lower than in the EU. Hence their capacity to influence wages or affect unemployment is in theory below than that of western European trade unions.

But, how does the power of European trade unions affect unemployment? Some claim that since unions generally only represent those in work and not those out of work, their interests coincide with those of the employed workforce and not with those of the unemployed. Consequently their main aim is to increase the wages of those in work even at the risk of generating greater unemployment. Although this may be a somewhat old-fashioned vision of the role of trade unions, it is true that in the past collective bargaining based mainly on wages may have resulted in an increase in unemployment. The objective of keeping wages high, especially in relatively centralized collective bargaining systems such as those found in the EU, could have contributed to limiting the expansion of the labour market. As Esping-Andersen puts it

the relationship between collective bargaining and labour market performance is often depicted as a 'hump-shaped' curve. In this view, desirable collective goals, such as price stability and low unemployment are more likely to result if unionism is either very weak (hence market forces will predominate) or very strong (consensual solidarity will predominate). (1999: 19)

However, it is not clear to what extent—if at all—the power of trade unions in western Europe has contributed to keeping unemployment rates high. As in the case of taxes on labour, the relationship between the power of trade unions and unemployment is highly imperfect. High rates of union membership and extremely centralized collective bargaining systems in countries like Austria, Denmark, or Sweden have not been translated into the highest unemployment rates in the EU. Low rates in the UK have also yielded relatively low unemployment levels, whereas contrasting levels of unionization in the south of Italy (high) and Spain (low) are associated with high unemployment.

A third factor linked to the regulatory framework which is regarded as a possible source of persistent unemployment in the EU is the minimum wage. For some, the existence of minimum wages in the EU is pricing workers with low skills out of the job market. This assertion is however questionable, especially in light of the negligible impact on unemployment rates of the introduction of a minimum wage by the Labour government in Britain. More important than the mere existence of a minimum wage is the level at which the minimum wage is set. Whereas a low minimum wage may have no impact on employment, high minimum wages may contribute to increasing unemployment, since the higher the cost of manual workers, the greater the incentive to opt for labour substitution investments. Most western European countries have relatively high minimum wages in comparison to the US. Many of the countries with high minimum wages are often those which have endured high unemployment. In a certain sense there seems to be a trade-off between unemployment and income inequalities, as far as the level of the minimum wage is concerned. On the one hand, in countries with low or non-existent minimum wages, such as the UK or the US and Canada, unemployment has been kept at relatively low levels but income inequalities have risen sharply. On the other, in countries where the minimum wage has been traditionally high, as is the case in most of Continental Europe, income inequalities have remained relatively low, but unemployment rates have escalated during much of the 1980s and 1990s (Krugman, 1994).

Two final regulatory factors which have been blamed for the persistence of high unemployment in the EU are high social benefits and worker rights. Social benefits, such as a high reservation wage and tax-wedge, have been accused of entrapping people in unemployment or welfare assistance (Esping-Andersen, 1999). This implies that the higher the social benefits, the lower the incentive to search for jobs, leading often to a spiralling 'poverty trap', by which people are better off unemployed that in work. Worker rights also tend to be much higher in Europe than elsewhere in the developed world, since they reflect the situation at the peak of the trade union bargaining power of the early 1970s (Crouch, 1999).

However, as in the cases of other factors related to the regulation of the labour market, the connection between the combination of high social benefits and worker rights and unemployment in Europe is not straightforward. Italy, which has by far the lowest unemployment benefits in western Europe, endures stark internal differences in unemployment and has a national unemployment rate similar to that of many of its neighbours. And generous unemployment benefits in Denmark and the Netherlands have not resulted in higher unemployment rates.

Although the rigidity of the labour market regulatory framework in the EU in comparison to other developed societies could to a certain extent be blamed for persistently high unemployment, regulation alone does not explain the whole story. Overall, countries which score highly in labour market rigidity rankings (see OECD, 1997), such as Italy, Spain, Belgium, or Germany, also have higher unemployment rates. But this trend does not hold for every country in the EU. Portugal, despite having a labour market almost as rigid as those of Italy and Spain, has traditionally had much lower unemployment rates. The same could be said of Austria, where strong rigidity has not been matched by high unemployment rates. And similar levels of labour market rigidity in the Scandinavian countries have yielded different jobless rates.

Hence, the causes of persistently high unemployment have to be looked for not only in the level of regulation of European labour markets, but also outside. The increasing mismatch between educational supply and labour demand is a factor affecting the employability of European workers. Educational structures vary enormously across European countries and there is little in common between the educational systems of Sweden and Greece. However, if one thing has characterized education systems across the EU, it has been their expansion during the last three decades of the twentieth century. Secondary education has become almost universal and the coverage of university education in the relevant age group has expanded from levels of around 15 per cent in the early 1970s to more than 40 per cent in many European countries (OECD, 1996). This expansion, which has contributed to the formation of a better skilled workforce, is however generating a serious problem of mismatch between educational supply and labour demand. Due to the slow reaction of educational structures across Europe to economic and social changes, many of the skills taught in European education systems have either become obsolete or are not demanded by the market. In addition, the participation of European firms in the educational process, although variable from country to country, has been lacking. The result has been an increasing number of European graduates with a series of skills which are hardly marketable and many companies with a shortage of individuals with the appropriate skills for their vacancies (Johnes, 1993).

Finally, higher unemployment rates may also be the consequence of the existence of divided markets across the EU until the implementation of the Single Market. Nationally divided markets, with national champions, monopolies, and oligopolies created a series of inefficiencies which have probably had a negative impact upon the job market (see Chapter 1).

In brief, there are multiple factors behind the persistence of high unemployment rates in the EU, and this multiplicity of factors makes tackling unemployment from a European perspective extremely difficult, since any measure aimed at curing it may only have a partial impact or may prove to be more effective in one area of the EU than in others.

5.3.1 Measures aimed at tackling unemployment

The persistence of high unemployment in the EU has forced the governments of the member states to act and to adopt measures to counter it. Most of these measures have had one common denominator: to make European labour markets less regulated and more flexible. Flexibility has become the key word in labour market discourses (Teague and Grahl, 1998). Labour markets have to become more flexible in order to increase European competitiveness and thus solve the employment problem. Flexibility means greater job mobility, but also, as underlined by Crouch,

making employees more disposable, in the senses of: easier and cheaper to dismiss; less covered by constraining agreements and regulations over conditions in which they can be required to work; less protections offered to their health, safety, and security; less controls on the extent to which they can be ordered to take on different kinds of work. (1999: 78)

This is generally known as 'numerical' or 'defensive' flexibility. Other measures linked to work flexibility are 'pay-related'. Worker's pay can, as a result of the deregulation in the labour market, be increasingly linked to their productivity or the number of hours worked. Finally, a third perception of flexibility is 'functional' or 'adaptive' flexibility. This sort of labour market flexibility is related to the adoption of active labour market policies aimed at training the unemployed and providing them with the necessary skills to allow them to perform a variety of tasks. It may also mean the inclusion of teamworking and co-operation in the production process (Crouch, 1999). Although most European countries have simultaneously adopted 'numerical', 'pay-related', and 'functional' measures of flexibility, 'numerical' and 'pay-related' measures have often taken centre stage.

In contrast to what happened with other challenges such as competitiveness or cohesion, the European reaction to the unemployment challenge has been neither cohesive, nor simultaneous. There has been no common EU strategy or policy to fight unemployment. Governments have been left to fend for themselves. As a result, the timing and depth of the adoption of flexible labour market reforms has varied from country to country. The reasons for such disparate reactions are related to the government and social structures in each country and to different concepts of what labour market flexibility means. Britain and the Netherlands were the first movers, although their schemes differed greatly. In Britain, labour market flexibility has been closely associated with the economic liberalism of the Thatcherite years. In this context, flexibility has implied thorough labour market deregulation. Other governments have been more reluctant to go down the 'flexibility' road. In most of Continental Europe, labour market flexibility has been linked to the reform of specific labour market laws and of the welfare state. In these cases, flexibility has implied a much less radical and traumatic reform of labour market structures than in the UK. The slow pace of reform in many southern European countries is also linked to the fact that a majority of the population with stable and protected jobs had a vested interest in maintaining the status quo. Family support for the unemployed, together with a relatively developed welfare system and the existence of a large underground economy, further contributed to making high unemployment something that could be tolerated by the system for relatively long periods of time.

In the end almost all EU governments have, however, succumbed to flexibility and deregulation. The main thorough reforms of national labour markets in Continental Europe came in the mid-1990s. Greece introduced legislation allowing employment to become more flexible in 1992; Germany in 1994; and France and Spain, which had been progressively introducing minor reforms since the 1980s, passed major reforms of their labour markets in the second half of the 1990s.

5.4 The impact of labour market flexibility on unemployment

At first sight the introduction of policies to flexibilize and deregulate European labour markets can be considered a success. The UK and the Netherlands, the first countries to introduce flexibility measures, have enjoyed lower unemployment levels than the rest of the EU since the late 1980s. Their unemployment rates have remained several points below the EU average. In 2000 unemployment in the UK was at 5.6 per cent of the active population, well below the 8.4 per cent average of the EU. The Netherlands, with an unemployment rate of only 2.6 per cent, was even below the US and Japan (4.1 and 4.9 per cent respectively).

The decrease in European unemployment in the late 1990s coincided with the passing of flexibility laws in many European countries. Economies which had been noted for their incapacity to create jobs during most of the 1980s and early 1990s have been creating jobs at a much faster rate than before the reforms. Half of the new jobs in the EU between 1997 and 2000 were created in Spain, whose unemployment rate fell from 22 to 14.2 per cent during that period. France also fared well and Germany recovered from the high rate of unemployment of the mid-1990s. With unemployment rates of 9.8 and 9.3 per cent respectively in 2000, they were well below their peaks of 1996–7. Similarly Sweden and Denmark enjoyed low levels of unemployment and even Italy and Belgium, two of the countries more reluctant to introduce labour market reforms, were starting to improve their position.

There is however one important factor which casts doubt on the effectiveness of reforms aimed at flexibilizing western European labour markets. The timing of most reforms has coincided with a period of economic expansion, and, in the past, economic booms have been associated with reductions in unemployment rates. It is therefore difficult to determine to what extent the reduction in unemployment rates in the second half of the 1990s is a direct result of the flexibilization of European labour markets, or simply the consequence of changes in the economic cycle.

5.4.1 Labour market flexibility, atypical employment, and social polarization

Even if we accept that labour market flexibility is responsible for a large part of the reduction in unemployment rates in western Europe, labour market reforms are unlikely to lead to a similar reduction in social exclusion and social polarization. If high unemployment in the EU generated a serious problem of social exclusion, mainly reflected in high rates of long-term unemployment, the recent flexiblization of the labour market may be reducing long-term unemployment, but at the cost of creating an increasing segmentation in the work force. Although, as Andersen, Haldrup, and Sorensen (2000) argue, there is still little evidence of a 'race to the bottom' and of an overall deterioration of labour standards, a large proportion of the new jobs being generated as a consequence of greater flexibility in the labour market differ substantially from the stable, relatively well-paid, and protected jobs of the post-war industrial period. Numerical and pay-related labour flexibility has favoured the emergence of different forms of atypical employment, forcing workers to resort to hitherto unusual employment forms. These range from part-time and temporary employment, homeworking and self-employment, to the rise of informal and disguised employment and of the underground economy (Bettio and Villa, 1989; Büchtemann and Quack, 1989; Meager, 1993).

One of the rising forms of atypical employment is part-time work. Changes in the legislative framework have allowed employers and employees to make use of flexible forms of work by which employees agree to work for less than 30 hours a week. Although part-time work has always existed, its incidence in the labour market before the crisis of the industrial model was almost negligible. Within the EU part-time work only exceeded 10 per cent of all employment in Denmark and Sweden prior to the 1970s. The percentage of part-time employment was higher in the US and Japan. Greater flexibility in the labour market has allowed part-time work to grow everywhere in the EU, with the only exception of Scandinavia, where its share has remained more or less stable. Countries which flexibilized their labour markets earlier—the UK, Ireland, and, especially, the Netherlands—have witnessed the greatest growth in part-time work. Sizeable increases have also occurred in Belgium, France, Italy, and Portugal, although the share of part-time workers in these countries is only slightly above 5 per cent of the employed population.

There is a clear gender divide in part-time work. Women make up the great majority of those willing or forced to work part-time. In most European countries the number of women working part-time is triple that of men. In some cases the difference is even higher: in Austria, Germany, and the UK, the difference is between six and seven times higher; in Belgium ten times higher. The extreme feminization of part-time work may be due to the fact that greater flexibility in and a reduced number of working hours allows more time to be devoted to childcare (a large percentage of part-time workers are mothers). Thus, from a certain point of view, part-time work contributes to the reconciliation of paid work and family life. However, the increasing importance of part-time work can also be seen as widening the gap between genders and condemning women in part-time jobs to the bottom of the employment scale and often to a life of economic dependency on their part-ners or on the state. In this sense it is important to note that Denmark and Sweden, the two countries where part-time work has remained stable in recent times, are also those with the greatest gender equality. The view of part-time work as promoting social polarization and social exclusion is reinforced by the fact that male part-time working is concentrated among the young and the over 55s (Crouch, 1999).

Another form of atypical employment which has expanded considerably as a result of the introduction of greater flexibility in the labour has been tem-porary or limited-contract work. This form of employment has reduced the cost of hiring and firing employees and allowed firms to dispose of less effi-cient employees and to adapt their workforce to shifts in demand (Crouch, 1999: 80). It has also reduced the level of job security of the post-war decades. Many EU countries have witnessed significant increases in temporary working during the 1990s, but nowhere have the increases been higher than in Spain and France. Labour market reform in these two countries has implied that the majority of the new jobs created have been temporary, with most of them concentrated among women and the young.

Self-employment is a third form of atypical employment which has grown with labour market reforms. Whereas self-employment declined in Europe during the post-war decades, its growth has clearly outpaced that of depend-ent employment since the beginning of the crisis of the industrial system (Meager, 1993). In contrast to part-time and temporary work, self-employment is basically a male phenomenon. But the gender difference does not imply that the growth of self-employment escapes the tendency towards greater social polarization that European labour markets are experiencing. Rather than heralding the emergence of a new entrepreneurial class, the growth of self-employment has been fundamentally concentrated in low pro-ductive and marginal sectors, among workers with lower educational attain-ment, immigrant groups, and ethnic minorities and in the countries with high unemployment rates, such as Spain, or a large agricultural sector (Greece, Ireland, Portugal, and Spain) (Meager, 1993). The growth of self-employment is also related to changes in the structure of large firms, increasingly willing to outsource production tasks in order to reduce the risk of changes in demand.

Finally, European labour markets have witnessed a phenomenal develop-ment of the informal or shadow economy. Some of the increase in the informal economy is linked to the expansion of legal work which is not recorded as formal economic activity, with family work being the most important form of this type of informal economy. The rest is related to the growth of the underground economy and of criminal and other illegal forms of economic transactions (Schneider and Enste, 2000). As a consequence of the lack of formal records, calculating the dimension of the informal economy

Table 5.2 The evolution of the size of the informal economy in the EU, the US, and Japan as a percentage of GDP, 1990–2000

	Average 1989/90	Average 1999/2000	Increase 1990–2000
Austria	6.9	9.8	2.9
Belgium	19.3	22.2	2.9
Denmark	10.8	18.0	7.2
Germany	11.8	16.0	4.2
Greece	22.6	28.7	6.1
Finland	13.4	18.1	4.7
France	9.0	15.2	6.2
Ireland	11.0	15.9	4.9
Italy	22.8	27.1	4.3
Netherlands	11.9	13.1	1.2
Portugal	15.9	22.7	6.8
Spain	16.1	22.7	6.6
Sweden	15.8	19.2	3.4
UK	9.6	12.7	3.1
US	6.7	8.7	2.0
Japan	8.8	11.2	2.4

Source: Schneider (2001).

is difficult. Estimates of the dimension of the informal economy in various European countries vary widely, but all indicators point towards an increase in recent years. Estimates of the evolution of the shadow economy by Schneider (2001) highlight that not a single country in the EU has experienced a contraction of its shadow or informal economy between 1990 and 2000 (Table 5.2). According to Schneider (2001), the informal economy expanded notably in the north of Europe (Denmark), the centre (France), as well as in the south (Greece, Portugal, and Spain). In 2000 it represented more than 20 per cent of GDP in Greece, Italy, Portugal, Spain, and Belgium and it was also high throughout Scandinavia (Table 5.2). The core countries of the EU had smaller informal economies, but, with the exception of Austria, larger than in the US and Japan (Schneider, 2001). The causes behind the expansion of the shadow economy in western Europe are the tax burden and the levels of social security contributions, the degree of regulation and social transfers, and the relative rigidity of European labour markets (Schneider and Enste, 2000). Given the nature of the shadow economy, those involved in the informal sector are likely to be women (family work) and ethnic minorities and immigrants (under-ground economy). The scarcity of work permits is also forcing most illegal immigrants to join the ranks of the informal sector (see Chapter 4).

The concentration of atypical employment forms among women, the young, the elderly, ethnic minorities and immigrants, and among the less skilled is contributing to a further segmentation of society. Whereas persist-ently high unemployment rates in western Europe had generated an 'A-team' of relatively highly qualified and stable wage-earners, and a large underclass of unemployed, the introduction of flexibility in the labour market has not been capable of solving the problem of social exclusion. In many senses it is con-tributing to a greater social polarization, where the class of stable wage-earners is not just opposed by an underclass of those excluded from the labour market, but also by an increasing army of unstable and precarious workers. For this army of less-skilled women, young people, immigrants, and ethnic minorities, work stability is becoming a luxury, since the norm is to alternate periods of low-paid marginal jobs (often known as McJobs) with occasional periods of 'idleness', due to unemployment or staying out of the labour force. As Harvey (2000) points out, this emerging social structure represents a return to the period prior to the mid-century social compromise, with a widening process of 'proletarianization' and employers increasing their con-trol over working conditions to the detriment of work stability and the rights of employees. In sum, flexibility and deregulation in the job market have brought about a profound reshuffling for the worse of the social structure established during the industrial era.

Although such a pessimistic view about the consequences of recent changes in the labour market is debatable, there is widespread evidence that flexibility in the job market is one of the factors behind the rise of social inequalities in the EU and much of the developed world. Greater precariousness in the labour market, the emergence of atypical forms of work, and, in some cases, the persistence of long-term unemployment are reducing the ranks of the middle classes and enlarging those of the underclass, on the one hand, and of the upper classes, on the other. Whereas the period between the end of the Second World War and 1970 saw a reduction in income inequalities, since the mid-1970s the trend has been reversed (Gottschalk and Smeeding, 1997). The increase in income dispersion has basically occurred at two levels: managerial and executive wages have been rising at a greater rate than those of stable employees, and the gap between the income of stable employees and those in a more precarious situation has also been widening. Those losing out most have been precisely those most affected by the expansion of atypical forms of employment. Education is also becoming one of the key factors behind the increase of inequalities. Those with lower skills are being relegated to atypical forms of employment and condemned to lower salaries.

The rise in income inequalities in the EU has also had a differential territorial impact. The countries which undertook an earlier or more profound reform of their labour markets have undergone the greatest increase in income inequality. Top of the list is the UK, where inequalities rose as much as in the US or Canada (Gottschalk and Smeeding, 1997). No other EU member state has experienced a similar polarization in wages or the creation of such a large underclass. The Netherlands and Sweden also saw wage inequalities rise sharply. Finally, many of the countries in Continental Europe have only witnessed moderate increases in inequalities. This may be the result of keeping a relatively rigid labour market until later. But, as mentioned earlier, in France or Germany there has been a trade-off between income inequalities and unemployment: an increasing army of unemployed was the cost paid for keeping the rise in wage inequalities for the majority of the population at bay. But once unemployment reached levels that forced these countries to flexibilize their labour market, anecdotal evidence suggests that wage inequalities have started to increase at a greater pace.

5.5 Conclusion

Socio-economic restructuring, economic globalization, and European integration have put the social and employment systems developed during the post-war era under considerable strain. The post-war social compromise based on job stability, workers' rights, and a developed welfare state has been challenged since the mid-1970s by the need to maintain economic competitiveness in a more integrated world. Although there has been no common European response to these challenges, two different phases can be identified. In the first phase, western European countries decided to stick to the inherited labour market framework. The consequence was persistently high unemployment across the EU and the emergence of a first form of social exclusion and polarization, mainly represented by those permanently cast out of the labour market: the long-term unemployed. The second phase has been characterized by the reform of labour markets. The Netherlands and the UK led the way in this direction in the second half of the 1980s. Most other EU member states have followed in their footsteps in the 1990s. The reform of the labour markets has almost inevitably meant the introduction of policy measures aimed at flexibilizing employment. The labour market reforms have—although, as we have seen, this is still debatable—managed temporarily to curb unemployment, but the new jobs being created differ enormously from those generated in the industrial era. Stable and relatively well-paid jobs have been substituted by atypical employment forms, ranging from part-time and temporary to self—and disguised employment. This may have helped to bring the unemployment rate down, but has aggravated the problem of social exclusion and polarization. As a result, the long-term unemployed are being substituted by a new underclass made of unstable and badly paid precarious workers drawn from the less privileged groups of society.

III
POLITY

6

Enlargement

6.1 Introduction

The fall of the Berlin Wall in November 1989 marked the beginning of the end of the polarized world that had emerged from the ashes of the Second World War. The collapse of the socialist regimes to the east of the Iron Curtain and the dire economic conditions most of these countries were in made central and eastern Europe look immediately towards the prosperous and democratic West. Membership of the EU became for central and eastern European countries (CEECs) an indicator of future stability and prosperity. As a result, most post-socialist regimes made their intentions of joining the EU clear early on, and joined a series of other applicants, such as Cyprus, Malta, and Turkey, which had been knocking at the EU's doors for some time. The EU, despite warm words towards the new applicants, has been slow to react to the challenge. Negotiations under way have divided applicant countries into several groups: those on the fast track to join the EU, or 'first wave' states (Cyprus, Czech Republic, Estonia, Hungary, Poland, and Slovenia); those on the slow track or 'second wave' (Bulgaria, Latvia, Lithuania, Malta, Romania, Slovakia); the special case of Turkey, that was finally accepted as candidate at the Helsinki summit in December 1999; and, finally those with which negotiations have not even started. But even in the case of the fast track countries negotiations are taking longer than expected. The reasons behind the slow EU reaction relate to both to the economic and political situation of a series of countries which are undergoing profound transitions to democracy and free market systems and which are trying to redefine their place in the world, and to the level of internal transformation that such a large enlargement entails for the EU.

This chapter studies the implications of the possible enlargement to the East for the applicant countries and the EU. The remainder of the chapter is divided into three sections. Section 6.2 examines change in central and eastern Europe. Section 6.3 focuses on the different forms of transition in CEECs. Section 6.4 concentrates on the possible impact of enlargement for the candidate countries and the EU.

6.2 Change in central and eastern Europe

To a large extent, the European Communities were the result of the post-war division of Europe. The early stages of European integration only involved stable capitalist democracies. Other democratic states west of the Iron Curtain joined the process in the 1970s (Denmark, Ireland, and the UK) and 1990s (Austria, Finland, and Sweden). In the case of the former dictatorships of southern Europe (Greece, Portugal, and Spain), membership of the then European Communities was only achieved once their transition to democracy had been completed. The few states in western Europe which have remained outside the process of European integration have done so of their own free will. Norway—which has rejected European integration twice in referenda—and Switzerland represent the main examples.

To the east of the Iron Curtain, economic and political integration with the countries of western Europe was simply not an option. The Cold War division into two politically opposed blocs meant that CEECs could not participate in the process of European integration. The tight political and economic grip that the Soviet Union held over these countries also prevented milder forms of collaboration with the EU. The existence of different and even opposing economic regimes was an additional barrier to collaboration. The European Communities were (and are) basically an association of democratic and capitalist countries in which socialist and centrally planned economies are not welcomed.

As a result, the perspective of east–west collaboration in Europe—let alone of economic and political integration—during the Cold War was just a pipe dream. The situation changed radically, however, in the late 1980s and early 1990s, with the collapse of the communist regimes of central and eastern Europe. The arrival of Mikhail Gorbachev in power in the Soviet Union in 1985 triggered a succession of events which in a few years led communist regimes to the east of the Iron Curtain to fall like dominoes. Gorbachev's policies of *perestroika* (reconstruction) and *glasnost* (transparency), together with the hint that, in contrast to what had happened in the past, the Soviet Union would refrain from intervening in the internal affairs of other eastern bloc countries, contributed to the rapid deterioration, opening, and/or collapse of former communist regimes across central and eastern Europe and eventually of the Soviet Union itself.

Hungary and Poland were the first countries to introduce thorough reforms. They were followed by East Germany. The fall of the Berlin Wall in November 1989 and the later demise of the former German Democratic Republic marked the high point of the changes in central and eastern Europe.

Czechoslovakia, Romania, Bulgaria followed and the breakdown of the Soviet Union represented the end of the Cold War.

In some cases the transition and/or collapse of the communist regimes happened more or less peacefully. Hungary's and Poland's transitions from a communist to a democratic regime took place gradually and without bloodshed. The fall of the Berlin Wall and Czechoslovakia's 'velvet revolution' were also peaceful events, as was the downfall of the communist regime in Bulgaria. The partition of Czechoslovakia into the Czech Republic and Slovakia was also achieved peacefully.

In other cases changes were not as smooth. The Romanian revolution initially involved skirmishes between pro-democracy demonstrators and the feared *securitate*, the communist regime's secret police, which later developed into clashes between the army (mainly supporting pro-democracy demonstrators) and the *securitate*. The relatively short period of armed conflict ended with the capture and execution by the army of the communist dictator, Nicolae Ceausescu, and his wife. In Albania, after an initially peaceful demise of the Stalinist regime of Ramiz Alia, the country plunged into anarchy, with numerous warring factions confronting each other. And the former Soviet Union was also not spared from conflict. The demise of the communist system brought the division of the country into fifteen republics, many of which have witnessed the emergence of armed strife, if not outright military conflicts, like the two wars in Chechnya.

However, the greatest transformation occurred in Yugoslavia, a country where the collapse of the system built by Tito resulted in the break-up of the country and inter-ethnic conflict. Many of the former Yugoslav republics have become independent, and, in most cases, independence has been achieved by war. Slovenia led the field after a war that lasted barely more than a week. A more serious and devastating armed conflict sanctioned Croatia's independence, and the separation of Bosnia-Hercegovina from Yugoslavia was only achieved after prolonged armed conflict and the cruellest war Europe has seen since the end of the Second World War. Inter-ethnic conflict involving the Muslim, Serb, and Croat communities and ethnic cleansing became the norm during the years of the war, and only international military intervention succeeded in re-establishing peace. The insurrection of the Albanian majority in Kosovo and the brutal reaction by the Serbs also brought about military intervention. Macedonia is the only ex-Yugoslav republic that achieved independence through peaceful means. Peace in Macedonia has, however, been under constant threat from neighbours and, especially, from the possibility of ethnic conflict between Albanians and Slavs within its borders.

6.3 The different transitions in central and eastern Europe

The fall of the Iron Curtain and of former communist systems and centrally planned economies left countries across central and eastern Europe facing a series of transitions which exceeded any sort of transition previously experienced by western European countries since the end of the Second World War. Whereas countries like Greece, Portugal, or Spain underwent in the 1970s a political transition from dictatorship to democracy, the transition in central and eastern Europe has been much more complex. In addition to the political transition from communist dictatorships to democracies, most CEECs have undergone or are undergoing three other simultaneous transitions, the first being the economic transition from centrally planned to market economies. The second is a diplomatic and international relations transition from being members of the Warsaw Pact and the Council for Mutual Economic Assistance (CMEA) to knocking on the EU's and NATO's doors. And, finally, what Kopecky and Mudde (2000) call the 'third transition', that is the identity transition in many of the newly independent countries, from being nationals of Czechoslovakia to being simply Czech or Slovak citizens, or from being Soviet citizens to being Estonians, Ukrainians, or Russians. The different forms of transition are explained in the following sections.

6.3.1 Political transition

Since the fall of the Berlin Wall, CEECs have undergone a rapid process of political change. The starting stage in this transition was in all cases a communist one-party state with a tight grip on society. The right to freedom of speech was limited and political opposition banned or tightly controlled. In almost all cases—bar Yugoslavia and, to a lesser extent, the Soviet Union—the communist regime also implied a strongly centralized government, with little or no territorial autonomy. The intended end stage of the political transition is the creation of stable democracies similar to those existing in western Europe.

Although in all CEECs the process of political transition has been accompanied by some degree of political upheaval and unrest, the outcomes of the process are characterized by its variability. Whereas in some cases there has been incomplete transition or even a reversion to authoritarian politics, other countries have been much more successful at reaching the end stage (King, 2000). This is the case of the Czech Republic, Hungary, Poland, and Slovenia. Within a few years of the demise of their former communist regimes, these countries had managed to set up the solid foundations of a democratic system. All basic democratic institutions are in place. Parliaments are elected democratically and there is a bustling political life, with opposition parties playing an important role in the political debate. Democratic legal systems have been developed, with an independent judiciary. The rule of law prevails. The fact that these four countries are ethnically homogeneous has also contributed to prevent the minority problems which have affected other CEECs.

The Baltic states (Estonia, Latvia, and Lithuania) have almost reached the final stage. They possess democratically elected legislative chambers, a relatively independent judiciary, and lively—if somewhat inexperienced—executives. Questions marks have been raised, however, about the treatment of the large Russian minorities that live in these three countries, and especially about the limitations imposed on these minorities to access citizenship.

In most other cases the political transition is still far from its final stage. Bulgaria has made the greatest progress in that direction, although it still cannot be considered a fully-fledged democracy: electoral volatility is still extremely high and the party system still not consolidated. In Romania, Russia, Slovakia, and the Ukraine, democratically elected leaders have often adopted undemocratic means to repress opposition or have tried to limit freedom of speech using different means and especially by ensuring control of the media. The resort to populism and nationalism has also been frequently used (i.e. by former populist leaders such as Vladimir Meciar in Slovakia or Boris Yeltsin in Russia) as a means to cling onto power. Populism and nationalism have also had a negative influence on respect for the rights of minorities. Hungarians in Romania and Slovakia, numerous minorities in Russia, and, to a lesser extent, Russians in the Ukraine, have seen their rights threatened by rising nationalism and, in some cases, by relatively hostile legislation about minorities. A poor economic performance in all these countries, bar Slovakia, has further contributed to making political reform unstable (Intriligator, 2000).

In the former Yugoslavia (with the exception of the above-mentioned Slovenia) political transition has been strongly mediated by nationalism, ethnic conflict, and war. Many of the countries emerging from the collapse of the former Yugoslavia have been ruled by former communist *apparatchiks*, who have used the nationalist and populist card as a means to preserve their power, even at the expense of war. Franjo Tudjman in Croatia but, especially, Slobodan Milosevic in Yugoslavia were the two main archetypes of this class of politicians that flourished in the republics of the former Yugoslavia during the transition period. The death of the former and the downfall and prosecution for war crimes of the latter may mark the beginning of a real transition to democracy in these countries, although the process is by no means likely to be easy.

Finally, in Belarus political transition has been from a communist dictatorship to a nationalist dictatorship. And in Albania, after a brief and relatively democratic spell which followed the resignation of the last communist leader, Ramiz Alia, the country plunged into anarchy from which it is struggling to recover.

6.3.2 Economic transition

Economic transition is proving to be even harder to achieve than political transition. As Petrakos, Maier, and Gorzelak argue, 'the process of transition may have removed the political and military divide in Europe, but it has not so far removed the economic one' (2000*b*: 12), since even the countries which have been more successful at developing complete democratic systems are encountering serious difficulties in transforming centrally planned socialist economies into capitalist systems.

The reasons behind these difficulties are manifold and have to do with the scale of the change. The passage from a communist to a capitalist economic regime entails a wholesale reform not only of how the economy is run, but also of the attitudes and habits of all economic agents. Transition to capitalism involves macroeconomic stabilization and the privatization of production means in societies where private property had, until then, been the exception rather than the rule. It also entails the end of central planning, of state support and subsidies, and the introduction of numerous market institutions such as competition and profit as the main purpose of economic exchange. Production and trade have to be restructured according to the new system (Hare, 1997). A system of trade basically based on barter among CMEA countries and responding to a centrally planned logic had to be opened up to competition from the rest of the world. In addition, the introduction of market institutions represents a significant psychological change for economic actors. In a society where most individual needs were catered for—albeit in a rather imperfect manner—by the state, the institution of capitalism brings risk and uncertainty into everyday life. Where once full employment and employment for life were the norm, transition to capitalism has brought about the risk of unemployment. Where once the state was the main—if not the only— entrepreneur, capitalism has entailed the need to transform normal individuals into entrepreneurs.

The main consequence of having to undertake mammoth economic changes in a relatively short period of time is that the transition to capitalism has in all cases been a difficult one, regardless of the transition model adopted by different countries. Two alternative approaches to economic transition have prevailed. Some countries implemented what is known as shock therapy, that is the rapid demise of socialist economic institutions and their replacement by market institutions. This fast track to capitalism involved comprehensive and often hasty processes of privatization and the end of state subsidies, as well as thorough reforms of the tax and banking systems. Poland is perhaps the best-known example of the implementation of a shock therapy, although the existence in Poland during the Cold War of some production means in private hands and of a certain level of entrepreneurship contributed to easing the shock. Other countries, in contrast, adopted a more cautious approach to economic transition. The transformation of socialist institutions into capitalist ones took place in a gradual and incremental way, with the state playing an important role in the process. The Czech Republic, at least in the early stages of transition, adopted this approach.

None of the alternative approaches to economic transition to capitalism has yielded magical results for countries that according to Fischer, Sahay, and Végh (1997) had given away about one generation's worth of income during the socialist era. In all CEECs transition has uncovered the fundamental weaknesses of the former socialist economies, and especially that of the lack of competitiveness of their economic fabric. Obsolete and strongly polluting heavy industries, inefficient industrial plants for consumer production, and ineffective and backward collective farms crumbled like card castles in the first years after the demise of communism. The consequence of this collapse was a severe recession in all CEECs and an even greater decline in employment levels (European Commission, 1999). Figure 6.1 represents the evolution of GDP during the 1990s in candidate countries to join the EU. The figure shows that, with the exception of Turkey, which did not have to undergo a process of economic transition, economic decline in all other countries has been the norm during much of the decade. 'First wave' countries (the Czech Republic, Estonia, Hungary, Poland, and Slovenia) experienced the strongest decline in the first half of the 1990s. In 1991 the Czech Republic, Hungary, Poland, and Slovenia saw their economies decline by between 5 and 15 per cent. The economic decline was even higher in the ex-Soviet republic of Estonia, which suffered a reduction in its economic output of almost a quarter in 1992 alone (Figure 6.1). The second part of the decade has been characterized by economic recovery. Rates of economic growth in Poland, Slovenia, Hungary, and the Czech Republic caught up with those of the EU by 1993. In Estonia the harmonization of growth rates was achieved in 1995. Since then the economies on the fast track to join the EU have, with few exceptions, managed to keep up and even exceed the economic pace of the EU. Most of this growth has taken place in the metropolitan and western regions of these countries (Petrakos, 2001).

There has been less to cheer about with regard to the economic performance of the 'second wave' states. As Figure 6.1 indicates, the collapse of communism prompted a deep economic recession in all these countries. Bulgaria,

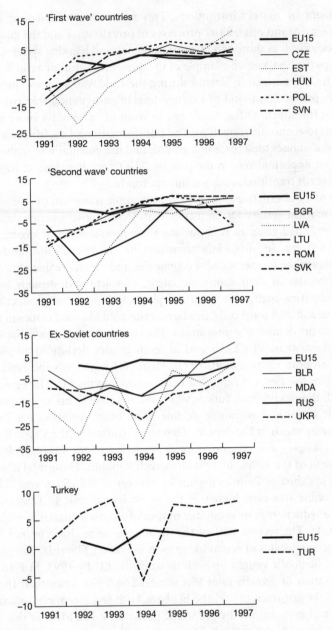

Figure 6.1 Evolution of GDP during the 1990s in different groups of candidate countries

Note: CZE, Czech Republic; EST, Estonia; HUN, Hungary; POL, Poland; SVN, Slovenia; BGR, Bulgaria; LVA, Latvia; LTU, Lithuania; ROM, Romania; SVK, Slovakia; BLR, Belarus; MDA, Moldova; RUS, Russia; UKR, Ukrania; TUR; Turkey.

Source: Own elaboration with World Bank World Development Indicators (2000) data.

Romania, and Slovakia witnessed their economies contract at rates of between 5 and 15 per cent in 1991 and 1992. The economies of the Baltic states of Lithuania and Latvia almost halved between 1990 and 1993. In Latvia the economy fell by more than a third just in 1992. As in the case of the 'first wave' economies, economic recovery has been the norm since 1995. However, and in contrast to the fast-track economies, the economic recovery has been less consistent and full of ups and downs. A relatively early recovery in Romania was halted in 1996 and since then the economy has lagged behind that of the other countries in the group. The fact that the country has failed to implement many of the harsh but necessary reforms needed to achieve a full transition to a market economy is a key explanatory factor of Romania's poor economic performance. A similar failure to implement thorough economic and political reforms in the early stages of transition in Bulgaria also resulted in sub-par economic growth. Their final introduction, from 1996 onwards, led to strong economic decline, at first, followed by a fragile economic recovery towards the end of the 1990s. Only Slovakia and the Baltic states of Latvia and Lithuania have managed to keep up with the economic pace of the EU since 1995 (Figure 6.1).

But the worst performers of all have been the republics emerging from the breakdown of the former Soviet Union, with the exception of the Baltic states. Political instability, widespread corruption, and the failure to reform the economy have jeopardized growth prospects in these countries and, in some cases, resulted in an economic debacle. As Figure 6.1 shows, the economic recovery experienced by the 'first' and 'second wave' economies is nowhere to be seen in the ex-Soviet republics. GDP in Belarus, Moldova, Russia, and the Ukraine fell almost year on year during the early 1990s. In Moldova GDP shrunk by more than 30 per cent in 1992 and 1994. The Ukraine was not far behind Moldova. And economic growth in Russia, the best performer in the group, was well below those of Bulgaria and Romania, the worst performers among the economies on the slow track to join the EU.

Among the candidates to join the EU, the best economic performances are found in those countries without a communist past and which, as a result, have not had to deal with the problems of transition. Cyprus, Malta, and Turkey have converged towards the EU during the 1990s. Figure 6.1 shows Turkey's growth performance. With the exception of 1994, Turkey's growth has exceeded that of the EU by several points.

The consequence of poor economic performance in the CEECs has been a loss of economic weight of the countries knocking at the EU's door with respect to the current member states. If in 1990 the economies of the CEECs for which complete series of data exist represented 14.79 per cent of the EU economy, in 1997 this ratio had shrunk to 11.01 per cent (Table 6.1). That is, the size of the fifteen countries included in Table 6.1 put together represented less than the joint size of the Dutch and Spanish economies. However, as mentioned earlier, there have been significant differences in the economic trajectories of the CEECs. The bulk of the economic decline has taken place in the ex-Soviet republics, whose relative economic size has shrunk from 9.16 per cent of the economy of the EU in 1990 to a mere 4.96 per cent in 1997 (Table 6.1). Economic decline has been greatest in Moldova and the Ukraine. The relative size of their economies with respect to the EU's economy in 1997 was well below half what they represented in 1990.

The 'second wave' economies also suffered a relatively strong decay in the early stages of transition. Between 1990 and 1994 the relative size of the economies of Bulgaria, Latvia, Lithuania, Romania, and the Slovak Republic shrunk from levels of 1.07 per cent of the EU's GDP to just 0.88 per cent.

Table 6.1 GDP at market prices (measured in 1995 US$) with respect to European GDP, 1991–1997

	1991	1994	1997
EU15	100.00	100.00	100.00
'First wave'	2.73	2.73	2.96
Czech Republic	0.63	0.58	0.61
Estonia	0.08	0.06	0.06
Hungary	0.56	0.53	0.54
Poland	1.24	1.35	1.53
Slovenia	0.22	0.22	0.23
'Second wave'	1.07	0.88	0.88
Bulgaria	0.17	0.15	0.12
Latvia	0.14	0.08	0.08
Lithuania	0.14	0.08	0.09
Romania	0.40	0.37	0.36
Slovakia	0.22	0.20	0.22
Turkey	1.83	1.91	2.21
Ex-Soviet	9.16	5.87	4.96
Moldova	0.08	0.04	0.03
Belarus	0.35	0.25	0.24
Russian Federation	6.67	4.40	3.84
Ukraine	2.06	1.19	0.85

Source: Own elaboration with World Bank World Development Indicators (2000) data.

Since then the gap between these countries and the EU has remained more or less stable (Table 6.1).

Only the economies on the fast track to join the EU and Turkey have managed to catch up. Turkey, although still only representing 2.21 per cent of the EU's economy in 1997 is the largest candidate country in economic terms. The five CEECs on the fast track to join the EU represent a mere 3 per cent of the EU's economy, an increase of one quarter of one per cent since 1991 (Table 6.1).

The length of the process of economic stabilization has so far not contributed to raising the standard of living in these countries. The CEECs and Turkey—whose joint economies, as we have seen, barely represent 11 per cent of that of the EU—have a population which is roughly similar to that of the fifteen member states of the EU (Table 6.2). The 'first wave' countries have 16.7 per cent of the EU's population but only represent 3 per cent of its economy, a ratio of 5.6 to one. The ratio in the slow track economies is almost thirteen to one and in the countries of the former Soviet Union, 11.5 to one. In Turkey the ratio is 7.7 to one.

Such a gap between the economic and demographic size of the countries to the east of the former Iron Curtain makes of all these countries economic laggards in comparison with the EU member states. None of the candidate countries has GDP per capita which exceeds that of any of the current members of the EU. The richest country among those queuing up to join the EU, Slovenia, has a GDP per capita measured in PPS which is five points below that of the poorest member of the EU, Greece. Slovenia and the Czech Republic are the only two CEECs whose GDP per capita is higher than half that of the EU average (Table 6.3). A second group of CEECs have GDP per capita levels between 60 and 70 per cent below the European average. Slovakia, Hungary, Poland, and Turkey belong to this category. Bulgaria, Romania, most countries emerging from the collapse of the former Soviet Union, and the countries of the former Yugoslavia for which data are available have a GDP per capita close to or below one quarter of that found in the EU. Croatia and Estonia are slightly above the 25 per cent threshold, whereas all the others have GDP levels between 15 and 25 per cent of the EU average (Table 6.3). Finally, at the bottom of the poverty league, we find Ukraine and Moldova, whose GDP per capita is respectively one tenth and one fourteenth of the European average (Table 6.3).

There are few encouraging signs in the evolution of the GDP per capita of these countries. If Turkey—the only state in Table 6.3 without a communist past—is excluded, all countries for which complete series of data are available have suffered a significant relative decline in their GDP per capita since 1980. Even in the case of the most prosperous members of the group, the relative decline with respect to the EU exceeds 20 per cent. The GDP per capita of the

Table 6.2 Population change in candidate countries and eastern Europe, 1980–1997

	1980	1985	1990	1994	1997
EU15	355 271	358 678	364 559	371 003	374 225
Cyprus	611	648	681	726	747
Czech Republic	10 232	10 335	10 363	10 336	10 304
Estonia	1 480	1 536	1 571	1 499	1 459
Hungary	10 707	10 579	10 365	10 261	10 155
Poland	35 578	37 203	38 119	38 544	38 650
Slovenia	1 901	1 973	1 998	1 989	1 986
'First Wave'	60 509	62 374	63 097	63 355	63 300
as a % of EU15	17.03	17.36	17.31	17.08	16.91
Bulgaria	8 862	8 941	8 718	8 435	8 312
Latvia	2 544	2 621	2 671	2 548	2 465
Lithuania	3 413	3 545	3 722	3 721	3 706
Romania	22 201	22 725	23 207	22 731	22 554
Slovakia	4 984	5 193	5 283	5 347	5 383
'Second Wave'	42 004	43 025	43 601	42 782	42 420
as a % of EU15	11.82	12.00	11.96	11.53	11.34
Turkey	44 484	50 286	56 126	60 572	63 745
as a % of EU15	12.52	14.02	15.40	16.33	17.03
Bosnia and Hercegovina	4 092	4 316	4 450	2 941	2 346
Croatia	4 588	4 701	4 778	4 777	4 768
Macedonia	1 889	1 969	1 903	1 947	1 997
Yugoslavia	9 780	10 211	10 529	10 519	10 614
Former Yugoslavia	20 349	21 197	21 660	20 184	19 725
as a % of EU15	5.73	5.91	5.94	5.44	5.27
Moldova	4 002	4 192	4 362	4 348	4 312
Belarus	9 643	9 975	10 260	10 356	10 267
Russian Federation	139 010	143 858	148 292	148 336	147 307
Ukraine	50 043	50 917	51 892	51 921	50 698
Ex-Soviet	202 698	208 942	214 806	214 961	212 584
as a % of EU15	57.05	58.25	58.92	57.94	56.81

Note: Data in thousands.

Source: World Bank World Development Indicators (2000) data.

Table 6.3 GDP per capita in CEECs and Turkey with respect to the EU, 1980–1997

	1980	1986	1992	1996	1997
EU15	100.00	100.00	100.00	100.00	100.00
'First wave'					
Czech republic	—	64.68	51.16	51.94	50.70
Estonia	—	—	25.19	23.41	25.28
Hungary	43.96	43.55	35.50	34.26	34.73
Poland	38.51	33.39	27.34	30.58	31.45
Slovenia	—	—	53.72	56.72	56.92
'Second wave'					
Bulgaria	27.37	29.19	24.96	21.41	19.34
Latvia	34.00	35.73	21.74	18.28	19.01
Lithuania	—	—	26.68	19.97	20.36
Romania	34.00	34.76	21.50	23.01	20.79
Slovakia	—	—	36.09	37.40	38.16
Turkey	27.37	28.31	30.32	29.88	30.63
Former Yugoslavia					
Croatia	—	—	23.70	23.80	25.32
Macedonia	—	—	20.55	15.94	15.48
Ex-Soviet					
Moldova	—	—	13.16	7.42	7.24
Belarus	—	—	31.27	21.66	23.40
Russian Federation	—	—	33.35	21.71	21.08
Ukraine	—	—	23.29	11.25	10.56

Source: Own elaboration with World Bank World Development Indicators (2000) data.

Czech Republic underwent a relative decline of 27 per cent between 1986 and 1997. The economic downturn in Hungary was 26 per cent between 1980 and 1997 and that of Poland, the fastest growing economy among the CEECs, 22 per cent in the same period. The widening of the gap with respect to the EU elsewhere was stronger. Bulgaria lost 41 per cent of GDP, whereas in Romania and Latvia the decline with respect to the European average was 64 and 79 per cent respectively (Table 6.3).

The panorama improves marginally if the years of the collapse of the former communist regimes are taken as the starting point. Since 1992 Croatia, Estonia, Poland, Slovakia, and Slovenia have managed to reduce the gap with the EU. They are however still the exceptions and not the rules. In most other cases the picture is that of slight decline or, in the case of most of the republics of the former Soviet Union, serious decay (Table 6.3).

Overall, it can be said that the economic transition from planned to market economies in the CEECs has been more complicated than the political transition from socialism to democracy. Whereas stable democracies have emerged in many central European countries and the Baltic states and, with the exception of Belarus, all the remaining countries enjoy some degree of political freedom, few CEECs have managed to achieve a full transition to a market economy. If anything, the first years of transition have led to a widening of the gap between the EU and the CEECs, on the one hand, and among CEECs, on the other (Petrakos *et al.*, 2000*b*). Poland and Slovenia are the most successful cases in this respect, followed by the Czech Republic, Estonia, Hungary, and, to a lesser extent, Slovakia. However, the economic distance that separates these countries from the poorest members of the current EU is still considerable. Poland, the largest and best performing country among the CEECs, has a GDP per capita which is still roughly half of that of Greece. Even if these countries in the future consistently outperform those of the EU, it will take a long time for them to catch up (Fischer *et al.*, 1997). In the case of the other CEECs and the republics of the former Soviet Union, the economic situation is even worse. Their level of production and of economic welfare is still well below what it was during the heyday of the planned economy and the outlook is not particularly good. The failure to implement thorough economic reforms and to guarantee an adequate and safe environment for business mean that it will take a long time before these economies take off.

6.3.3 Identity and diplomatic transitions

In addition to the political and economic transitions, many of the countries knocking at the EU's door are facing two other types of transition. The first of these two additional types of transition is the identity transition. The crumbling of the world order established at the end of the Second World War not only stands for a radical change in the political and economic governance of all CEECs, in many cases it also represents a change in identity. It is not just that citizens who were used to being governed by a one party state and to operating in a world where the public ownership of economic assets dominated have had to adapt themselves to democracy and free-market economies, but also that, in many cases, they have had to adapt to having a new nationality. The 1990s have witnessed the disintegration of several states in the region (Hare, 1997: 127). One state has disappeared (the former German Democratic Republic) and many others have only recently gained independence. The former Czechoslovakia split peacefully into the Czech Republic and Slovakia.

Five states (Bosnia-Hercegovina, Croatia, Macedonia, Slovenia, and Yugoslavia) have emerged from the breakdown of the former Yugoslavia and seven (Belarus, Estonia, Latvia, Lithuania, Moldova, Russia, and the Ukraine) from what was the European part of the former Soviet Union. Some of these new states, and most notably Russia, have long historical traditions. In other cases their previous history as independent states has to be traced back to the Middle Ages, or, as in the cases of Estonia and Latvia, is basically limited to the period between the two world Wars. Finally, some states, such as Belarus, Bosnia-Hercegovina, Macedonia, and Moldova, and experiencing their first period as independent states.

Recent access to independence means that the issue of national identity is frequently still not well defined. National identity is not a problem in the countries with relatively long histories as independent states (Bulgaria, Hungary, Poland, Romania, Russia) or in those with relatively homogeneous populations, a common and distinctive language, and a history of nationalist movements (the Czech Republic and Slovenia). When some of these features are missing, nation-building and the forging of a national identity is not straightforward (Kopecky and Muddle, 2000). Although the Baltic states have distinctive national languages and powerful nationalist movements, the presence of large Russian minorities, especially in Latvia and Estonia, has made national identity and citizenship key issues during the whole transition period. In other cases the presence of a strong neighbour with a similar culture has also brought the question of national identity to the fore. Are the inhabitants of Moldova Moldovans or just Romanians? And are the Belorussians simply Russians? In the case of the Ukraine, the issue of national identity splits the country: whereas Ukranian nationalism is robust in the western part of the country, an area which only came under Russian influence in the Soviet period, the eastern part of the country, where large Russian contingents live, is intensely russophile. The former Yugoslav republics of Bosnia and Hercegovina and Macedonia are also strong cases of lack of collective identity. The presence of large and since the civil war hostile Muslim, Serb, and Croatian groups in Bosnia-Hercegovina and of a large Albanian minority in Macedonia may jeopardize the viability of both states and ultimately lead to the division of both countries.

The last form of transition is the diplomatic transition or the integration or reintegration of CEECs into a 'Western-dominated' international system. More than forty years of communism had led to an almost complete severing of multilateral diplomatic ties between countries on opposing sides of the Iron Curtain. With the exception of the United Nations (UN) and its related organizations, there were relatively few fora where representatives of the opposing blocs met. Parallel and often antagonistic organizations had been set up in the East and West. Military co-operation was co-ordinated by the

Warsaw Pact in the East and the North Atlantic Treaty Organization (NATO) in the West. The CMEA acted as the opposite of the European Communities.

The fall of the Berlin Wall led to the crumbling of the Warsaw Pact and of the CMEA. Many of the CEECs felt that these organizations had been more of a Soviet imposition than organizations representing and/or protecting their own national interest. Hence, the 1990s have been a period in which all CEECs have had to completely re-orientate their international relations. On the one hand, this has meant some countries joining international organizations, such as the International Monetary Fund (IMF), the Organization for Economic Co-operation and Development (OECD), or the World Trade Organization (WTO), which have a much greater economic content that the UN. On the other hand, the diplomatic transition also stands for an integration into 'western' international organizations. In contrast to what has happened in other parts of the world, there has been limited interest in the development of regional economic and political co-operation. The Central European Free Trade Area (CEFTA), established in 1991, was basically intended as a way to prepare CEECs for EU membership and never really got off the ground. The Commonwealth of Independent States (CIS), which included most of the former Soviet Republics, currently has little economic and political clout.

The reason for this lack of interest in regional economic, military, and political co-operation is the attraction that the EU and NATO exert on these countries. Rather than rekindling and revamping previously existing organizations or promoting regional integration, the main international aim of CEECs has been to become 'western' societies, and membership of the EU and NATO are regarded as essential steps by the citizens of these countries in this drive towards the West. As a result, aiming for membership of NATO and the EU has the overwhelming support of the population of these countries, despite the scepticism of certain groups such as farmers and pensioners (Cichowski, 2000). This support is rooted in the belief—that also permeated previous expansions of both organizations—that membership of the EU is a synonym for democratic stability and economic prosperity in a free-market environment. 'EU membership would provide the CEECS with a safeguard against internal opponents of democracy and capitalism' (Baldwin, 1997: 80). Membership of NATO is regarded as a deterrent against the possible renewal of imperialism in Russia. The integration into 'western' organizations also has powerful symbolic connotations, since it represents for most of central and eastern Europe overcoming the world order established in Yalta and Soviet domination. To a certain extent, it can be said that this 'drive towards the West' epitomizes a return to the world order of the beginning of the twentieth century in which the economies and politics of many CEECs were firmly ingrained in those of central Europe, and especially interlinked with those of Germany and Austria.

Yet, despite the fact that membership of both organizations is often associated in the collective imagination, NATO and the EU have behaved in a rather different way with regard to enlargement. Where the EU has dithered, NATO has reacted much faster. The Czech Republic, Hungary, and Poland are already members of NATO and others may join in the near future, once Russian distrust is overcome. In contrast, the EU has dragged its feet and, despite starting negotiations with most CEECs and other countries over the issue of membership, progress towards enlargement has been slow and full of internal obstacles. What are the reasons for the slow progress in the field of enlargement? The next section will deal with the challenges that enlargement poses to European integration as a whole as well as to candidate countries.

6.4 Enlargement and European integration

The pattern in the EU over the last forty years has been towards greater economic and political integration. The European Communities have evolved from a free trade area in the late 1950s to an economic and monetary union at the beginning of the twenty-first century. As seen in Chapter 1, the best part of this transformation took place in the last two decades of the twentieth century. Hence the collapse of the Soviet bloc and transition in central and eastern Europe coincided in time with the peak of European integration. At the time of the fall of the Berlin Wall in 1989 the then EC was engaged in completing the Single Market and preparing for economic and monetary union. The sudden change of the geopolitical panorama on its eastern border presented the EU with a fundamental dilemma: whether to give priority to the process of integration already under way, or to concentrate on preparing for the foreseeable enlargement of the EU to the East.

The debate between these two strands was during the 1990s known as the *widening* versus *deepening* debate (Preston, 1997). Deepening the EU represented the old agenda of steaming ahead with greater economic integration, before opening the gates of the EU to new members. Widening the EU implied a halt in the integration process in order to allow CEECs and other possible candidates to join in quickly and then proceed with integration. The adoption of one option or the other had important implications. Deepening the EU would make it more difficult for candidate countries to join, since the number of norms, rules, and regulations which govern the EU—and which are known by the French term of *acquis communautaire*—would have expanded considerably. Widening the EU from fifteen to twenty or twenty-seven members, without a prior and thorough reform of its institutions, would make it more difficult to achieve the needed consensus to proceed with economic and political integration. The *widening* versus *deepening* debate also split member states. On the one hand, France, fearing the increasing influence of Germany in an enlarged EU, was firmly on the deepening side. Its allies were the Benelux countries and Portugal and Spain, who saw important benefits from achieving greater economic integration before new members were allowed in. In addition, there was the general fear of upsetting Russia if the issue of enlargement was taken too early or pushed too far. On the other hand, Britain led the supporters of widening the EU before deepening it. A Conservative government, wary of giving up greater sovereignty to Brussels and supported by a largely Eurosceptic population, saw enlargement as an effective way of preventing greater integration. Germany, Greece, and Italy were in two minds. They all wanted to deepen European integration, but also had a strong geopolitical and commercial interest in European enlargement to a series of countries with which they shared common borders. The deepening side won the debate. The EU immediately after 1989 proceeded with the integration agenda and relegated enlargement to the background. The admission in 1995 of three more pro-widening countries (Austria, Finland, and Sweden) came once the integration agenda had been almost totally completed.

The consequence of this outcome is that progress on enlargement has been slow. The early response by the Community was limited to an Action Plan (October 1989), followed by a series of aid programmes and trade and co-operation agreements with individual countries. The main aid programme has been the Phare programme (Pologne-Hongrie: Assistance à la Restructuration des Économies). This technical assistance programme, initially designed to aid Poland and Hungary, was quickly extended to other applicant countries. Trade and co-operation agreements with Hungary, Poland, and the former Czechoslovakia were signed in 1991 and followed by others with Bulgaria and Romania in 1993 and with the three Baltic republics and Slovenia in 1995–6.

This rather ad hoc way of dealing with applicant countries has been progressively substituted by a more structured—albeit still haphazard—policy framework that has emerged from successive European summits (Baldwin *et al.*, 1997; Sedelmaier and Wallace, 2000). The Copenhagen summit in June 1993 was the first in a long stream of European summits dealing with the issue of enlargement. It set a series of conditions, known as the 'Copenhagen criteria' that candidate countries must meet in order to become members of the EU. These include:

a) stable institutions guaranteeing democracy, the rule of law, the protection of minorities, and human rights;

b) a functioning market economy, capable of coping with an increasingly competitive market pressure

c) an institutional framework capable of assuming the obligations of the *acquis communautaire* in its entirety.

The Essen summit of December 1994 commissioned a White Paper with the intention of making it a guide to accession for the candidate countries. The Madrid summit of December 1995 set off the process of reforming EU policies—mainly the CAP and the Structural Funds—and of assessing the level of fulfilment by the candidate countries of the 'Copenhagen criteria'. This document, known as the Agenda 2000, was published in July 1997 and included a framework strategy for enlargement, an assessment of the candidates, an impact study, and a new financial perspective. The Luxembourg summit of December 1997 divided the applicants into 'first wave' and 'second wave' countries according to their level of fulfilment of the Copenhagen criteria. Negotiations finally started with the 'first wave' countries in April 1998. The 'second wave' countries followed after the December 1999 Helsinki summit (Sedelmaier and Wallace, 2000). Finally, the 2000 Nice summit made a first attempt at a much need institutional reform of the EU in order to cope with enlargement.

The process of preparing for enlargement has throughout the 1990s played second fiddle to that of economic and political integration. Proceeding with economic and political integration has had significant consequences for the future enlargement of the EU, making it more difficult both for the candidate countries to adjust to and assimilate the *acquis communautaire*, as well as for the EU and its current members to endure the economic and institutional reforms needed for doubling the numbers of the member states of the EU. The next two sections will look at the problems of enlargement, first from the perspective of the candidate countries, and then from that of the EU.

6.4.1 The challenge of enlargement for candidate countries

For countries that since the fall of the Berlin Wall and the collapse of the Soviet Union have had to face profound transformation, membership of the EU represents an even greater leap into the unknown. As mentioned earlier, these countries associate the EU with democratic stability and economic prosperity and thus popular support for membership runs high. But EU membership also implies swallowing the bitter pill of thorough economic, institutional, and political reform. In many ways, the need for adjustment in CEECs in order to join the EU is greater than it was for any of the current member states of the EU for several reasons.

The first reason is related to the greater economic and political gap of current candidates in comparison with former candidates at the time they joined the EU. In economic terms the CEECs and other candidates, such as Turkey, are much poorer than any of the current members of the EU at the time they joined. Some of the previous enlargements of the EU involved states whose GDP per capita was similar—if not well above—that of the EU. That was the case with the 1973 enlargement (with the exception of Ireland) and that of 1995. Even the Mediterranean enlargements of the 1980s posed less of a problem from an economic point of view. When Greece joined the EC in 1981, its GDP per capita measured in PPS was 61.8 per cent of the European average. Spain had, at the time of joining in 1986, a GDP per capita of 70.5 per cent of the EU average, and the poorest country ever to join before the end of the twentieth century was Portugal, with a GDP per capita of 55.1 per cent of the EU average. If we compare these indicators with the GDP per capita of the current candidates we find that only one country, Slovenia, is in a slightly better position than Portugal when it joined the EC. Most other countries are well below this threshold. The two largest candidates outside the former Soviet Union, Poland and Turkey, whose joint population represents more than one quarter of that of the current EU, only make up 3.8 per cent of the economy of the EU and have GDP per capita rates that barely exceed 30 per cent of the European average. And, as described earlier, the economic situation of many of the 'second wave' countries and among the ex-Soviet Republics is even worse. In addition, the thorough economic reforms needed to set the foundations for joining the EU are likely to provoke greater economic hardship in the short term, as was the case for Hungary and Poland in the early 1990s or Bulgaria in the second half of the 1990s.

The second reason behind the greater need for adjustment is related to the fact that the *acquis communautaire* is bigger and much more complex than it was when previous candidates joined. The Mediterranean enlargement took place before the Single European Market and EMU Union were completed. The EU was also in the early stages in terms of social and political integration. The Schengen Convention was in the making and co-operation in the areas of foreign policy, security, and justice and home affairs was still very much a dream. A smaller *acquis* facilitated the adjustment of poorer countries like Greece, Ireland, Portugal, and Spain (Baldwin *et al.*, 1997). CEECs and other candidate countries have been required, under the Copenhagen criteria to assimilate the *acquis communautaire* in its entirety when they become members. But assimilating this *acquis* is proving difficult. First, EU regulations and policies have been designed for the well-developed west European economies rather than for the economies of transition countries, whose institutional structure is much weaker and whose policy and legal needs are often very different from those of the core countries of the EU (Grabbe and Hughes, 1998). Second, trying to assimilate the *acquis* during the 1990s has become like trying to shoot a moving target. EU regulations and policies have continued to expand at a relatively high pace since the CEECs expressed their intention to join the EU. Moreover, assimilating the *acquis communautaire* has been made even more difficult for CEECs by the fact that, in contrast to what happened even in the 1995 enlargement, candidate countries are being required to incorporate the whole European *acquis* without the possibility of opt-out clauses and with strong restrictions on transitional periods which would allow new members to adapt to EU rules and regulations from within.

Finally, current applicants are being assessed not just on their capacity to assimilate EU legislation, but also on the stability of their democracies and on their success at implementing market reforms. These conditions, contained in the Copenhagen criteria, are behind the division of applicants into different groups. Countries which have performed better in this triple transition have been 'rewarded' by being promoted to the fast track to membership. In contrast, countries that have failed to fulfil these conditions have been 'banished' to the slow track. It can thus be said that for current candidates the conditions for EU membership are more far-reaching and complex than just the simple assimilation of legislation.

6.4.2 The challenge of enlargement for the EU

In many ways the challenge of eastern enlargement is almost as demanding for the EU as it is for candidate countries. Enlargement will increase the heterogeneity of the EU and therefore it requires a rethinking of European institutions and policies if it is to succeed (European Commission, 1999). In this sense enlargement is affecting every domain of EU policies and its institutional arrangements (Sedelmeier and Wallace, 2000: 428). The Treaty of Rome set up a series of governing institutions for the EC with only six member states in mind. These institutions have managed to cope with successive enlargements, but in a EU of fifteen member states they are already showing signs of strain. The EU is increasingly accused of suffering from a democratic deficit and of having institutions that are not transparent and democratically accountable. On a day to day basis, decision-making has also become difficult. Unanimous decisions, which were the norm in the early stages of the EC, are now increasingly rare and even qualified majority voting has come under scrutiny. Despite thorough discussion about the reweighting of votes of countries in the Council, the 2000 Nice Treaty came up with a compromise that changed little and is likely not to solve the problem in the long run. Discussions on issues such as the number of EU commissioners per country or on whether each member state should be allowed to have one commissioner have been common in recent years.

It is thus widely accepted that enlargement from fifteen to twenty or twenty-seven members (if 'first' and 'second wave' applicants are considered) entails an unprecedented scale of institutional reform in many areas. The first area goes beyond the simple reweighting of member state votes in the Council or the number of commissioners and concerns the whole governance of the EU. The current institutional structure of the EU deters not just day to day decision-making, but also the adoption of a long-term vision and of coherent strategies. The absence of a democratically elected and accountable EU government, and the need to reach unanimous decisions, in some areas, and to resort to qualified majorities, in others, makes progress difficult. This process is further burdened by tactical trade-offs among countries across policy dimensions. Only a thorough revision of the current institutional framework will prepare the EU for the institutional shock of enlargement. The first steps have been achieved at the Nice summit in 2000, but, as mentioned earlier, these steps are far too timid to cope with the challenges ahead.

Enlargement also has important budgetary implications. The accession of countries with GDP per capita levels well below the European average and with large agricultural sectors would put a European budget dominated by agricultural, regional development, and cohesion funds under serious strain (Baldwin, 1997; Armstrong and Taylor, 2000). One possible option would be to increase the European budget in order to accommodate the needs of the new members. However, given the economic problems of the candidate countries, this would mean a significant expansion of the budget, something that the main contributors are hostile to. Denmark, Germany, the Netherlands, and Sweden have already expressed their opposition to any budgetary expansion that would lead to a sizeable increase in the EU's budget. Another alternative would be to reduce agricultural and cohesion expenditure in current member states and concentrate it in the new countries. This option would take on two of the most powerful interest groups in the EU: farmers and poor regions (Baldwin, 1997). The member states that stand to lose out as a result of such changes have already made their position clear. France, one of the main beneficiaries from the CAP, has never been a fervent advocate of enlargement and has dragged its feet in the reform of the CAP (Smith, 2000: 123). The Cohesion countries, led by Spain, have tried to link enlargement to the preservation of the current level of aid for their territories.

The final option is a thorough reform of EU policies in order to adapt them not only to the impact of enlargement, but also to changes in the economic and political environment since the policies were first implemented. Both the CAP and the Structural Funds cannot cope with enlargement without reform, since the increase in expenditure would bankrupt the EU (Begg, 1997; Tangermann, 1997). An attempt at reforming EU policies has been presented in the Agenda 2000. However, the proposals to reform the CAP, the Structural and Cohesion Funds, and to revise the European budget to cover the needs of enlargement fall short of the thorough reform needed to address the possible impact of the expansion of the EU towards the East. And despite their timidity, the implementation of the policy reforms in both areas has continued at a slow pace (Smith, 2000).

Finally enlargement may revive the large flows of east–west migration of the early 1990s, although, as Begg (1997) acknowledges, the probable impact of enlargement on migration is difficult to estimate.

6.5 Conclusion

Enlargement is one of the key challenges the EU has to face in the near future. The assimilation of a series of countries whose combined population, if the European republics of the former Soviet Union are included, exceeds that of the current EU, but whose economies put together make up slightly more than one tenth of that of the EU, is inevitably going to transform the EU. On the one hand, enlargement is likely to increase political and economic stability on the European Continent. The precarious economic conditions and the political and, sometimes, armed strife which have engulfed many of the countries emerging from the collapse of the Iron Curtain are likely to give way to greater democracy and prosperity. Greater stability and prosperity could help preclude massive east–west migration in the future. The experience of previous enlargements of the EU seems to point in that direction. The emergence of new and stable markets for trade is a further reward of enlargement. On the other hand, the sheer scale of enlargement may cost the EU dear. Enlargement will increase the budget burden, especially in the areas of structural and agricultural spending and may encourage east–west migration in the early stages of membership. Furthermore, it may jeoparzide further integration, lead to institutional paralysis, and tilt the balance of power within the EU—much to the chagrin of the French—in Germany's favour.

For enlargement to be successful it requires, however, a thorough reform of the economies, policies, and institutions of the applicant countries in order to guarantee a smooth transition from the current EU to one with double the number of member states. But it is as important as reform in applicant countries for the EU to face its own institutional and policy reform in order to sort out some of the problems that are already besieging the day to day operation of the EU, before they become endemic in an enlarged Community. And these reforms need to be undertaken fast. Candidate countries have had to wait for almost ten years between the fall of the Berlin Wall and the opening of formal negotiations on membership. Further delays will only undermine support for EU membership in candidate countries and contribute to accentuating some of the governance problems in the EU in the last few years. In Baldwin's words 'the CEECs and the EU are now engaged, but the wedding date has not been set and the bride price could pose a problem' (1997: 73).

7

Regionalism and regionalization

7.1 Introduction

European integration is not the only challenge to the power of the nation state in Europe. A potentially more powerful challenge is emerging from below. In recent decades most European countries have witnessed a revival or an emergence of nationalist and regionalist tendencies. In many cases the revival of nationalism and regionalism in Europe has triggered processes of regionalization and devolution which have radically transformed the map of Europe since the 1970s. Apart from Austria, Germany, and, outside the EU, Switzerland, all other European states had, to a greater or lesser extent, a unitary political system before the end of the 1960s. Nowadays the trend has been reversed and centralized states are increasingly becoming the exception to the rule. Regionalization and devolution are so prevalent that talk about the existence of a 'Europe of the Regions' has become commonplace.

In this chapter I will analyse how and why the process of regionalization came about, what it represents for the European nation state, and whether we are witnessing the emergence of a 'Europe of the Regions'. The chapter is divided into four further sections. Section 7.2 deals with the process of regionalization itself. Section 7.3 presents the transfer of power from the nation states to the regions. Section 7.4 looks for the roots of the process in the emergence of a new type of regionalism across Europe, whereas Section 7.5 discusses whether this process has led to the emergence of a 'Europe of the Regions'.

7.2 Regional devolution in Europe

At the end of the 1960s the territorial structure of most of the present member states of the EU—and even of many countries outside it—was remarkably similar. The great majority of the states in Europe were heavily centralized, characterized by a powerful central administration and solid but territorially small—especially in the cases of France and Spain—local authorities. There was relatively little or no transfer of power to other territorial administrations. Regions, wherever they existed, were mere administrative divisions with neither political importance nor decision-making power. Policies beyond the local dimension were the exclusive prerogative of the state. The only exceptions to the dominance of centralized governments were the three federal states of Austria, Germany, and Switzerland. And even in the cases of Austria and Germany the federal model of territorial administration was relatively recent. It was imposed by the Allies after the end of the Second World War, with the introduction of the federal states (known in German as *Länder*) as a way to counter the concentration of political power in Berlin during the Nazi period. Italy was also on paper a decentralized state. Its 1948 constitution had provided for the formation of 'special' and 'ordinary' status regions. The 'special status' regions were established in those areas of the country with linguistic minorities and in the islands of Sardinia and Sicily, whereas the rest of Italy was to be divided into 'ordinary status' regions. However, the decentralization process, with the exception of the 'special status' regions, did not get off the ground until the 1970s.

At the beginning of the twenty-first century the picture has changed radically. Despite still representing about half of the states in the EU and most of those of central and eastern Europe, strong central governments are on the retreat. Moreover, the centralized form of government is increasingly confined to relatively small and homogeneous states. Among the centralized states, Denmark, Finland, Greece, Ireland, Luxembourg, and Sweden have less than 10 million inhabitants and none of them—perhaps with the exception of Finland—has any significant national or linguistic minorities. The Netherlands is the largest centralized state in the EU, but despite a Protestant–Catholic cleavage and a Frisian minority, its 15 million inhabitants make a much more homogeneous group than the population in neighbouring states.

The challenges to the centralized state have been widespread in larger and less homogeneous countries. In some cases these challenges have led to the partition of former plurinational states. As mentioned in Chapter 6, central and eastern Europe has seen the division in the 1990s of Czechoslovakia, the Soviet Union, and Yugoslavia into a series of states. Czechoslovakia was peacefully partitioned into the Czech Republic and Slovakia. War led to the emergence of Bosnia-Hercegovina, Croatia, Macedonia, and Slovenia out of the former Yugoslavia. And the process of disintegration in Yugoslavia seems still under way, with Kosovo and a large percentage of the population of Montenegro demanding independence. The collapse of the Soviet Union saw the birth or rebirth of Belarus, Estonia, Latvia, Lithuania, Moldova, Russia, and the Ukraine in its European part. Not always has the national or regional issue east of the former Iron Curtain led to state division. Poland, a more homogeneous national state, has embarked in the late 1990s in a, so far, limited process of regionalization.

In the EU, the challenges to the nation state from below have been more peaceful and have not (yet) led to the disintegration of states. Nevertheless, the emergence of the regions as political actors has been a general process which has left none of the larger and less homogeneous countries of the EU unscathed.

The regionalization process has adopted different forms across the EU, leading to the establishment of multiple political and administrative territorial regimes. These territorial regimes can be grouped into four different categories (Rodríguez-Pose, 1998: 67):

a) *Federal states*: The regions or federal states enjoy a considerable level of autonomy, with the power of the state normally confined to the realms of foreign policy, defence, and a few areas of economic policy. Within the EU, Austria, Belgium, and Germany belong to this group.

b) *Regional states*: Regions in a regional state traditionally enjoy a lower level of autonomy than those in a federal state, although in some cases—as in the case of many Spanish regions—there is little difference. The process of regionalization in regional states is achieved, in contrast to federal states, without a profound restructuring of the state. Italy and Spain belong to this category.

c) *'Regionalized states'*: The 'regionalized state' represents a less advanced form of decentalization. 'Regionalized states' are often in a transition stage towards a regional or a federal state. This stage generally entails the definition of the regions and regions tend to have fewer powers than in more advanced forms of regionalization. France, Portugal, and the UK can be included in this category.

d) *Centralized or unitary states*: Centralized or unitary states lack an intermediate tier of government between central and local governments. Regions, wherever they exist, tend to be mere administrative entities with little or no political significance and no decision-making powers. Most areas of public policy are still in the hands of the central government. There are currently seven centralized states in the EU (Denmark, Finland, Greece, Ireland, Luxembourg, Netherlands, and Sweden).

The picture of territorial politics in the EU is rendered more complex if differences in the level of autonomy between regions within states are taken into account. Not all devolved countries in the EU have homogeneous self-government regimes for all its regions. This is only the case in the three federal states and France. Italy, Portugal, Spain, and the UK have undergone processes of what is known as 'asymmetrical devolution', by which some regions enjoy greater levels of autonomy than others. In Italy and Spain, greater powers have been transferred to the so-called 'special status' regions and 'historical nationalities' than to the remaining regions. In the cases of Portugal and the UK, parts of the country have devolved powers while others are still directly ruled by the central government (Table 7.1).

7.2.1 From regionalism to regionalization in the EU

As mentioned earlier in the chapter the regionalization process is relatively recent. With the exception of Austria and Germany, the emergence of regions as political actors has taken place since the late 1960s and early 1970s. During this period formerly centralized states across western Europe have witnessed the emergence of subnational movements and regional demands which have spurred the regionalizaton debate everywhere in the EU and, in some cases, have contributed to the reform of the state and to the emergence of a regional tier of government. Keating (1998) identifies two waves of regionalism and regionalization in western Europe. The first one occurred in the 1960s and 1970s with the upsurge of national and regional movements in those areas with a more deeply rooted identity. After a relative lull during the late 1970s and early 1980s a second wave of regionalism—the so-called 'new regionalism'—took place in the late 1980s and throughout the 1990s, although in this case it was a more widespread form of regionalism than in the previous wave, and more often based on economic rather than on identity grounds. The revival of regionalism during this period has been associated with the renewed devolution of powers to the regions across Europe. This section of the chapter looks at what forms the re-emergence of regionalism has adopted and at how is regionalism is linked to the process of regional devolution in different EU countries.

Austria and Germany are the two EU countries with the longest established regional governments. Although—at least in the case of Germany—federalism is deeply rooted in the traditions of a country which was only unified in the 1870s and which had erected its Empire and the Weimar Republic as federations, the establishment of post-war federal states in Austria and Germany owes more to their defeat in the war than to any other reason. The Allies were keen to prevent the re-emergence of Germany as a strong military power and one of the ways devised to achieve this was the adoption of a federal form of government (Keating, 1993). The 1949 German Basic Law established a clear division of power between the Federation and the ten federal states or *Länder* and the city of West Berlin. After the German reunification in 1990 the number of *Länder* increased to sixteen. The aim of the

Table 7.1 Level of regional autonomy across the EU

	Level of autonomy			
	High	Medium	Low	Non-existent
Federal states				
Austria	The whole country			
Belgium	The whole country			
Germany	The whole country			
Regional states				
Italy		'Special status' regions	'Ordinary status' regions	
Spain	Andalusia, Basque Country, Canary Islands, Catalonia, Galicia, Navarre, Valencia	The rest of the country		
'Regionalized' states				
France		Possibly Corsica	The whole country	
Portugal		Azores, Madeira		Continental Portugal
UK	Scotland	Northern Ireland, Wales	London	English regions
Centralized states				
Denmark				The whole country
Finland				The whole country
Greece				The whole country
Ireland				The whole country
Luxembourg				The whole country
Netherlands				The whole country
Sweden				The whole country

Source: Own elaboration.

Allies to disrupt traditional institutions and power bases in Germany becomes more evident when the configuration of the *Länder* is analysed. Only Bavaria and the Hanseatic cities of Bremen and Hamburg in West Germany and Saxony in the former East Germany existed as states in the pre-unified Germany. All other *Länder* were artificially constructed from the merger of pre-existing states, as in the case of the union among the southwestern former Catholic Kingdom of Baden, the former Protestant Kingdom of Württemberg, and a third smaller state into Baden-Württemberg, or else were the result of the partition of Prussia into smaller states. Indeed, the regional structures of the German states were established in a territorial setting which was fundamentally defined by the occupation zones (Benz, 1993). The imposition of a federal system by the Allies together with the massive migrations which followed the end of the Second World War—which contributed to the homogenization of the German population—means that regional identity as a driver of regional devolution in Germany has been much less of an issue than elsewhere in western Europe.

The Allies played a similar role in Austria. Although the country, given its size, represented much less of a potential threat than Germany, the existence of four occupation zones in Austria helped to shape the *Länder*, which do not conform to any pre-existing political structure. With the exception of Burgenland, which was part of Hungary in the Austro-Hungarian Empire, the remaining *Länder* are subdivisions of the old Kingdom of Austria.

In most other EU countries the process of regionalization took place later. The deepest transformation has occurred in Belgium, which in a period of twenty-three years has travelled from a unitary to a regionalized state, in 1970, and to a fully federal state by 1993 (De Rynck, 1998). This voyage from a centralized to a federal state can only be understood by looking at the evolution of the Belgian state since independence. Belgium seceded from the Kingdom of the Netherlands in 1830. The grounds for secession were founded on the religious cleavage between the Catholic Belgians and the mainly Protestant Dutch. But, besides sharing a common religion, there was little else that united the inhabitants of the new country. Fundamental linguistic and cultural cleavages divided the new state. The southern part of the country is occupied by the French-speaking Walloons, whereas the north of the country is inhabited by the Dutch-speaking Flemish. This division was reflected in the initial problems on agreeing a common name for the territory. The name of Belgium—the appellation the Romans gave the tribes living in the area and the name of the province they later created—had to be rescued from the history books. If Belgium emerged as a unitary state after independence it was mainly due to the economic and political supremacy of the Walloons at the time. During the nineteenth and the beginning of the twentieth century, the agreement between the Walloon elite and a 'frenchified' Flemish urban bourgeoisie made French the language of politics and the economy. The Flemish, however, started to rebel against the control of the country's institutions by the French-speaking, asking first, for Dutch to be granted equal status to French, and later, for the establishment of a Flemish autonomous region.

This was not achieved until the late 1960s. A series of additional factors contributed to an increasing tilting of the balance in favour of Flemish interests. First and foremost was the economic decay of Wallonia. Wallonia, the richest region in Europe just after the Second World War, has seen its coal mines and heavy industries suffer a steep decline since the 1950s. The traditionally more rural and agricultural Flanders experienced a more successful transformation of its economy towards services and trade. The contrasting economic trajectories of the two main Belgian linguistic communities contributed to a reversal of the roles and, by the time the country was regionalized in 1970, Flanders was already well ahead of Wallonia in GDP per capita. Another factor supporting the interests of Flemish nationalism was their greater demographic dynamism *vis-à-vis* the Walloons.

The strength and vigour of Flemish nationalism triggered a response by the Walloons in the form of a Walloon nationalism (De Rynck, 1998). Tension between both communities peaked in the 1960s and ultimately led to the regionalization of the country in 1970. The institutional reforms which followed in 1980, 1988–9, and 1993 transformed Belgium into a *sui generis* Federal State. In contrast to other federal states, the division of power follows two different criteria. The first criterion is language and led to the establishment of a Flemish- (or Dutch-) speaking, a French-speaking, and a German-speaking community. The second criterion is identity and has led to the division of the country into three regions: Brussels, Flanders, and Wallonia. The Flemish Community and Region have merged into one entity, with Brussels as its capital.

Today Belgian decentralization rivals that of the most decentralized states, although the presence of five territorially overlapping subnational entities makes Belgium the most complex and arguably the most difficult-to-handle state in the EU.

Spain has also undergone a profound territorial transformation. It was one of the most centralized states in Europe until the death of General Franco in 1975, but the advent of democracy brought about a parallel process of asymmetrical decentralization which has entailed a transfer of power from the centre to the regions similar to that of many federal states. The roots of the Spanish decentralization process have to be traced back to the formation of the Spanish state in early modern times. The creation of Spain in 1492 was the consequence of the merger of four Medieval Kingdoms, either as a result of military conquest or dynastic alliance. All of the former Medieval Kingdoms kept their laws and privileges in modern Spain. From the beginning of the eighteenth century the Bourbon dynasty tried, as was being done in France, to create a greater sense of nationhood in Spain by suppressing regional laws and privileges. However, the nation-building experiment failed: the suppression of regional privileges was only achieved in the Kingdom of Aragon—whereas the Kingdom of Navarre and the Basque Provinces managed to hang on to their privileges until the present—and the whole process of centralization fuelled considerable resentment in the peripheral nations of Spain. The Second Spanish Republic (1931–9) tried to address this resentment by granting autonomy to Catalonia and the Basque Country, the regions with the strongest identity. This effort was thwarted by the Spanish Civil War and the repression of national and regional identities by the Francoist regime. But once again the attempt to curb nationalism and regionalism only contributed to generating a greater yearning for regional autonomy (Pérez Díaz, 1990). As a result, the restoration of democracy in the late 1970s went hand in hand with a process of decentralization and regional autonomy.

Contrary to what happened in Belgium and in other federal states, the Spanish devolution model was not homogeneous across regions. The powers of the Autonomous Communities—as the regions are known in Spain—vary according to the way in which they achieved devolution (Heywood, 1995). The Spanish constitution of 1978 did not provide for a single way of accessing regional autonomy. The achievement of greater or lesser autonomous powers thus depended on the interpretation of the strength of local identity (Rodríguez-Pose, 1996). Large autonomous powers were transferred from the centre to regions with their own language and rich cultural traditions, such as Catalonia, the Basque Country, and Galicia, in a relatively short period of time. Navarre, which had kept its own Medieval privileges also achieved high autonomy. Other regions such as Andalusia, the Canary Islands, and Valencia followed suit. The powers of many of these regions are similar to or even greater than those of states in federations.

The remaining ten regions achieved a much lower level of autonomy during most of the 1980s and early 1990s, although the gap has significantly narrowed in the second half of the 1990s with greater transfers of powers to these regions.

The regionalization process in Italy has been less radical than in Belgium or Spain. As in the case of Spain, the origins of regionalization can be traced back to imperfect nation-building. Since the end of the Roman Empire the Italian peninsula had been politically divided. Multiple states—often city-states—coexisted and fought each other for centuries. Foreign powers took advantage of this situation and often established themselves on parts of Italian soil. This situation only came to an end in 1870, when the troops of the northwestern Kingdom of Sardinia entered Rome, thus completing the process of unification they had started a decade earlier. A century of an Italian unitary state did not suffice, however, to smooth out the differences generated by centuries of political and economic division among Italian regions. Although the efforts of the Italian state to promote the Italian language to the detriment of local and regional dialects has been successful, other differences have proved much harder to eradicate. The most important of all is the economic imbalance between a rich and industrial north and a relatively poor and agricultural south. This problem, known in Italy as the *Questione Meridionale* (or the question of the south), has been at the heart of Italian politics over the last half century. Policies aimed at curbing the gap between the north and the south have not been successful (Padoa-Schioppa, 1993) and regionalism in the south and increasingly in the north of the country has been linked to economic arguments.

Another factor which has favoured the emergence of regional movements and regionalist demands in Italy has been the existence of linguistic minorities in border regions. The German-speaking minority of the Alto Adige—or South Tirol, as it is called by the Austrians—represents the largest of these groups. Annexed from Austria only after the First World War, the inhabitants of Alto Adige have been fighting to preserve their German language and culture. The French-speaking minority in the northwestern mountainous region of the Valle d'Aosta shares the same goal as the German-speakers. And the inhabitants of Friuli, with a powerful and well-established dialect and a non-negligible Slovenian minority, have also been active on the regionalist front.

The unitary state's failure to even out regional particularities was to a certain extent acknowledged by the 1948 constitution, which provided for the creation of 'special status' regions in those areas with the strongest regional identity: Sardinia, Sicily, Trentino-Alto Adige, and Valle d'Aosta. A fifth 'special status' region was created in 1963 in Friuli-Venezia Giulia. In addition, the Constitution also established fifteen 'ordinary status' regions in the rest of Italy. However, until 1970, when the regional councils were first instituted, the 'ordinary' regions only existed on paper. And significant powers were not transferred to the regions until 1976. Since then, the level of autonomy of Italian regions—both 'special' and 'ordinary' status—has expanded considerably (Keating, 1993).

Regional devolution in the UK came rather late and has, so far, only affected the peripheral nations of the country. Once again, an imperfect process of nation-building is at the root of the regionalization process. The conquest of Ireland, the incorporation of Wales into English governance structures, and the Act of Union of 1707, by which the English and Scottish parliaments were united, were steps towards the formation of what is known as a 'union state' in Britain (Tomaney, 2000). British identity proved fragile and nationalist and regionalist movements soon appeared. Pressures to reform the structure of the

UK were rife in Ireland during most of the nineteenth century, a factor which eventually led to the partition of the island in 1921. Nationalistic tension in Scotland and Wales was also latent during the late nineteenth and throughout the twentieth century. The permanence of a separate Scottish legal and educational system, as well as the establishment of the Secretary of State for Scotland, a Scottish Office and, much later, of a Secretary of State for Wales, contributed to reinforcing the separate identity in Scotland and Wales. The presence of nationalist parties in both areas of the UK and of a Welsh-speaking community in Wales were additional factors pushing towards devolution.

The first wave of devolution took place, as in many other EU countries, during the late 1960s and the 1970s. The only difference is that in this case it failed to achieve the decentralization of the state. The electoral growth of the Scottish National Party (SNP), which achieved 30 per cent of the Scottish vote in the 1974 general election, pushed the Labour government of the time to introduce legislation to create a Scottish and a Welsh assembly. Devolution referenda were held in Scotland and Wales. The Scottish electorate favoured devolution by the narrowest of margins, but low turnout meant that the yes votes did not reach the 40 per cent of the electorate required to achieve devolution. Devolution was emphatically rejected by the electorate in Wales (Tomaney, 2000).

The Thatcherite period represented a break in the aspirations of nationalist movements in Scotland, Wales, and Northern Ireland. The Thatcherite idea of a strong state was at odds with any form of territorial devolution of power. Only the advent of the Blair government and of New Labour in 1997 put the question of devolution firmly back on the political agenda. Referenda on devolution were held in 1997 and 1998 in Scotland, Wales, and Northern Ireland and the return of powers to the regions was approved everywhere (although in Wales by the slightest of margins). Regional Assemblies were established in Northern Ireland and Wales, and a parliament with tax varying powers was elected in Scotland. London became the fourth area of the UK to achieve some form of self-government. In a 1999 referendum Londoners voted in favour of the appointment of an elected mayor and of a Greater London Assembly.

This partial and asymmetric devolution process has left the UK as a country with a highly complex territorial structure. It has regions with a high degree of autonomy (Scotland), regions with relatively intermediate (Wales and Northern Ireland) and low (London) powers, and still the majority of its territory (England) directly ruled from Westminster. In addition, regional autonomy has already been suspended and then reinstated by the central government in Northern Ireland. This highly complex territorial arrangement means that the regional question is likely to resurface in the UK in the future. The so-called

'English question' may be the next step in the devolution process (Tomaney and Ward, 2000). English regions hit by strong economic decline, such as the North East, the North West, and Yorkshire, have set up Constitutional Conventions with the aim of achieving devolution. But opposition to any further form of devolution is also strong in other areas of England.

France, despite being considered as the paradigm of the European centralized nation state and the most successful case of nation-building through secular political intervention, has not been immune to the devolution process. The territorial structure of France before the French Revolution was not dissimilar to that of Spain and the UK. Numerous regions which had been annexed by the Kingdom had kept their own laws, institutions, culture, and languages. Occitan and Provençal dialects were strong in the south of the country and significant Breton, German-speaking, Flemish, and Basque communities existed within its territory. The French Revolution and the regimes that followed it represented an attempt to homogenize and eliminate all vestiges of local cultures. France became a centralized country. The only politically meaningful territorial division was between the central and the 36,000 local governments (Keating, 1993). The departments—the intermediate division—were nothing more than administrative entities with little real power.

The process of cultural and linguistic homogenization of France was relatively successful in comparison to what happened in Spain and the UK. All old regional privileges were lost, peripheral languages regressed considerably everywhere, Occitan and Provençal almost disappeared, and a solid national identity was forged. Regionalism was almost confined to Corsica, and, to a lesser extent, to Brittany and the Basque Country.

Hence, when twenty-two regions were established in 1972, the process of regionalization had little connection—as was the case in Belgium, Spain, the UK, and even in Italy—with the vigour of regionalist movements. Regionalization in France was much more the result of economic planning than of disintegrating forces (Balme, 1998). French regions were devised as the appropriate territorial units for the implementation of certain public policies, most notably in the fields of education, culture, and economic development. Regions were granted some powers from the centre, but almost no means to carry out any autonomous policies. The direct election of Regional Councils from 1986 has granted French regional governments greater legitimacy, but their level of autonomy remains well below that of regions in most neighbouring countries (Rodríguez-Pose, 1998).

During the late 1990s and early twenty-first century there have been increasing signs of a new regionalist wave in France. Regional movements have become stronger in the Basque Country, Brittany, and, especially, in Corsica. The question of granting greater autonomy to these regions is appearing increasingly on the political agenda, and Corsica seems destined to be the first French region to attain a high level of devolution.

7.2.2 The bastions of centralism

Not all western European countries have been pushed towards decentralization. As shown in Table 7.1, seven out of the fifteen member states of the EU are still centralized countries. As mentioned earlier, they tend to be small—their joint population only represents around 13 per cent of the total population of the EU—and relatively homogeneous countries. The presence of Lapp communities concentrated in the north of Finland, of a Frisian minority in the north of the Netherlands, or of Vlach and Albanian groups in Greece has not sufficed to trigger regionalist movements in these countries. Their small numbers and, in some cases, the protection of their cultural rights and heritage within the existing political and legal framework have acted as a deterrent for any aspirations of autonomy.

This does not mean, however, that these countries have been completely immune to the decentralization debate. The convenience of establishing intermediate or meso levels of government has been debated in several countries. One such case has been the Netherlands where the regionalization question has always been in the background but has never become an important national political issue. The diminishing importance of the religious cleavage in the country between a Catholic south and south east and a Protestant north and south west, together with the lack of any significant territorial inequalities and the relatively small size of the country, have contributed to keep regionalist demands at bay. The result is a country with strong central and local governments in which provinces—the main intermediate administrative level in the Netherlands—carry little political weight (Toonen, 1998).

But perhaps the most meaningful case of resistance to decentralization comes not from a unitary country but from an already 'regionalized' country. Portugal granted regional autonomy to the archipelagos of the Azores and Madeira in its 1976 constitution. The distance between these groups of islands and the Portuguese mainland, as well as their social, cultural, and economic particularities, led to the widespread belief in the islands and among the Portuguese political elite that autonomy was the most adequate way of tackling the archipelagos government and development problems. The decentralization plan was however not to be limited to the islands. Discussions took place about the convenience of regionalizing the Portuguese mainland. The Portuguese Socialist Party—in government during much of the 1990s—supported regional devolution. The argument behind the drive towards devolution was that regional institutions would be more adept at tackling planning and investment issues, and therefore regional devolution could contribute to reducing the economic gap between the more developed Atlantic coast and the impoverished interior. Plans to proceed with regionalization of the Portuguese mainland came to an abrupt end however when the Portuguese electorate comprehensively (with 63 per cent of votes against) rejected devolution in 1998.

7.3 The transfer of power from the nation state to the regions

The European regionalization process has brought about important changes in governance and policy-making structures across the EU. Few countries in the EU have been spared from transferring greater powers from the centre to subnational governments. The regions have been the main beneficiaries of these transfers. Even regions with a low level of autonomy, such as the French regions, are responsible for a considerable array of policies, such as regional economic development, culture, parts of secondary and higher education, vocational training, and the environment.

Italian regions have a greater level of autonomy and this is reflected in their legislative powers. Regions in Italy have traditionally had a say in areas such as the health service and vocational training. Their regional powers have progressively increased since the late 1970s. A significant step in this direction has been the approval of the Bassanini law in 1997, which, under the principle of subsidiarity, encourages the transfer of powers traditionally reserved for the Italian state to the regions and local authorities. As a result of this expansion, most 'ordinary status' regions have established a series of departments dealing, among other things, with agriculture, tourism, regional planning, environment, economic development, etc. 'Special status' regions enjoy greater powers. Among the powers transferred to a 'special status' region such as Friuli-Venezia Giulia we find agriculture, hunting and fishing, industry and trade, craftsmanship, public utilities, regional transport and infrastructure, urbanism, culture, and university education.

Spanish regions have many of the competences transferred to the Italian regions and more. The low autonomy regions, whose powers were until recently limited to economic development, regional planning and infrastructure, tourism, and agriculture, have grabbed education and health from the central government during the 1990s. Regions with high levels of autonomy, such as Catalonia, the Basque Country, and Galicia, have long held these powers. But in some cases their competences extend beyond these limits and include aspects such as policing, taxation and fiscal affairs, and even some form of foreign policy (Rodríguez-Pose, 1996).

In Belgium the coexistence between regions and communities has created a complex division of powers. Communities are mainly responsible for culture, education, sports, and youth, while regions have powers that cover fields such as the economy, the development of SMEs, research and development, transport, energy, planning, the environment, social affairs, health, transport, and employment and training.

In the case of the countries with the greatest level of devolution—Austria, Belgium, Germany, and the highly autonomous regions of Spain—the powers amassed by the regions have limited the functions of the state to little more than defence, foreign affairs, and macroeconomic matters.

The expansion of regional powers has not always been matched by a similar increase in regional financial budgets. Table 7.2 reports the evolution of the share of government expenditure by different tiers of government between 1980 and 1997. Lack of data for the share of expenditure of regional governments in many of the countries which have undergone recent processes of devolution prevents us from getting a complete picture of the evolution of the financial power of the regions across the EU. However, it could be said that, with the exception of Spain, the expenditure balance between the central and the regional and local governments across the EU has remained relatively stable between 1980 and 1997 (Table 7.2)

Austria is one of the examples of this stability. The central government has remained by far the biggest public spender, with more than two thirds of total government expenditure. Regional governments have marginally increased their share from 13 to 15 per cent, but this increase has been mainly achieved at the expense of local governments rather than of the national government. In Germany both regional and local governments have lost out to the national government. The budgetary effort linked to German reunification has contributed to reinforcing the financial supremacy of the Federal State. Even in countries which have experienced recent regionalization processes, such as Belgium, France, or Italy, the share of expenditure of the central government has not suffered significant change (Table 7.2). This has left many of the regional governments across the EU with insufficient economic resources to undertake all their functions. This is the case of Italian regions, 90 per cent of whose revenue was until recently in the form of grants by the central government and most of it was earmarked for specified expenditures, especially on health (Keating and Loughlin, 1997). A similar grant system was the main source of revenue for all the Spanish regions without tax varying powers. And at the beginning of the 1990s expenditure by French regions was just 8.2 per cent of the expenditure of all subnational governments (Balme, 1998).

The situation is slowly starting to change. The tax varying powers accorded to the Scottish parliament provide Scotland with a significant capacity to raise revenue. During the 1990s Spanish regions whose budget depended on central

Table 7.2 Share of total government expenditure by different tiers of government, 1980–1997

	1980			1990			1997		
	Central government	Regional government	Local government	Central government	Regional government	Local government	Central government	Regional government	Local government
Austria	68.7	13.3	18.0	69.8	13.5	16.7	69.4	15.4	15.2
Belgium	85.9	—	14.1	88.9	—	11.1	89.1	—	10.9
Denmark	47.5	—	52.5	55.6	—	44.4	56.0[a]	—	44.0[a]
Finland	61.6	—	38.4	60.2	—	39.8	61.4	—	38.6
France	84.0	—	16.0	82.5	—	17.5	82.5	—	17.5
Germany	56.4	25.5	18.0	59.0	24.0	17.0	62.5[c]	23.7[c]	13.9[c]
Ireland	—	—	—	76.3	—	23.7	74.7[b]	—	25.3[b]
Italy	—	—	—	77.2	—	22.8	76.7[c]	—	23.3[c]
Luxembourg	—	—	—	83.4	—	16.6	85.5	—	14.5
Netherlands	74.7	—	25.3	76.7	—	23.3	78.3	—	21.7
Portugal	—	—	—	92.2	—	7.8	89.9	—	10.1
Spain	89.0	0.3	10.7	70.0	16.8	13.2	69.0[b]	19.3[b]	11.7[c]
Sweden	63.2	—	36.8	63.3	—	36.7	64.1[c]	—	35.9[c]
UK	74.2	—	25.8	74.9	—	25.1	77.7[c]	—	22.3[c]

Notes:
[a] 1995
[b] 1996
[c] 1998

Source: Own elaboration with IMF Public Government Finance Data.

government grants, have been given access to 30 per cent of the income tax revenues generated within their respective territories. And the introduction in 1998 of new forms of regional taxation, such as the IRAP—*imposta regionale sulle attività produttive* or regional tax on productive activities—reflects the increasing fiscal federalism within the Italian context.

However, despite recent progress, the financial capacity of regions to develop and implement their own autonomous policies remains crippled. Even in the country that has witnessed the greatest regional financial revolution, Spain, the expenditure of regional governments in 1997 was less than 20 per cent of total government expenditure (Table 7.2). And most Spanish regional governments were heavily indebted. In Germany, regional expenditure was below one quarter of total expenditure and in Austria, it represented only 15 per cent. Central government expenditure represented more than half of total government expenditure everywhere, and it is worth noting that it tended to be lower in centralized than in regionalized countries. Local authorities in heavily centralized countries such as Denmark, Finland, and Sweden enjoy the greatest financial autonomy in the EU.

7.4 The roots of the regionalization process

What are the factors behind the regionalization process in Europe? Why have so many countries in the EU decided to go regional in a period of just three decades? The roots of the process of regionalization and regional devolution have to be searched for in the revival of nationalism and regionalism across Europe since the 1960s. Having languished after the end of the second World War, nationalist and regionalist movements experienced a regeneration in the 1960s and 1970s, which led some researchers to consider the 1970s as the decade of regionalism and regionalization (Mény, 1982). The factors behind this regeneration were fundamentally of a historic, linguistic, and cultural nature. National or regional movements in regions—or nations within regions—with a particular historical character, with their own language or dialect, or with a clear-cut cultural collective identity were at the forefront of the first wave of regionalization. This was the case with the historical regions of the Basque Country, Catalonia, and, to a lesser extent, Galicia in Spain; Scotland and Wales in the UK; Flanders and Wallonia in Belgium; Brittany or Corsica in France; or even Sardinia and Sicily in Italy. Regional movements brandished historical, linguistic, cultural, and even ethnic discourses in order to justify their demands for autonomy and devolution. Nationalist and regionalist movements in these areas were strong and active. Demands for regional autonomy were frequently centred around the need to protect and promote the local culture, language, and identity *vis-à-vis* what was regarded as the dominance or even the 'aggression' of the national cultures and languages. And the way to achieve this protection was by transferring powers from the centre to the regions and by allowing regions to elect their own parliaments and assemblies, to pass their own laws, and to set up their own governments. The presence of regionalist movements in regions with a strong collective identity combined with the absence or weakness of similar movements in regions lacking this sense of identity often resulted in asymmetrical devolution. Most of the regions with a strong collective identity have achieved regional autonomy sooner rather than later. The 'special status' regions of Italy and the Belgian regions started the process. The Spanish 'historical' autonomous communities followed later and the process has been almost completed in the 1990s with the devolution of power to Scotland, Wales, and Northern Ireland in the UK and the discussions to grant Corsica greater autonomy in the French context. Regional autonomy in the 'special status' regions of Italy, in the historic communities of Spain, and in Scotland, Wales, and Northern Ireland was also achieved earlier than in the rest of each country.

Resorting to economic arguments as a way to achieve regional devolution or autonomy was rare. During the first wave of regionalism, regional autonomy and devolution were above all a question of identity, and economic issues—if present at all—were relegated to the background. However, and after a period of relative calm in the early 1980s, a new and different wave of regionalism has emerged in western Europe (Keating, 1998). This new regionalism no longer resorts to the traditional arguments of former waves, but puts the economy at the heart of its discourse. Authors such as Keating (1998) and Scott (1998) have underlined that regionalism at the end of the twentieth century is more related to the processes of globalization and socio-economic restructuring than to identity, culture, language, or religion. According to the 'new regionalist' literature, the greater mobility of production factors linked to economic globalization and European integration and the transfer of powers to supranational bodies triggered by economic integration are undermining the capacity of nation states to control economic development processes within their territories. Technological advances, greater access to information, and the development of infrastructure are contributing to solve some of the bottlenecks which prevented subnational areas from having access to factors of production and from achieving economic development. The greater capacity of regions to participate in the global economy, together with the increasing inability of nation states to govern it, are supposedly transforming the region into a key actor in economic policy (Keating, 1998). In contrast to what was the norm during the post-war period, when national economies grew at a very high rate (e.g. the so-called 'German miracle'), examples of dynamic economies are nowadays increasingly concentrated at the sub-national level: the Silicon Valley in the US, the Cambridge area in Britain, Veneto in Italy, and Baden-Württemberg in Germany.

However, the processes of globalization and European integration are not only providing new opportunities for regional economic development. They are also presenting a series of challenges. Regions can no longer rely on national cohesion policies as was earlier the case. The greater mobility of capital and labour, together with the budgetary constraints linked to the process of European economic integration, are pushing regions to adopt more pro-active development strategies. Regions and cities are forced to compete with each other in order to attract capital, technology, firms, or labour (Cheshire and Gordon, 1998), as well as to set up their own development policies in order to enhance their economic potential (Storper, 1997; Scott, 1998). From this point of view, regional success in a globalized world depends on the capacity of each region to adopt pro-active policies and to form a complex web of public and private institutions generating local synergies (Keating, 1998). Consequently, the 'new regionalism' sees the regional devolution in the EU not only as a way of preserving and developing local identity and culture, but almost as a way of guaranteeing economic survival in an increasingly competitive world.

Greater regional economic visibility and clout have inevitably led to greater demands for devolution and transfers of power to subnational tiers of government. Regions and regional movements have not shied away from using the economic argument as a political card. One of the most notorious examples in this direction has been the emergence of the Northern League in the rich regions of northern Italy. This secessionist and protest movement started its life as different regional groups—Lega Lombarda, Lega Veneto, Lega Piemonte—and as rather conventional regionalist movements. Their early discourse, based on linguistic and ethnic arguments, did not gain them much support. It was only after their merger into the *Lega Nord* or Northern League in 1989 and their resort to the economic argument that their support multiplied (Diamanti, 1993). The Northern League's rhetoric, although still impregnated with ethnic and even racist nuances (see Chapter 4), goes beyond the traditional discourse of nationalist and regionalist parties and movements. It is mainly founded around a critique of the capacity of the central government to manage local resources effectively. The Italian central government is accused by the Northern League of profligacy and of being 'dominated by southerners', who use the capital generated by the north in order to subsidize the south of the country and to support a public service full of 'parasites'. It also claims that the taxes levied in the north of the country contribute to finance government malpractice and clientelism in Rome and the south of the country (Gallagher, 1994: 460). This discourse has made the Northern League increase its electoral support exponentially. During the 1990s they repeatedly achieved more than a quarter of the votes in several northern provinces at local, regional, and national elections (and in some cases gained the support of almost 10 per cent of the total electorate in national elections), and this support made them a key actor in the extremely fragmented Italian political panorama. They also played an important role in local politics by winning local elections in numerous northern cities, including Milan (Giordano, 2000).

The success of this type of rhetoric has been noted by more traditional and 'respectable' nationalist parties and movements. One such party has been the moderate Catalan nationalist Convergència i Unió, which has been the ruling party in Catalonia since devolution. Party leaders began during the 1990s to adopt an economic discourse and to resort to the argument that Catalonia was not receiving from the Spanish state what 'she deserved' both from an economic and an identity perspective. Convergència i Unió also implied that the region and its regional government are more capable than the central government of managing their own resources, and therefore the control of the majority of local resources and tax revenues should be in the hands of regional governments.

In view of the power of this new form of economic regionalism, many European states have succumbed to devolution processes or have granted greater transfers of powers to the regions. As was mentioned earlier, despite keeping the bulk of government expenditure, in cases of the greatest levels of devolution the powers of the state have become more of less restricted to the areas of defence, foreign affairs, and macroeconomic management. Yet, these are precisely areas of power which European integration is taking away from the nation state. EMU has taken away from member states a considerable margin of macroeconomic manoeuvre and progress has been made towards setting up European-wide foreign and defence policies.

7.5 Towards a 'Europe of the Regions'?

Some claim that the combination of greater transfers of powers to supranational and subnational bodies with the emergence of regions as key economic actors in a globalized world has contributed to a 'hollowing-out' of the state. From this perspective, the state has been starved of more and more of its powers by the twin challenges of subnational and supranational forces (Amin and Tomaney, 1995; Tomaney and Ward, 2000) and the main areas of economic management and policy-making are no longer in the hands of the state, but in those of Brussels and of the regions. The supranational and subnational levels of government seem to be pushing towards the demise of the nation state as we know it. The presence of an EU regional development policy has forced even governments with a centralized system of government to think in regional terms. Taken to its limits, this argument suggests that in the European context the state no longer matters (O'Brien, 1992; Ohmae, 1995); that in the future the main economic and political issues are going to be those of Europe at large, on the one hand, and those of regions and cities, on the other: in sum, the emergence of what has been popularly known as the 'Europe of the Regions'.

But does this 'Europe of the Regions' really exist? Is the relevance of the nation state really dwindling in favour of subnational levels of government? Although it is undeniable that subnational entities and institutions have been gaining weight in the both at a national and EU level, as reflected by the creation of the Committee of the Regions (Christiansen, 1996), the emergence of a 'Europe of the Regions' is a more controversial process. Not everyone agrees that the combined forces of regionalization and European integration are heralding the demise of the nation state. According to Alan Milward (1992) in his highly controversial *The European Rescue of the Nation-State*, European integration has not only not weakened the nation state, but, on the contrary, it has reinforced its powers by giving current EU member states a capacity to shape matters that go beyond their national boundaries. The states in the EU are the main drivers of European integration and make up the European Council. Many EU summits during the 1990s have been conducted in a climate of reasserting national interests and, as a result, the European Commission and the regions are forced to dance to the tune played by the member states. Hirst and Thompson (1995) have also underlined that, although recent changes have altered the traditional functions conducted by nation states, these changes do not imply a waning influence, but a profound transformation of their role. States are becoming power brokers between subnational and supranational levels of government, a role which is granting them a whole new array of functions in a more complex system of governance.

From an economic point of view, several studies have also cast doubt upon the emergence of an economic 'Europe of the Regions'. Despite the increasing use of economic arguments in order to justify demands for greater transfers of powers to the regions, most analyses highlight that the economic performance of regions is still very much embedded in that of the state they belong to (Rodríguez-Pose, 1998). Although regions have often been heralded as the new emerging economic spaces in a globalized world, economic growth rates, productivity or unemployment rates in the industrial declining north of France are still closer to those of the south of France than to those of neighbouring and equally declining Wallonia. The same can be said for growth rates in the south and north of Italy.

In sum, although western European regions have been gaining greater power, the configuration of a true 'Europe of the Regions', in which the national tier of government is engulfed by the powers of regions from below and those of the EU from above, is still very much a pipe dream. We are probably closer to what Leonardy (1993) has defined as a 'Europe *with*, not *of*, the regions', a Europe 'where the growth of initiatives and competences on regional and European levels is accompanied, in many instances, by a reassertion of national states and bureaucracies' (Borrás-Alomar *et al.* 1994: 24).

7.6 Conclusion

The revival of regionalism in European states during the last decades of the twentieth century has brought the regional dimension to the fore. The reply to regionalism has been a profound transformation of the territorial organization of many western European states and the emergence of regions as active political entities in the European arena. Processes of regional devolution have certainly addressed long-repressed demands for self-government and have contributed to preserving and promoting national and regional languages, cultures, identities, and economies. However, the shift from a 'Europe of the nation states' to a 'Europe with the regions' entails numerous risks which may jeopardize other European achievements. The current resort to economic arguments in order to justify regional differences in levels of devolution has provoked a large asymmetry in the capacity of different regions to develop their own autonomous policies. This is evident among EU countries and within those countries such as Italy, Portugal, Spain, or the UK, where the regionalization process has been asymmetrical from the start. But the functioning of regional administrations is creating even greater diversity in regional policies and regional efficiency everywhere. Diverse powers and institutional capacities are generating a myriad of diverse—when not openly competitive—policies. The multiplication of regional policies is not necessarily bad. Regional governments can function as 'democracy labs' and implement policies which are 'closer to the people' (Donahue, 1997). Regional administrations can also contribute to generating a more transparent link between governments and the people and lead to greater public efficiency. However, such differences in policy-making and policy efficiency are likely to be achieved to the detriment of economic and social cohesion. As shown by Putnam (1993) in the case of Italy, regional administrations in the north of the country tend to be much more transparent and efficient than those of the south. This means that regions with greater powers and a more dynamic administration are in a better starting position to adopt the 'active competition policies' demanded by a globalized world. Regions with lesser powers or less efficient administrations risk being left out of the process. In any case, the likely outcome is an escalation in territorial competition and regional conflict, as has been the case in the US or Brazil.

It is difficult to foresee what is going to be the future development of the regionalization process and regional governments in the future. There are multiple possible scenarios, ranging from a generalization and a deepening of the process of regionalization at the European level which results in a true 'Europe of the Regions', to a backlash against devolution in many European countries, although the former, without greater co-ordination at the national or European level of regional policies may generalize inter-regional competition and conflict, and the latter may be neither feasible, nor desirable.

References

AMIN, A., and TOMANEY, J. (eds.) (1995), *Behind the Myth of European Union: Prospects for Cohesion* (London: Routledge).

ANDERSEN, T. M., HALDRUP, N., and SORENSEN, J. R. (2000), 'Labour market implications of EU product market integration', *Economic Policy*, 30: 105–42.

ARMSTRONG, H. W. (1995), 'Convergence among regions of the European Union: 1950–1990', *Papers in Regional Science*, 74: 143–52.

—— and TAYLOR, J. (2000), *Regional Economics and Policy*, 3rd ed. (Oxford: Blackwell).

ASCHAUER, D. A. (1989), 'Is public expenditure productive?' *Journal of Monetary Economics*, 23: 177–200.

BALASSA, B. (1961), *The Theory of Economic Integration* (London: Allen & Unwin).

BALDWIN, R. E. (1989), 'The growth effects of 1992', *Economic Policy*, 9: 247–81.

—— (1997), 'Concepts and speed of an eastern enlargement', in Siebert, (1997: 73–88).

——, FRANÇOIS, J. F., PORTES, R. , RODRIK, D., and SZEKELY, I. P. (1997), 'The costs and benefits of eastern enlargement: the impact on the EU and Central Europe', *Economic Policy*: 125–76.

BALME, R. (1998), 'The French region as a space for public policy', in Le Galès and Lequesne (1998: 181–98).

BARRO, R. J. and GRILLI, V. (1994), *European Macroeconomics* (Basingstoke: Macmillan).

—— and SALA-i-MARTÍN, X.X. (1991), 'Convergence across states and regions', *Brookings Papers on Economic Activity*, 1: 107–82.

BAUMGARTL, B., and FAVELL, A. (eds.) (1995), *New Xenophobia in Europe* (London: Kluwer Law International).

BECK, U. (2000), *What is Globalization? (Cambridge: Polity Press)*.

BECKER, G. (1981), *A Treatise on the Family* (Cambridge, Mass.: Harvard University Press).

BEGG, I. (1997), 'Interregional transfers in a widened Europe', in Siebert (1997: 189–203).

BENHABIB, J., and SPIEGEL, M. M. (1994), 'The role of human capital in economic development: Evidence from aggregate cross-country data', *Journal of Monetary Economics*, 34: 143–73.

BENZ, A. (1993), 'German regions in the European Union: from joint policy-making to multi-level governance', in Le Galès and Lequesne (1998: 111–29).

BETTIO, F., and VILLA, P. (1989), 'Non-wage work and disguised wage employment in Italy', in Rodgers and Rodgers (1989: 149–78).

BIGO, B. (1994), 'The European internal security field: Stakes and rivalries in a newly developing area of police intervention', in M. Anderson and M. den Boer (eds.), *Policing across National Boundaries* (London: Pinter).

BOER, M. DEN, and WALLACE, W. (2000), 'Justice and home affairs: Integration through incrementalism?' in Wallace and Wallace (2000: 493–522).

BORRÁS-ALOMAR, S., CHRISTIANSEN, T., and RODRÍGUEZ-POSE, A. (1994), 'Towards a

"Europe of the regions"? Visions and reality from a critical perspective', *Regional Politics and Policy*, 4: 1–27.

BOYER, R. (2000), 'The political in the era of globalization and finance: Focus on some regulation school research', *International Journal of Urban and Regional Research*, 24: 274–322.

BÜCHTEMANN, C. F., and QUACK, S. (1989), ' "Bridges" or "traps"? Non-standard employment in the Federal Republic of Germany', in Rodgers and Rodgers (1989: 109–48).

BUDAPEST GROUP (1999), 'The relationship between organised crime and trafficking in aliens' (Budapest: Budapest Group).

BURDA, M., and WYPLOSZ, C. (1993), *Macroeconomics: A European Text* (Oxford: Oxford University Press).

CECCHINI, P. (1988), *The European Challenge 1992: The benefits of a Single Market* (Aldershot: Wilwood House).

CEPII (1997), 'Trade patterns inside the Single Market' (Paris: CEPII, Working Paper 97–07). http://www.cepii.fr/ANGLAIS/DOCW9707.HTM.

CHATTERJI, M. (1998), 'Tertiary education and economic growth', *Regional Studies*, 32: 349–54.

CHESHIRE, P., and GORDON, I. (1998), 'Territorial competition: Some lessons for policy'. *Annals of Regional Science*, 33: 321–46.

CHRISTIANSEN, T. (1996), 'Second thoughts on Europe's "third level": the European Union's Committee of the Regions', *Publius*, Journal of Federalism, 26: 93–116.

CICHOWSKI, R. A. (2000), 'Western dreams, eastern realities: Support for the European Union in central and eastern Europe', *Comparative Political Studies*, 33: 1243–78.

COLEMAN, D. (ed.) (1996*a*), *Europe's Population in the 1990s* (Oxford: Oxford University Press).

—— (1996*b*), 'New patterns and trends in European fertility: International and sub-national comparisons', in Coleman (1996*a*: 1–61).

COOLS, H. (1995), 'Fragile national identity(s) and the elusive multicultural society', in Baumgartl and Favell (1995: 28–45).

CROUCH, C. (1999), *Social Change in Western Europe* (Oxford: Oxford University Press).

CROXFORD, G. J., WISE, M., and CHALKEY, B. S. (1987), 'The reform of the European Regional Development Fund: A preliminary assessment', *Journal of Common Market Studies*, 26: 25–38.

DARBY, J., HALLETT, A. H., IRELAND, J., and PISCITELLI, L. (1999), 'The impact of exchange rate uncertainty on the level of investment', *Economic Journal*, 109: C55–C67.

DE GRAUWE, P. (1997), *The Economics of Monetary Integration*, 3rd ed. (Oxford: Oxford University Press).

DE LA FUENTE, A., and VIVES, X. (1995), 'Infrastructure and education as instruments of regional policy: Evidence from Spain', *Economic Policy*, 20: 11–40.

DE RYNCK, S. (1998), 'Civic culture and institutional performance of the Belgian regions', in Le Galès and Lequesne (1998: 199–218).

DICKEN, P. (1998). *Global Shift*, 3rd ed. (London: Paul Chapman).

DIAMANTI, I. (1993), *La Lega: Geografia*, Storia e Sociologia di un Nuovo Soggetto Politico (Rome: Donzelli).

DONAHUE, J. D. (1997), *Disunited States: What's at Stake as Washington Fades and the States take the Lead* (New York: Basic Books).

DOTY, R. L. (1996), 'Immigration and national identity: Constructing the nation', *Review of International Studies*, 22: 235–55.

EBBINGHAUS, B., and VISSER, J. (1999), 'When institutions matter: Union growth and decline in Western Europe, 1950–1995', *European Sociological Review*, 15: 135–58.

—— —— (2000), *Trade Unions in Western Europe since 1945* (Basingstoke: Macmillan).

EL-AGRAA, A. M. (1998), *The European Union: History*, Institutions, Economics and Policies, 5th edn. (Hemel Hempstead: Prentice Hall).

EMERSON, M., AUJEAN, M., CATINAT, M., GOYBET, P., and JACQUEMIN, A. (1988), *The Economics of 1992* (Oxford: Oxford University Press).

ERMISCH, J. (1996), 'The economic environment for family formation', in Coleman (1996a: 144–62).

ESPING-ANDERSEN, G. (1990), *The Three Worlds of Welfare Capitalism* (Cambridge: Polity Press).

—— (1999), *Social Foundations of Postindustrial Economies* (Oxford: Oxford University Press).

EUROBAROMETER 48 (1997), http://europa.eu.int/comm/dg10/epo/eb/eb48/eb48.html6

EUROPEAN COMMISSION (1980a), *Regions in Europe: First Periodic Report on the Social and Economic Situation and Development of the Regions of the Community*, (Brussels–Luxembourg: OPOCE).

—— (1980b), *Les Européens et leur Région* (Brussels–Luxembourg: OPOCE).

—— (1985), *Completing the Internal Market: White Paper from the Commission to the European Council* (Brussels: Commission of the European Communities).

—— (1994), *Competitiveness and Cohesion: Trends in the Regions: Fifth Periodic Report on the Social and Economic Situation and Development of the Regions in the Community* (Brussels–Luxembourg: OPOCE).

—— (1999), *Sixth Periodic Report on the Social and Economic Situation and Development of the Regions of the European Union* (Brussels–Luxembourg: OPOCE).

—— (2000), *Structural Actions 2000–2006* (Brussels–Luxembourg: OPOCE).

EUROPEAN ECONOMY (1999), *Mergers and Acquisitions*. Supplement A. No. 2. February 1999.

FABBRO, R. DEL (1995), 'A victory of the street', in Baumgartl and Favell (1995: 132–47).

FAVELL, A., and TAMBINI, D. (1995), 'Clear blue water between "us" and "Europe"', in Baumgartl and Favell (1995: 148–63).

FIELDING, A. (1993), 'Migrants, institutions and politics: the evolution of European migration policies', in King (1993a: 40–62).

FISCHER, S., SAHAY, R., and VÉGH, C. A. (1997), 'How far is eastern Europe from Brussels?' in Siebert (1997: 97–122).

FUJITA, M., KRUGMAN, P., and VENABLES, A. J. (1999), *The Spatial Economy: Cities, Regions and International Trade* (Cambridge, Mass.: MIT Press).

GALLAGHER, T. (1994), 'The regional dimension in Italy's political upheaval: role of the Northern League 1984–1993', *Parliamentary Affairs*, 47: 456–68.

GAUTHIER, A. H. (1996), *The State and the Family: A Comparative Analysis of Family Policies in Industrialized Countries* (Oxford: Clarendon Press).

—— (1999), 'Historical trends in state support for families in Europe (post-1945)', *Children and Youth Services Review*, 21: 937–65.

GIORDANO, B. (2000), 'Italian regionalism or "Padanian" nationalism: The political project of the Lega Nord in Italian politics', *Political Geography*, 19: 445–71.

GOLDTHORPE, J. H. (1992), 'Employment, class, and mobility: A critique of liberal and Marxist theories of long-term change', in Haferkamp and Smelser (1992: 122–46).

GOTTSCHALK, P., and SMEEDING, T. M. (1997), 'Cross-national comparisons of earnings and income inequality', *Journal of Economic Literature*, 35: 633–87.

GRABBE, H., and HUGHES, K. (1998), *Enlarging the EU Eastwards* (London: Cassell/The Royal Institute of International Affairs).

GRAY, J. (1998). *False Dawn* (London: Granta Books).

GUSTAFSSON, S. S., WETZELS, C. M. M. P., VLASBLOM, J. D., and DEX, S. (1996), 'Women's labor force transitions in connection with childbirth: A panel data comparison between Germany, Sweden and Great Britain', *Journal of Population Economics*, 9: 223–46.

HAFERKAMP, H., and SMELSER, N. J. (eds.) (1992), *Social Change and Modernity* (Berkeley: University of California Press).

HANTRAIS, L. (1997), 'Exploring relationships between social policy and changing family forms within the European Union', *European Journal of Population*, 13: 339–79.

—— (2000), *Social Policy in the European Union*, 2nd edn. (Basingstoke: Macmillan).

HARE, P. (1997), 'The distance between eastern Europe and Brussels: Reform deficits in potential member states', in Siebert (1997: 127–45).

HARVEY, D. (2000), *Spaces of Hope* (Edinburgh: Edinburgh University Press).

HAUSER, H. (2001), 'Nothing ventured, nothing gained', *EIB Papers*, 6: 101–7.

HECKMAN, J. J., and WALKER, J. R. (1990), 'The relationship between wages and income and the timing and spacing of births: Evidence from Swedish longitudinal data', *Econometrica*, 58: 1411–41.

HEYWOOD, P. (1995), *The Government and Politics of Spain* (Basingstoke: Macmillan).

HIRST, P., and THOMPSON, G. (1995) 'Globalization and the future of the nation-state', *Economy and Society*, 24: 408–42.

HITIRIS, T. (1998), *European Union Economics* (London: Prentice Hall).

HOEM, B. (1993), 'The compatibility of employment and childbearing in contemporary Sweden', *Acta Sociologica*, 36: 101–20.

HUYSMANS, J. (2000), 'The European Union and the securitization of migration', *Journal of Common Market Studies*, 38: 751–77.

INTRILIGATOR, M. D. (2000), 'Democracy in reforming collapsed communist economies: Blessing or curse?' *Contemporary Economic Policy*, 16: 241–6.

JEFFREY, C., and STURM, R. (eds.) (1993), *Federalism*, Unification and European Integration (London: Frank Cass).

JOHNES, G. (1993), *The Economies of Education* (Basingstoke: Macmillan).

JOSHI, H. (1998), 'The opportunity costs of childbearing: More than mothers' business', *Journal of Population Economics*, 11: 161–83.

KALWIJ, A. S. (2000), 'The effects of female employment status on the presence and number of children', *Journal of Population Economics*, 13: 221–39.

KANG, N. H., and JOHANSSON, S. (2000), 'Cross-border mergers and acquisitions: Their role in industrial globalisation' (Paris: OECD, STI Working Papers, Directorate for Science, Technology and Industry).

KEATING, M. (1993), *The Politics of Modern Europe: The State and Political Authority in the Major Democracies* (Cheltenham: Edward Elgar).

—— (1998), *The New Regionalism in Western Europe: Territorial Restructuring and Political Change* (Northampton, Mass.: Edward Elgar).

—— and LOUGHLIN, J. (eds.) (1997), *The Political Economy of Regionalism*. London: Frank Cass.

KEEBLE, D., OFFORD, J., and WALKER, S. (1988), *Peripheral Regions in a Community of Twelve Member States* (Brussels–Luxembourg: OPOCE).

KING, C. (2000), 'Post-postcommunism. Transition, comparison, and the end of "eastern Europe"', *World Politics*, 53: 143–67.

KING, R. (ed.) (1993a), *Mass Migration in Europe: The Legacy and the Future* (Chicester: John Wiley and Sons).

—— (1993b), 'European international migration 1945–90: A statistical and geographical overview', in King (1993a: 19–39).

—— LAZARIDIS, G., and TSARDANIDIS, C. (eds.) (1999), *Eldorado or Fortress? Migration in Southern Europe* (Basingstoke: Macmillan).

KOPECKY, P., and MUDDLE, C. (2000), 'What has eastern Europe taught us about the democratisation literature (and vice versa)?' *European Journal of Political Research*, 37: 517–39.

KOSINSKI, L. (1970), *The Population of Europe* (London: Longman).

KOSTAKOPOULOU, D. (2000), "The 'protective Union": Change and continuity in migration law and policy in post-Amsterdam Europe', *Journal of Common Market Studies*, 38: 497–518.

KRUGMAN, P. (1994), 'Europe jobless, America penniless', *Foreign Policy*, 95: 19–34.

—— and VENABLES, A. J. (1996), 'Integration, specialization, and adjustment', *European Economic Review*, 40: 959–67.

Le GALÈS, P., and LEQUESNE, C. (eds.) (1998), *Regions in Europe* (London: Routledge).

LEONARDI, R. (1995), *Convergence, Cohesion and Integration in the European Union* (Basingstoke: Macmillan).

LEONARDY, U (1993), 'The Länder and the Federation in German Foreign Relations', in Jeffrey and Sturm (1993: 119–35).

LÓPEZ-BAZO. E., VAYÁ, E., MORA, A. J., and SURIÑACH, J. (1999), 'Regional economic dynamics and convergence in the European Union', *Annals of Regional Science*, 33: 343–70.

MARTINIELLO, M. (1995), *Migration, Citizenship, and Ethno-National Identities in the European Union* (Aldershot: Avebury).

MASON, K. O., and JENSEN, A. M. (eds.) (1995), *Gender and Family Change in Industrialized Countries* (Oxford: Clarendon Press).

MEAGER, N. (1993) 'Self-employment and Labour Market Policy in the European Community' (Berlin: WZB, WZB Discussion Paper FIS 93: 201).

Mény, Y. (ed.) (1982), *Dix Ans de Régionalisation en Europe* (Paris: Cujas).

Milward, A. S. (1992), The European Rescue of the Nation-State (Berkeley: University of California Press).

Montanari, A., and Cortese, A. (1993a), 'South to North migration in a Mediterranean perspective', in King (1993a: 212–33).

—— —— (1993b), 'Third world immigrants in Italy', in King (1993a: 275–92).

Mouritsen, P. (1995), 'The agonies of innocence', in Baumgartl and Favell (1995: 88–105).

Murphy, M. (1993), 'The contraceptive pill and women's employment as factors in fertility change in Britain (1963–1980): A challenge to the conventional view', *Population Studies*, 47: 221–43.

Neven, D., and Gouyette, C. (1995), 'Regional convergence in the European Community', *Journal of Common Market Studies*, 33: 47–65

O'Brien, R. (1992), *Global Financial Integration: The End of Geography* (London: Royal Institute of International Affairs).

OECD (1996), *Education at a glance* (Paris: OECD).

—— (1997), *Economic Outlook* (Paris: OECD).

Ohmae, K. (1995), *The End of the Nation-State: The Rise of Regional Economies* (New York: The Free Press).

Overman, H., and Puga, D. (1999), 'Unemployment clusters across European regions and countries' (London: CEPR, discussion paper 2255).

Padoa-Schioppa, F. (1993), *Italy, the Sheltered Economy: Structural Problems in the Italian Economy* (Oxford: Clarendon Press).

Pérez Díaz, V. M. (1990), 'Governability and the scale of governance: Mesogovernments in Spain' (Madrid: Instituto Juan March de Estudios e Investigaciones, WP 1990/6).

Petrakos, G. (2001), 'Patterns of regional inequality in transition economies', *European Planning Studies*, 9: 359–83.

—— Maier, G., and Gorzelak, G. (2000a), *Integration and Transition in Europe: The Economic Geography of Interaction* (London: Routledge).

—— —— —— (2000b), 'The new economic geography of Europe: An introduction', in Petrakos *et al.* (2000a: 1–37).

Pinelli, A. (1995), 'Women's condition, low fertility, and emerging union patterns in Europe', in Mason and Jensen (1995: 82–104).

Preston, C. (1997), *Enlargement and Integration in the European Union* (London: Routledge).

Puga, D. (2000), 'European regional policy in light of recent location theories' (London: CEPR, discussion paper 2767).

Putnam, R. D. (1993), *Making Democracy Work: Civic Traditions in Modern Italy* (Princeton: Princeton University Press).

Quah, D. (2001), 'ICT clusters in development: Theory and evidence', *EIB Papers*, 6: 85–100.

Rasmussen, H. K. (1997), *No Entry: Immigration Policy in Europe* (Copenhagen: Copenhagen Business School Press).

Rodgers, G., and Rodgers, J. (eds.) (1989), *Precarious Jobs in Labour Market Regulation: The Growth of Atypical Employment in Western Europe* (Geneva: ILO).

RODRÍGUEZ-POSE, A. (1996), 'Growth and institutional change: the influence of the Spanish regionalisation process on long term growth trends', *Environment and Planning C: Government and Policy*, 14: 71–87.

—— (1998), *Dynamics of Regional Growth in Europe: Social and Political Factors* (Oxford: Clarendon Press).

—— (1999), 'Innovation prone and innovation averse societies: Economic performance in Europe', *Growth and Change*, 30: 75–105.

—— (2000), 'Economic convergence and regional development strategies in Spain: The case of Galicia and Navarre', *European Investment Bank Papers*, 5: 89–115.

—— (2001), 'Is investment in R&D in lagging areas of Europe worthwhile? Theory and empirical evidence', *Papers in Regional Science*, 80: 279–95.

SALA-I-MARTÍN, X. X. (1996), 'Regional cohesion: Evidence and theories of regional growth and convergence', *European Economic Review*, 40: 1325–52.

SALT, J. (1989), 'A comparative overview of international trends and types, 1950–80', *International Migration Review*, 23: 431–56.

—— (1992), 'The future of international labour migration', *International Migration Review*, 26: 1077–111.

—— and FORD, R. (1993) 'Skilled international migration in Europe: The shape of things to come?', in King (1993a: 293–309).

SCHNEIDER, F. (2001), 'The size and development of the shadow economies and shadow economy labour force of 18 Asian and 21 OECD countries: First results of the 90s' (Linz: Department of Economics, University of Linz).

—— and ENSTE, D. H. (2000), 'Shadow economies: size, causes, and consequences', *Journal of Economic Literature*, 38: 77–114.

SCOTT, A. J. (1998), *Regions and the World Economy: The Coming Shape of Global Production*, Competition, and Political Order (Oxford: Oxford University Press).

SEDELMEIER, U., and WALLACE, H. (2000), 'Eastern enlargement: strategy or second thoughts', in Wallace and Wallace (2000: 427–60).

SIEBERT, H. (ed.) (1997), *Quo Vadis Europe?* (Tübingen: J.C.B. Möhr).

SMITH, J. (2000), 'Enlarging Europe', *Journal of Common Market Studies*, 38: 121–4.

SOPEMI (various years), *Trends in International Migration: Continuous Reporting System on Migration* (Paris: OECD).

STORPER, M. (1997), *The Regional World: Territorial Development in a Global Economy* (London: Guilford).

TANGERMANN, S. (1997), 'Reforming the CAP: A prerequisite for an eastern enlargement', in Siebert (1997: 151–79).

TEAGUE, P., and GRAHL, J. (1998), 'Institutions and labour market performance in western Europe', *Political Studies*, 46: 1–18.

TOMANEY, J. (2000), 'End of the empire state? New labour and devolution in the United Kingdom', *International Journal of Urban and Regional Research*, 24: 675–88.

—— and WARD, N. (2000), 'England and the "new regionalism"', *Regional Studies*, 34: 471–8.

TOONEN, T. A. J. (1998), 'Provinces versus urban centres: current developments, background and evaluation of regionalisation in the Netherlands', in P. Le Galès and C. Lequesne (1998: 130–49).

TRAJTENBERG, M. (1990), *Economic Analysis of Product Iinnovation* (Cambridge: Cambridge University Press).

TRIANDAFYLLIDOU, A. (2000), 'The political discourse on immigration in southern Europe: A critical analysis', *Journal of Community and Applied Social Psychology*, 10: 373–89.

—— and MIKRAKIS, A. (1995), 'A ghost wanders through the capital', in Baumgartl and Favell (1995: 10–28).

TSOUKALIS, L. (1993), *The New European Economy: The Politics and Economics of Integration* (Oxford: Oxford University Press).

UBBIALI, G. (1995), 'Towards the institutionalisation of prejudice?' in Baumgartl and Favell (1995: 118–31).

UNITED NATIONS POPULATION DIVISION (2000), *Replacement Migration: Is it a Solution to Declining and Ageing Populations?* (New York: UN, http://www.un.org/esa/population/migration.htm).

VAN DE KAA, D. J. (1987), 'Europe's second demographic transition', *Population Bulletin*, 42: 1–57.

VAN DIJK, J., and FOLMER, H. (1999), 'Wage effects of unemployment duration and frequency', *Journal of Regional Science*, 39: 319–37.

VANHOUDT, P. (1999), 'Did the European unification induce economic growth? In search of scale effects and persistent changes', *Weltwirtschaftliches Archiv*, 135: 193–220.

—— MATHÄ, T., and SMID, B. (2000), 'How productive are capital investments in Europe?' *EIB Papers*, 5: 81–105.

WAKOLBINGER, E. (1995), 'The danger of populism', in Baumgartl and Favell (1995: 10–27).

WALLACE, H., and WALLACE, W. (2000), *Policy Making in the European Union* (Oxford: Oxford University Press).

WISE, M., and CROXFORD, G. (1998), 'The European Regional Development Fund: Community ideals and national realities', *Political Geography Quarterly*, 7: 161–82.

Index